兒時瑣憶

蔣彝

HSIEN-
(great-grand-

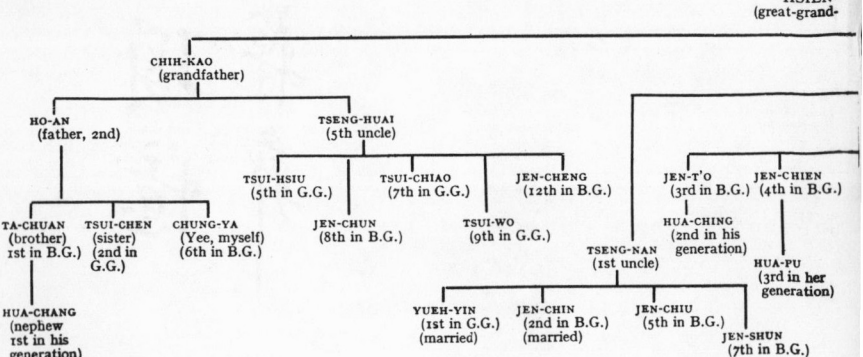

CHIH-KAO
(grandfather)

HO-AN
(father, 2nd)

TSENG-HUAI
(5th uncle)

TSUI-HSIU
(5th in G.G.)

TSUI-CHIAO
(7th in G.G.)

JEN-CHENG
(12th in B.G.)

JEN-T'O
(3rd in B.G.)

JEN-CHIEN
(4th in B.G.)

TA-CHUAN
(brother)
1st in B.G.)

TSUI-CHEN
(sister)
(2nd in
G.G.)

CHUNG-YA
(Yee, myself)
(6th in B.G.)

JEN-CHUN
(8th in B.G.)

TSUI-WO
(9th in G.G.)

HUA-CHING
(2nd in his
generation)

TSENG-NAN
(1st uncle)

HUA-PU
(3rd in her
generation)

HUA-CHANG
(nephew
1st in his
generation)

YUEH-YIN
(1st in G.G.)
(married)

JEN-CHIN
(2nd in B.G.)
(married)

JEN-CHIU
(5th in B.G.)

JEN-SHUN
(7th in B.G.)

NOTES.—(1) This table shows the relationships
(and a few important ones who were dead) when I
of my grandmother, my great-aunts or of my aunts;
wives of the members, which would have made the

(2) B.G. signifies Boys' Group and G.G. Girls'
in the Boys' Group, though my only brother was
my brother and me.

FAMILY

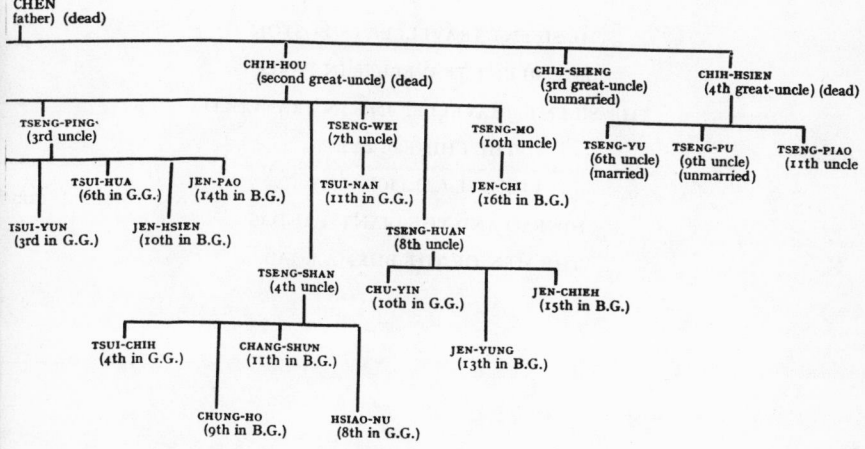

between the members of my family who were living
was fifteen years old. It does not include the names
I have not, that is to sày, attempted to include the
table too complicated.

Group. Thus I myself, "Chung-Ya," was the 6th
the 1st, because four boy-cousins were born between

By Chiang Yee

A CHINESE CHILDHOOD

by
CHIANG YEE

The Norton Library
W · W · NORTON & COMPANY · INC ·
NEW YORK

First published in the Norton Library 1963

TO

ALL MEMBERS
OF THE
HALL OF THREE FOOTPATHS

BOTH THOSE WHO ARE LIVING

AND THOSE WHO HAVE

' RIDDEN THE STORK '

Books That Live
The Norton imprint on a book means that in the publisher's
estimation it is a book not for a single season but for the years.
W. W. Norton & Company, Inc.
2 3 4 5 6 7 8 9

CONTENTS

INTRODUCTION

W<small>HEN I SIT</small> quiet and alone my thoughts drift back
to my childhood. Sometimes I find that the recollection
of some delightful happening has made me smile ; sometimes the memory of some less happy one brings a saddened
feeling to my heart, as though the untoward event were
really taking place now.

It would be nice to claim that my childhood was typical.
But China is a huge country ; habits and customs in it
differ widely from place to place, and naturally the lives
of individuals differ too. Not all Chinese families, for
example, are, as is often believed, very numerous. Some
consist only of husband, wife and perhaps one child ;
others comprise as many as thirty or forty people living
under one roof. I, as it happens, was brought up in one
of the big families ; but I well remember how the stories
of my home which I told to my classmates in school and
college proved interesting to them because so many of
them had no experience of life in a large family.

I was an orphan, and I still have not forgotten my
feeling of loneliness when my cousins ran to their parents
to be comforted and petted. I see myself, a shy, uncom-
plaining, somewhat discouraged child, standing aloof from
these scenes of companionship, and the memory is still
bitter-sweet. But as a rule I was happy.

Change, however, puzzled me. I remember asking
my grandmother why something I had known or seen
before should be different, and she told me never to expect
anything to happen twice in exactly the same way. How
right she was ! I like to think that she knows that I am
now in a foreign land, and would feel neither surprise nor

regret at that change, too : though, were she alive, I do not know whether or not I should be here. What inscrutable purposes does the God of Change pursue? No one can say ; and probably I shall have many more changes to face before I join my grandmother.

Is it a good thing to dwell on the past? During the six years I have spent in England I have often heard praises of ' the old days ' and grumblings about the present. Many of my friends have argued that I ought to look more at the future and spend less time in thoughts of the past. ' This,' they say, ' is the Twentieth Century and a time of Progress.' But actually I do not dislike change. I take pleasure in watching one thing develop into another and in speculating about its future. But I do not always consider the new better than the old. And in regard to childhood, it is certain that nothing can replace *that* happiness, which it is surely sometimes sweet to recall.

This record of my childhood is neither chronological nor systematic. If I had tried to make it so, much of it would not have been comprehensible to Westerners. As it is, many of the details will seem very strange and curious. I have confined myself to the years between five and fifteen, when I was one of the family and had little concern with outside affairs. I am glad and proud to possess these recollections, for I am a conservative and obstinate person, and I believe that in spite of rapid and, alas ! often now catastrophic changes, Chinese life remains essentially the same. China has been changing for five thousand years, but whereas in the past the changes were as imperceptible as the seasons, now they seem to take place ' while you wait '. It is a matter of speed, that is all.

MY BIRTHPLACE

I WAS BORN in Kiu-kiang. It is a comparatively small district of the province of Kiangsi, but since the Later Han period (250 B.C. to A.D. 219) it has been the scene of many important historical events. The celebrated young general, Chou Yu of the Wu kingdom, made the capital city of the district his headquarters, and a lane was named after his beautiful wife, Hsiao Chiao, younger cousin of the wife of the Emperor Chao Lieh of Shu (about A.D. 199 to 256). Kiu-kiang has been connected with nearly all the changes of dynasty in our history. This is because of its position. The Yangtse River lies to the west, the famous Lu mountain to the south, and a little farther down on the south-east is Lake P'oyang, one of the five biggest lakes of China. The founder and first emperor of the Ming dynasty (A.D. 1369–1643) fought many fierce battles around this place, traces of which, I believe, are still to be seen on Lu mountain ; but I have never tried to remember events connected with war and I have not bothered to see these traces.

To me the most interesting aspect of the place has always been its associations with famous Chinese poets and painters. I cannot record them all here, but I would like just to mention the names of a few who hold important positions in our literature and art and whose works are known to some extent in the West.

Tao Chien -of Ch'in dynasty (A.D. 265–419), many of whose poems have been translated into English and other languages, was born in the south-west corner of Lu mountain. I am not attempting to compare myself with him but merely to identify the district for my Western readers when I say that this is only fifteen miles from the house where I was born. Tao Chien was a thorough-going hermit and a poet of Nature. He admired and wrote about nothing except mountain scenery, the flowers of the chrysanthemum, and wine. It is due to his love of the chrysanthemum that this flower has ever since been called the hermit of flowers. We think that a hermit must possess a very strong character to be able to stand aloof from the vulgar vanity of society, and the chrysanthemum does not compete in colour and fashion with other flowers which bloom in the spring, but blossoms alone in the frosty autumn. We give the poet's name to the wild species of chrysanthemum which grows in the hedges of the river-banks and on the hills. Once Tao Chien was appointed to be the governor of the Peng-Tsê district. Upon being told to perform a certain ceremony of etiquette due from one of lower rank to his superior, he asked why he should bend his chest to earn a few pecks of rice, and promptly hung his seal of office on a central beam and ran away. In spite of his great poverty he enjoyed his cups to the full and wrote many poems about his easy life. He never entertained his friends, but if wine was provided he would come and sit among them just to drink it. When the wine was finished he would leave them without a word. He called himself Mr. Five Willows, because in front of his house there stood five such trees. He wrote of himself that he liked reading but did not try very hard to understand what he read—a statement which has since been quoted by thousands of students in excuse to their teachers! I too must plead guilty!

Another poet who came and went in this neighbourhood is Li P'o of T'ang dynasty (A.D. 618–905). Many of his famous poems describe the beauty of the waterfalls on Lu mountain. Su Tung P'o of Sung dynasty (A.D. 960–1276), too, must not be forgotten in connexion with Kiu-kiang,

because two lines of one of his poems have become pro-
verbial among literary circles : ' I cannot discern the true
features of Lu mountain, because I myself am always
engulfed in the mountain.'

P'o Chu-I, who lived later than Li P'o and earlier than
Su Tung P'o, has won our hearts by his ' Song of the
Guitar '. It was written after he had heard, while escorting
one of his friends along the river-bank, the sound of a
guitar from a junk. He was at this time Governor of
Kiu-kiang and several other districts. On learning from
the lady who was playing the guitar how in her youth she
had been famed for her beauty and admired by many a
young man, but when she became old and lost her youthful
charm had married an elderly business man who was always
away from her and had no thought of love, the poet was
reminded of how he had formerly been an officer at the
Emperor's court but was now far from the capital, having
lost the Emperor's favour. The feeling of the whole song
is very melancholy. The particular spot on the river-bank
at which the meeting between the poet and the lady took
place can still be pointed out by the natives of the city,
although for many years now a railway station has occupied
the site. Some time after the poet's death a bower with
the name ' Guitar ' was built near the spot in memory of
him. The meeting took place nearly a thousand years ago.
When I took office in the local government of the district
I gathered a group of workmen to repaint the bower. My
position and duty bore no comparison with those of P'o
Chu-I, but many of my friends still like to address me
by his official title, ' Master of Horses of Chiang Chou ',
because it sounds more poetical than the modern title of
the office.

A mountain admired by so many great poets for thousands
of years could hardly escape the attention of painters also.
Ku Kai-Ch'ih of the fourth century mentions the beauty of
Lu mountain in his writings on painting, but none of his
own landscape paintings is in existence. The very valuable

picture, ' A Snow Scene on Lu Mountain ' by Ching Hao
of the ' Five Dynasties ' (A.D. 905–960), is, however, still
in existence. Two other well-known landscapes of the
mountain, one by Sheng Chou of Ming dynasty (A.D. 1369–
1643) and the other by Kao Chi-Pei of Ch'ing dynasty
(A.D. 1644–1911), were shown at the International Exhibition of Chinese Art at Burlington House, 1935–6. These
details will give my readers some idea of the wealth of
artistic associations possessed by my birthplace.

I was born in the midst of the small city on the south
bank of the Yangtse River. Though I was not taken to
visit Lu mountain until I was fourteen years of age, I had
actually lived near the foot of it for a time, during the
Revolution of 1912 which changed China into a republic.
Countless times I walked along the river-bank, which I
could reach in less than a quarter of an hour from my
house. (If I walked the journey in the English manner it
would take five minutes exactly !) From the bank I could
see sails of all sizes. In windy weather they floated
picturesquely on the wrinkled surface of the water in a
way that I have seen nowhere else. The colour of the
Yangtse water is yellow, owing to the myriad particles
of fine sand which it carries. It is always milky, never
clear.

About twenty miles below the city lies Lake P'oyang.
The junction of river and lake is very interesting, the two
running together in straight lines as if divided by a knife.
The colour of the lake water is a very deep blue. Also
outside the south gate of the city wall lies a small but
beautiful lake called Kan-T'ang, divided into two by a
willow bank and a stone bridge. The description of its
beauty, which is very great, I will leave, however, till later,
when I come to mention some incidents which happened
to me there.

Nothing very particular is produced in the district of
Kiu-kiang, but many important things are exported from
its port. among them porcelain, cotton, tea, and China-

grass linen. Any Westerner who has been in Kiu-kiang will remember having bought porcelain on the ship or in the street. Though the city is very small, with only one main street, a portion of it is wholly lined with porcelain shops. This is because Ching-Tê-Chên, the place where every kind of Chinese porcelain has been manufactured since Han times, lies only a little more than fifteen miles from Kiu-kiang. All its products have for centuries been sent through Kiu-kiang to every part of the Chinese empire and the world.

Before I matriculated and went to college at Nanking I

OLD CITY WALL OF KIU-KIANG

had really no idea that there could be other places as beautiful as Kiu-kiang. A Chinese saying goes, ' All parents think their own child better than others,' and I am inclined to think that no person is not emotionally attached to his birthplace. I cannot remember exactly what the city looked like before the Revolution of 1912, but I was always told by my elders that, except for some Western buildings erected along a part of the river-bank after it was opened to Western nations as a Treaty Port, Kiu-kiang was not much changed. The old city was surrounded by a wall, and I spent many a joyful hour walking along the top of it, looking down into the courtyards of houses and at their exteriors, with the vast view of the illimitable river and the great mountain ranges on the other side. The wall was pulled down as useless about 1923, but I like occasionally to dream that I am walking there again.

FLOWER SELLER

2

THE CHIANG FAMILY

On the New Year's Eve of my twelfth year, immediately after the ceremony and the festival dinner (which I shall describe in a later chapter), my father called me into his study and sent me to ask my grandfather whether I might be shown the family clan book. It is traditional in China for a child to be told, on reaching a certain age, something of the history of his family. The age differs from family to family but is rarely under ten. My grandfather gave his consent, and as my grandmother expressed a wish to be present at the event, my father thought it best to exhibit the clan book in the central hall, where our ancestral shrine stood, so that all the members of the household could attend if they desired. Except for those who were too young, they all came ; for my father possessed great charm of manner and an excellent gift of story-telling. A painter by calling, he lived quite in his own way and seldom mingled with the other members of the family. In China an artist or scholar holds a privileged position and is not obliged to conform, as are others, to every domestic regulation. When my father did join in family gatherings his company was invariably appreciated by all.

It was a memorable evening. All the lanterns in the hall were lit, and my father, after changing his dress and burning incense at the ancestral shrine, climbed up a ladder and took down very respectfully the wooden case in which the clan books were kept. There were thirty or forty volumes. He put them on the square table specially placed in the middle of the hall. Grandmother sat with a screen behind her in her usual dignified seat under the shrine. Grandfather was not present; he was tired and feeling his age. All the rest of the family—perhaps twenty persons—sat around the walls of the hall. My father seated himself at the table, with me standing on his right hand and two cousins, one a girl only two months older than me, the other a boy eight months younger, on his left. We could all three read a little of the classics and it was time for us to be initiated into the mysteries of the clan book. We were

CENTRAL HALL WITH AN ANCESTRAL SHRINE ON THE TOP

wearing our new silk robes, as was usual on New Year's Eve. I had a blue satin jacket without sleeves, a garment called *Pei Hsin* in Chinese, over my red gown. At that time I did not understand that this jacket was not so dignified as the one *with* sleeves, called *Ma Kua* and usually made of black silk; I liked the blue colour and had no thought for its significance. We were offered seats but we preferred to stand in order to see the words in the book.

Father passed quickly over the first few pages, which I know now were an introduction or preface written by

some well-known person at the time when that edition of
the clan book was printed, but he raised his voice and made
a gesture of respect when the first name appeared. ' This,'
he said, ' so far as the records show, was our first ancestor.'
He did not speak the name, ' Hsu ', because it is not customary in China for a person to address or speak of an elder
by name; he called him ' Yuan-ching Kung '. Yuan-
ching was another name of our first ancestor, and Kung
a respectful term used in referring to elders. Actually the
first ancestor's full name was ' Chiang Hsu, also named
Yuan-ching '. No member of my generation would be
permitted to name him thus, and I only do so here to
make the matter clear to my readers. ' Yuan-ching Kung
lived,' continued Father, ' at the end of the first century
B.C. and was appointed by the Emperor Ai government-
inspector and Governor of Yen Chou (a place bigger than
the modern province). Unfortunately, this Emperor did
not reign very long (6–2 B.C.) and there was a great
disturbance in the time of his successor, when Wang
Mang, a powerful minister, made himself regent for the
boy-emperor. Yuan-ching Kung did not approve of
Wang's action. He resigned his post, owing to ill health,
and went back to his native place, "Tu Ling" (a place
near the modern capital city of Shensi province which,
in the Han dynasty, was Chang-An, the capital of China).
Yuan-ching Kung kept to the confines of his own house,
in front of which he made three footpaths through a
bamboo grove. Except for occasional visits to his two
intimate friends, Chiu Chung and Yang Chung, he met
nobody. One footpath he followed when he went to see
his friends, the other two footpaths were used by his friends
when visiting him. As they all became hermits their for-
gathering came to be a symbol of a poetic function; and
the name of " Three Footpaths " is often alluded to in later
literature in reference to our Yuan-ching Kung. He was
an upright and sincere man. His name was often mentioned
in the capital when he held office, and this caused the

unrighteous minister Wang Mang to be afraid of him and to try to do him injustice. Knowing he was no match for Wang, Yuan-ching Kung decided to become a farmer and desired all his offspring, too, to devote themselves to the cultivation of the fields. None of his literary works in book form has remained, but the rule he made for his family is printed in large characters in the clan book. It consists of only four words : " Benevolence ", " Righteousness ", " Sincerity ", and " Endurance ". He commanded that each member of the family should be trained in these four qualities. Since then our family has always been called " The Hall of Three Footpaths ".'

At this point my father paused, and a cup of tea was handed to him by one of our servants. We all had something to eat and drink, my cousins and I preferring cake to tea. I pondered what Father had been saying. He had explained that before Yuan-ching Kung's time there were no records of ancestors in our family. But according to the early history of China, one of the sons of Duke Chou, brother of the Emperor Wu Wang (1134–1120 B.C.), was made prince of a State called Chiang, and the descendants of this prince used the name of the State for that of the family. As time went on the family became scattered all over the kingdom. That is why there are to-day so many Chiang families in existence.

According to the clan book, Yuan-ching Kung had three sons and two daughters. The sons were all excellent farmers and made the family prosper and increase. The two daughters married farmers and brought up their children according to our family rule.

Turning page after page my father remarked on this and that ancestor, until he came to a page over which he sighed deeply. The time was the end of the Sung dynasty (A.D. 960–1276), when the Mongols were a scourge in the north of China, and there was also a serious epidemic in that region. Our ancestors decided to sell the land and move to the centre of China. That was how the family came to settle in Kiu-kiang. For a very long time they lived and farmed on the north side of the Yangtse River, the community growing until the members numbered thousands. Splitting up, they built many houses close to each other, forming a village all the inhabitants of which shared the family name of ' Chiang '. They subscribed and collected money to build a big ancestral temple, and a school which we call *I-Hsueh* of the Chiang family, in which all the children were educated. Then a member of the forty-seventh generation bought land on the south side of the river, where the modern city lies. As he had business in the city which occupied most of his time, he built a house on the south side and only crossed the river once a year to pay tribute to the ancestral temple. His house was considered an offshoot of the original Chiang family and a temporary shelter to facilitate business. Whether temporary or not, every dwelling should have an ancestral shrine so that tribute can be paid twice a month according to custom. My father went on to say that this temporary house was the one in which we were living. According to the records it had had fewer rooms at first, most of the space being devoted to the garden. Now the house had sheltered more than ten generations.

Continuing his story to the present generation, my father pointed out how one of the fifty-first generation who did not follow the family rule as laid down by the first ancestor brought the family into disgrace. He was a youngest son, and being neglected, was always getting into difficulties. This reflected on the elders of the family, who were considered to have failed in their duty of bringing him up well ; each member of the family therefore shared the shame. ' Though I must not criticize my elders,' my father went on, ' I think our grandmother would like all of you to know this fact, so long as you remember the proverb which says that the private shame of a family should not be made known to outsiders.' (Even as I write this I feel disloyal, though I address people of a different culture who will think none the worse of my family for the misdeeds of a remote ancestor !)   At last my cousins' names and mine appeared.   I was so excited and proud of being printed in the clan book that I moved nearer to Father's seat to have a good look at my own name.   There it was, with only the date of my birth beside it.   Father told me to step back again.   He said that my name was added when I was about three years old.   The latest volume of our clan book was reprinted every three years in order to keep it up to date.   The whole clan book was reprinted every ten years, so that each new branch of the family might acquire a copy of it.   The setting and printing were done entirely by members of the family and the whole set of woodblocks was kept in the ancestral temple.   Father indicated that in the coming autumn he would take us across the river to pay our first tribute at the ancestral temple.

After he had finished his recital we all had our New Year's Eve fun.   There were at that time in all more than fifty people, including a few servants, living in the house. No confusion existed in addressing one another, for we have special terms for elders and youngsters : *Pai* for Father's elder brother ;   *Shu* for his younger brother ; *Pai-mu*, wife of Father's elder brother ; *Shen*, wife of Father's younger brother ;   *Ku*, Father's sister ;   *Yi*, Mother's sister ; *Kê*, elder brother ;   *Ti*, younger brother ;   *Chieh*, elder sister ;   *Mei*, younger sister ;   *Sao*, brother's wife, &c. ·We address each other by the number of our position in the generation.   Those above my generation address me by the family name.   But those in the same generation I would address as ' The third *Kê* ' or ' The seventh *Mei* '.   Boys and girls are numbered in their own sex.   Thus I am the third and youngest son of my parents, the sixth in the boy group and the fifteenth in the whole generation.   My father's generation numbered eleven.   My youngest uncle was only one year older than me, and though he studied and played with us he was entitled to the respect and privileges of his generation.

As ours was not a wealthy family the elder members were kept very busy. There was not a special servant attached to each room in the house, as in most big Chinese families. The elder girls had to help their mothers with cleaning and washing, and the boys did some work for their fathers too. Any elder could order any younger member to do something for him, but it was not often that this right was implemented. Probably at that time my family could have afforded more servants than it had, but it was my grandmother's policy to make every one work to a certain extent. At festival times or on other important occasions the family joined hands with the servants. My memory of my grandmother, as she was in the days before I left home for college at Nanking, is that of a perpetually busy old lady, ever mindful of the family affairs and honour.

BASKET SELLER

3

THE HALL OF THREE FOOTPATHS

Every branch of the Chiang family bears the name 'The Hall of Three Footpaths'. In the house where I lived hung a big rectangular board on which a popular calligrapher, Liu Yun-chiao, had at some time written three large characters, *San Ching T'ang*, the equivalent of the name. The board hung on the central beam of the last hall, where the ancestral shrine was situated.

On the front gate of the house we hung every night a round oil-paper lantern. The same three characters were painted on it but in a much smaller size. And a number of small hand-lanterns bearing the same characters on one side were always ready for use at night, and a pair of large cylindrical lanterns with painted stands for special occasions. On festival days or for marriage ceremonies the lanterns would be red in colour with the three characters in gold. For a funeral ceremony the lantern was pure white with the characters in blue. I remember well how I tried to keep on friendly terms with the servants so that I could be allowed to light the candles in the lanterns. This was one of my special joys. I became very fond, too, of the open fire after my grandfather had told me that 'Fire' was the patriarch of our civilization and described how the Emperor Sui-Jen of more than five thousand years before had discovered how to strike fire from wood and taught the Chinese to cook food.

I never asked exactly when and how our house was built, but I think I can describe what it is like. We do not measure our houses by height (for they are of one storey only), but by 'depth' or area. Our house has three big square courtyards, called *T'ien Ching* or 'sky-wells', in the middle, with a hall between each. The halls, which

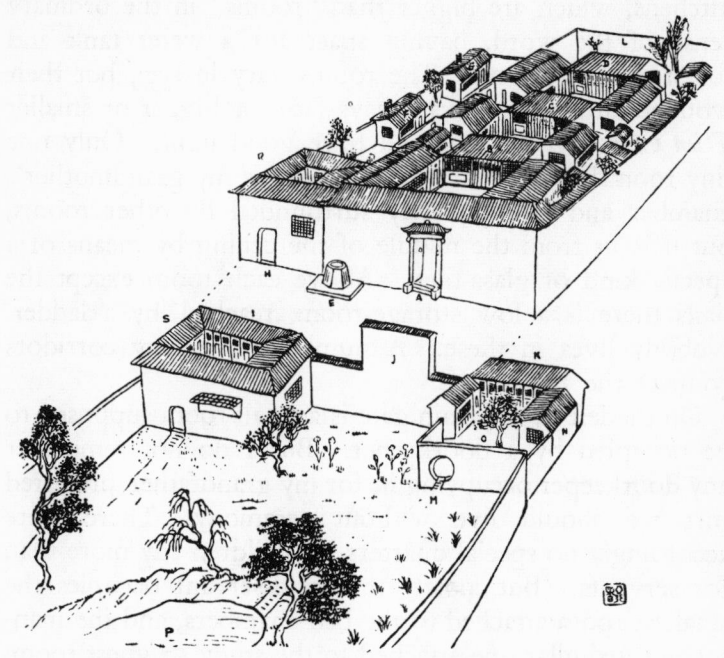

SKETCH PLAN OF THE HALL OF THREE FOOTPATHS

A.	MAIN ENTRANCE	L.	BACK GARDEN
B, C, D.	FIRST, SECOND AND THIRD HALLS	M.	MOON-GATE FROM SCHOOL TO GARDEN
E.	FAMILY WELL	N.	STORE FOR COFFINS
F, G.	TWO KITCHENS	O.	" TSENG " TREE
H.	SIDE DOOR	P.	POND
I.	ANOTHER DOOR (NOT VISIBLE IN SKETCH)	R.	FOURTH GREAT-UNCLE'S QUARTERS
J.	HIGH SCREEN-WALL	S.	THIRD GREAT-UNCLE'S QUARTERS
K.	ANOTHER DOOR (NOT VISIBLE IN SKETCH)		

THE DOTTED LINES CROSS THE ROAD WHICH BECAME KNOWN AS CHIANG'S LANE.

are extremely high, are supported on huge round wooden pillars cut from trees on Lu mountain. On both sides of each hall are suites of four large rooms always occupied by the elders of the family. To the right and left of these rooms are three further rooms. The arrangement might seem to be symmetrical but actually it is not so. In all there are about forty-two rooms, excluding the two kitchens, which are bigger than ' rooms ' in the ordinary sense of the word, having space for a water tank and for storing firewood. The rooms vary in size, but their wooden lattice windows always face the bigger or smaller *T'ien Ching*, so that they all have good light. Only one tiny room has no windows. It adjoins my grandmother's chamber and is completely surrounded by other rooms, but it is lit from the middle of the ceiling by means of a special kind of glass-tiles. Above each room except the halls there is a low storage-room, reached by a ladder. Nobody lives in these. A number of narrow corridors connect the rooms.

On the left of the main gate is a small room supposed to be occupied by a doorkeeper. But I do not remember any doorkeeper occupying it, for my grandfather preferred that we should live without ceremony. There were accordingly no special quarters for children any more than for servants. But mostly the maid-servant occupies the smallest room attached to the bed-chambers, and the man-servant a similar one attached to the study or guest-room.

At the front and back of each hall are screen-like doors divided into eight parts on each side. The upper half of each of the front eight has a design in wooden lattice-work which we paste over with thin paper ; the lower half is of plain wood. The middle four doors of the back eight are always closed on ordinary days. In front of these stands a long narrow shelf used as a mantel, with a square table beneath. On the shelf are ornaments such as a table-screen, a porcelain figure or a piece of *Yu-I* made of jade or wood, and a big flower vase. Two big chairs stand on either side of the table. Above the mantel-shelf hangs a picture with two pieces of calligraphy to right and left of it. These pieces we call *Tui-Tzu*. The picture in the middle is a landscape—a peony and birds, a stork and pines, the subject changing according to season, the peach blossoms and swallows of spring giving way to the lotus and kingfisher of summer, the chrysanthemums of autumn, and the winter-plum of winter.   It is not necessary to change the picture, but as my grandfather had in his younger days been a keen collector of paintings, and as my father was a painter himself, we had always plenty of pictures to choose from.   Indeed, my father liked to find a suitable subject for each month ; and it was a matter of pride to me that I was always called upon to do the business

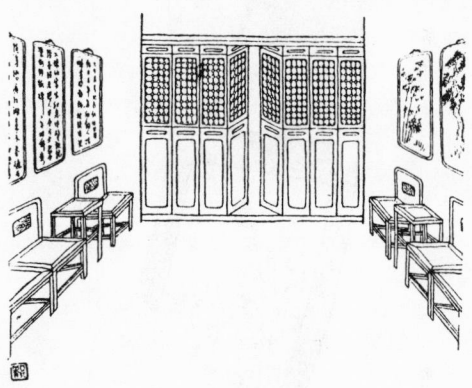

SCREEN-LIKE DOORS

of unrolling and rolling the pictures.   At first I was too small to be able to get them straight, and I had then the care of the boxes in which they were kept.   Father never asked any other of my generation or any of the servants to help him on these occasions, and the recollection of this distinction still brings a glow to me.

On the two walls of each hall there hang four pictures of the same size and four similar pieces of calligraphy.   In my house the pictures are always on the right and the calligraphy on the left.   There may have been a reason for this arrangement, but I do not know it.

A small landscape by a friend of Father's was hung in Grandfather's room, and a small flower-painting by Father in Grandmother's chamber. My sister had four small flower-and-bird paintings by Father. My brother preferred calligraphy in his study, and I remember him explaining to Father that he could not bear a brightly coloured flower-painting in his room because his young friends would laugh at him and accuse him of effeminacy, since flower-paintings were always hung in ladies' chambers. My father smiled.

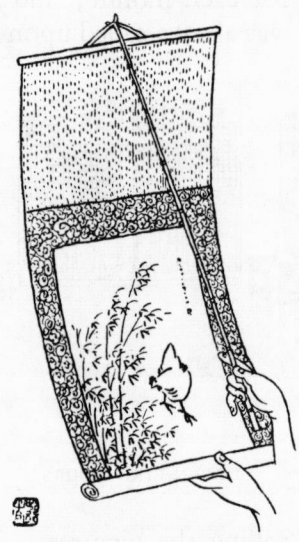

HANGING A PICTURE

My father was always busy making changes in the arrangement of his study. Occasionally he hung there one or two of the best works of well-known masters, but seldom any of his own among them. He might perhaps hang one or two of his paintings, but generally he quickly became dissatisfied even with these and took them down again.

Two guest-rooms were used for the closer friends of the family or for those who came on particular business. Visitors who came by introduction or were merely nodding acquaintances were generally received by the elders in the first front hall. In each hall there are eight chairs and four small tables, arranged symmetrically on either side, close to the walls, under the pictures and calligraphy. They are all arranged in the same way. In the middle of the first two halls is a space which can be occupied at festival times by four square dinner tables ; the last hall can contain five tables. Each table can seat eight people, two on either side, and some of them are made to fold up. On festive occasions all the eight parts of the screen-like doors were taken off, and the whole depth of the halls and sky-wells was revealed from the main gate. They are taken off in summer, too, to give more light and air.

Two big earthenware jars, four or five feet in diameter at the mouth and three feet high, stand in the middle of the two central sky-wells. They contain goldfish, and I remember how I used to bother my grandmother and my sister to lift me up to look at them. No grass grew in these sky-wells, which were paved with regular limestone blocks. At each corner were small round holes through which the rainwater could drain away. My father wanted to beautify even these holes, and he made three designs of a tortoise, a frog and a crab, and asked a stone-mason to carve them for him to the right size. He chose these three animals because their broad backs covered the holes while the water drained away between their legs. These designs were copied for the same purpose in Mother's own family and afterwards in my sister's family too. Once they were in position the elders soon forgot them, but they provided a perpetual source of entertainment for us youngsters. In other small sky-wells grew various plants, dwarf bamboos, palm trees, and many kinds of flowers in season.

To the right of the main house stood a smaller house, consisting of a little hall with two rooms on either side. My third great-uncle lived here. A similar cottage or lodge, just opposite, sheltered my fourth great-uncle's children. Attached to this cottage there was, oddly enough, a very big front garden, originally directly connected

with the main house and only cut off from it by my grandfather to allow of the passage of a thoroughfare. This
meant that in front of the main gate there was a well-
paved space where we youngsters could play. Only a
very low brick wall faced the main gate, so that, standing
at the gate, we could obtain a splendid view of the distant
blue range of Lu mountain. Unfortunately, some one
later bought the piece of land on the other side of our
front garden and erected a modernized three-storey
building which destroyed our view, thus, according to the
local theory of geomancy, jeopardizing the prosperity of
our family. To counteract this a very high brick screen-
wall was erected in place of the low one. On the upper
part of this screen-wall the workmen with their usual talent
wrought in bas relief some landscapes and some representa-
tions of popular stories about the three kingdoms—a
period just a little later than that of our first ancestor. In
the very middle my third great-uncle asked a popular calligrapher of the city to write one big character, *Fu*, which
means ' Happiness '. Carved on the central stone opposite
the main gate, it caused each of us as we came out to
face happiness !

To the left of the screen-wall stood a small house with
a hall and two large rooms which was built to be the
family school. I was not taken there till I was five years
of age, and although I did not begin really to learn anything until I was six, I loved to listen to the older children
chanting and reciting the classics. The central wall contained a small shrine for the written image of Confucius.
Our tutor occupied the two rooms. In front of the hall
was a small garden—one might call it another type of
courtyard—a part, actually, of the main front garden and
cut off from it only by a short wall. A moon-gate led to
the garden proper. A large thorny tree, called a *Tseng*,
belonging to the orange group, which grew in this little
garden, will always remain in my memory. None of
my cousins will forget it either, for it could be seen

from our desks in the hall, and our eyes were always fixed on it while we recited the classics to our tutor, especially if the recitation were difficult. It gave shade in the heat of summer, and when the tutor allowed us a little rest we would sit or play under it. It blossomed towards the end of May and was covered with tiny white flowers with a yellow spot in the middle, in shape like almond blossom but grouped more like the blossoms of the pear. When the petals fell it was our duty to sweep them away and bury them. This was our tutor's order, and we liked nothing better. A high wind would bring down thousands of the tiny fruits as well as the blossoms, and we always longed to finish our lessons so that we could pick them up and vie with each other in collecting the largest number. We used them for all sorts of games, such as making beads, throwing them to each other as snowballs, counting scores, and so on. And although the tree was full of thorns, the bolder of my cousins would climb up the trunk and try to beat down the fruits, which, as they grew larger and larger, turned greenish-yellow and then yellowish-brown in colour. They were no good for eating as they had not the quality of an orange and their juice was very sour. We used them as ornaments on our mantelpieces. About two or three hundred fruits matured every year and Grandmother used to distribute them as presents to our relatives, if possible with a few leaves still attached.

At the back of the main house was another garden, but smaller than the front garden and possessing no round pond. I was told that the water of the pond in the front garden ran through the main drainage of the High Street to the Yangtse River. For making tea, water from the river or from the mountain streams had to be bought every day, the water from our own well being unfit for making good tea. The well, however, supplied enough water for other daily uses. Originally it was situated inside the house, close to the kitchen, but Grandfather thought that we should let other people share its water, and it was resunk outside the house. This concession was a great convenience to our neighbours, but it made our own servants grumble incessantly, especially in summer when every family needed more water than usual and the well dried up for a short time. Grandmother suggested that we could draw our water late at night, but no servant liked this idea. They asked the elders to let them restrict the use of the well in summer-time for at least two hours every day. An iron was fitted to go through the well super-structure, but it vanished mysteriously and thick cords had to be substituted and a watch kept. Sometimes I was given the job of watching. But though my mind was determined and my heart hardened, when I faced a number of our neighbours waiting, bucket in hand, for water, I never could resist undoing the knot. Ultimately I was discovered and the servants lost faith in me as a watchman. I felt we ought to help others if we could, but logically I had not a leg to stand on.

MOUNTAIN WATER SELLER

AN UNSPOKEN DECREE

It was a new maid-servant, who up to the time that she took service with us had lived all her life in the country, who was the means of revealing the unspoken decree to us youngsters. She was very young and only helped occasionally with the washing and cleaning; she was employed chiefly to do shopping. She always spent a considerable time on her expeditions to the shops, for she found everything in the city strange and interesting. On her return she would tell us in her naïve way what she had seen. We naturally encouraged her to do so, for our elders did not go out much and we boys were not allowed outside the garden until we reached the age of ten, so that the city was interesting to us too.

One afternoon she came back full of excitement. I must have been about six years old at the time. It was the year 1909, when the Emperor Kuang Hsi, unofficially arrested by the Empress Dowager Tsu Hsi, died. As soon as school was over we gathered in the second hall, and as the grandparents lived in the third hall and the other elders were busy in their studies or boudoirs, our talk was not interrupted. First she described how she had seen a group of people standing in front of a *Tao-Tai Yamen*, a residence in which lived an official controlling ten districts, with his family and staff. The official was, as was usual at that time, a Manchurian, a member of the 'royal race'. Wondering what the people were doing there, our maid joined them. They were all gazing at the strange costumes and curious coiffure of the family of the Manchurian official. She then went on to tell us that one of the ladies wore a huge cap with two big artificial flowers on each side, and a brightly embroidered satin robe of peach-blossom colour. Another wore a deep green robe, and the third was a maid with a large silver hair-pin fastened in her hair in a most peculiar way. These details interested the girls more than the boys, and I remember that what I wanted to know was whether the faces of these curious people looked exactly like ours and whether they spoke the same language. I was too young to ask any other questions. I had often heard my elders discussing the Manchurians privately, but whenever I inquired the meaning of 'Chi Jen', which was the name by which we knew them, I was always stopped and ordered not to utter the words again. The maid, however, talked very freely and some of the older girls joined in, saying that they knew there were many more Chi Jen in Peking and that their habits were different from ours. I was very puzzled. Presently Grandmother came out of her chamber and approached us. Speaking sharply to the maid she said: 'Who are you that you should make such a noise here? Be off to your work!' And when the maid had gone, she went on to explain to my elder cousins that she did not like them to talk about the 'Chi Jen' and commanded all of us not to mention the subject again. Then she swept back into her chamber. We all felt downcast. Later I heard from my sister, who was nine years older than I, that it was only through Grandmother's pleading that the maid was allowed to stay on in our house, for Grandfather objected so strongly to the mention of Manchurians in the house that he wanted to dismiss the maid. That was the unspoken decree—not to mention the Manchurians!

MANCHURIAN HAIR-
DRESSING

Grandfather was about seventy-four at this time, and as a rule kept aloof from family affairs. His chamber was more or less isolated from the rest of the house, and he had a small sky-well of his own where he could hang his caged-birds on the trees. He was always good-humoured and very fond of his grandchildren, and I, being a favourite of his, played in his quarters more often than the others of my age. After the maid episode I did not dare to go there for some time. I had begun to realize his nature and to think that he might not like me to play, an idea which had never entered my head before. But I soon forgot the matter and went to play there as usual.

It was only three years later that China became a republic. By that time I had grown to realize that Grandfather's antipathy to the Manchurians was on account of their having overthrown the Ming dynasty in 1643! Though China had been ruled by the Manchus for more than two hundred years before his time, he still believed strongly that we should be ruled by our own race. He knew the history of the Ming dynasty in detail and had read a great deal about the sufferings of the real Chinese at the hands of the Manchus. Not that he had anything against Manchurians as human beings, but he resented the fact that an 'outside' tribe, untrained in our culture, should rule us and especially that the first emperor of the Manchu dynasty should have given every kind of privilege to the Manchurians. As members of the royal race, any Manchurian could claim support from the Government, and the most illiterate were often appointed to high positions as local governors. This upset the Chinese more than anything. As years went on the position was aggravated by the degeneration of the Manchurians, who came to rely entirely on the Chinese and to lose altogether their native language and habits. The Chinese naturally wished to get rid of them, and in Grandfather's lifetime there were many riots. My grandfather resolved never to have anything to do with Manchurians, and he often lamented that the great statesman Tseng Kuo-fan of Hunan had not made himself emperor of the Chinese empire after quenching the Tai-

p'ing Rebellion (1850–64). Grandfather was never a republican, but he preferred a republic to the degenerate
Manchurians.

I do not remember all that he told us in those days,
but one particular story lingers in my mind. He said that
the Emperor Chien Lung (1736–94) was of pure Chinese
blood and this is how he established the fact. When the
wife of the Emperor Yung Cheng (1723–34) was about to
give birth to her first child, she was afraid that if it was a
girl—who would not of course be able to succeed to the
throne—she should lose power. She had been very good
to the wife of a court minister named Chen, a Chinese of
Chekiang province, and when this woman bore a son two
days before the Empress expected her own baby, the
Empress saw a way out of her possible difficulty. Actually
the Empress was delivered of a girl, but arrangements had
been made with the royal doctors, court ladies and eunuchs,
and the Emperor was informed of the birth of a son. At
once two court ladies and two eunuchs were sent to the
house of Chen with the message that the Empress desired
to see the three-days-old baby. Strange as was the demand
it implied a great honour and the Chen family had no
alternative but to allow their baby to be taken to the palace.
Later they received in exchange the royal baby girl. As
the imperial family exercised supreme power in those days
no one was allowed to criticize them, upon pain of death.
The Chen family knew this only too well and kept silent.
But not long afterwards Chen was sentenced to death on
some pretext, and his wife and child too were not spared.
The court ladies, eunuchs and doctors involved in the plot
suffered a like fate. All this at the instigation of the
Empress. Probably the Emperor Yung Cheng never discovered the secret. When the ' son ', the Emperor Chien
Lung, had been on the throne some time he seemed to get
wind of the secret from some source, for he made several
trips from Peking to tour the south country, chiefly in
the provinces Kiangsu and Chekiang, a procedure that

had very seldom been followed by preceding emperors. According to my grandfather, Chien Lung was a great lover of beautiful scenery, and his tours in the south were partly for this reason and partly for the purpose of investigating his connexion with the Chen family, which of course had never been officially disclosed. Many stories exist of Chien Lung's wanderings in the south. It is said, for example, that he once dressed himself like a poor student and tried to rent a small room in a country inn, where he had a romantic affair with the daughter of the inn-keeper. The importance for us of proving that Chien Lung was a true Chinese lies in the fact that we do not consider the Manchurians are a cultured race fit to rule over us. But Chien Lung distinguished himself in our art and literature and so must have been a Chinese inheriting the love of learning—that is the idea. This story as told by my grandfather caught my fancy and I have since read many stories and books about Chien Lung.

It was no doubt due to Grandfather's unspoken decree that we youngsters knew so little about the Manchurians. Grandfather always considered himself to be a man of the Ming régime. He wore a sort of Ming costume, different from what other people wore at that time, and gathered his hair on the top of his head instead of in the so-called pigtail. He did not enter for any examination for public life, but he read a great deal. He was more an historian than any other type of scholar. His chief concern was to mind his own business and be a good farmer and something of a hermit. But he did not prevent other members of the family from going into public life, or from behaving and dressing according to the custom of their time, so long as the word 'Manchurian' was not mentioned in the house. His *shou-i*, or 'funeral clothes', were made in Ming fashion to his special order, and he himself examined them very carefully. I saw them first when they were laid out in the courtyard for airing the summer before his death.

The *Tao-Tai Yamen*, where our new maid had seen

Manchurians, is very close to our house. We could see it from our main gate and could reach it in less than one minute, but I was not allowed to go there until I had reached a certain age. I remember once crying so loudly at this prohibition that Grandfather came out of his chamber. He smiled and said : ' Don't cry, my treasure. When you grow up you will become the official and live in that house. Don't cry.' Grandfather never called me by name but always *pao-pao*, which means ' treasure '. Strangely enough I did become the official of the district, and was the first man to convert that Yamen into the local governor's residence (1930); throughout the Manchu dynasty no native had been appointed local governor in his own birthplace. Even more strange is it that my elder brother should have succeeded me in office and have occupied the same residence (1933). His administration covered a much wider area than mine.

But now Grandfather has been dead for more than twenty years, and my brother, who joined the Revolution in its early days, died last year, and Kiu-kiang is in the hands of the invader. No words can express my feelings.

FRUIT SELLER

5

A 'BOY-STUDENT' OF SIXTY-TWO

As GRANDFATHER had no objection to members of the
family entering public life, my second great-uncle decided
to follow some official career. But he did not get very
far. He spent his whole life trying to pass the first district
examination, and at sixty-two he had not succeeded.

He died while I was still in the cradle, so I do not remember him, but in later years I heard constantly of his
efforts and of the zeal with which he devoted himself to
the Eight-Legs style of writing favoured in imperial quarters
at that time.

Grandfather had a sense of humour and seemed to find
life pleasant; he loved flowers, birds and, of course, his
grandchildren. My second great-uncle was a totally different type of man. He wore a solemn and severe expression
and seldom spoke to any one without quoting a sentence
or two from the Confucian classics. If the person addressed
knew nothing of the quotation he would at once put an
end to the conversation. He considered himself a very
strict and faithful disciple of Confucius. In his study were
to be found nothing but the classics and explanations of
the classics. On the wall hung four strips of red paper
with a Confucian saying on each :

'LOOK NOT AT WHAT IS CONTRARY TO PROPRIETY.'
'LISTEN NOT TO WHAT IS CONTRARY TO PROPRIETY.'
'SPEAK NOT WHAT IS CONTRARY TO PROPRIETY.'
'MAKE NO MOVEMENT WHICH IS CONTRARY TO PROPRIETY.'

He was rarely to be seen outside his study, being guided

by the proverb *Shou-pu-shih-chuan, tsu-pu-chu-hu* (' One whose hand is never without a book and whose feet never step out of the gate' is a real scholar). When he walked his eyes were always fixed straight in front of him, again in conformity with a proverb : *Mu-pu-hsieh-shih* (' One who never looks sideways' is a genuine gentleman). He was wont to be scornful of youngsters who acted contrary to his conception of a gentleman.

Once I was told by Grandfather that had this second great-uncle lived on and succeeded in his first examination the organization and behaviour of our household would have been quite different. But in Grandfather's opinion the great-uncle would not have made a good administrator even if he had succeeded in his further examinations and been appointed some kind of governor, because he knew only the words of Confucius' classics and had not grasped the ideas they expressed. ' He was a good eater,' he said, ' but not a good digester, so we always called him a *Shu-tai-tzu*' (which means a silly man knowing nothing but books). And Grandfather went on to explain that Confucius did not expound many of his ideas in detail, but simply urged the necessity of being a man first in order that one can adapt oneself to circumstances. We must know what a man should be before we can enter into the society of men. ' The second great-uncle was wrong,' added Grandfather, ' in wanting to practise every word of the classics without penetrating to the meaning. For instance, Confucius would not have approved that the eyes of his disciples should be fixed so straight ahead as to prevent their noticing the Master approaching on the right or left. Now, boys and girls, I am very pleased that you are all able to read classics, but I hope you will not *shih-erh-pu-hua* (" eat but not digest ").' My brother and sister listened attentively, but I, who was only just beginning to study the classics, did not understand Grandfather's words and remained very puzzled as to why my second great-uncle should have failed so repeatedly in his examination.

One afternoon when I was about ten years old, Father took me for a long walk to a place near the east gate of the city wall, where he pointed out the former *kao-peng*, or 'Examination shelter'. It had fallen into ruin after the revolution which removed the Manchu dynasty, and there was nothing to prevent us going in and looking round. The grass was so abundant and tall that it was hardly possible even to walk along the main stone-paved road. The residence of the examiner was no longer in existence except for a segment of broken wall. Fortunately, some parts of the long shelter still remained undamaged, and I remember that this building extended on either side of the residence. The row included many small rooms divided by a thick brick wall. In each room there was just enough space for a table, a chair and even a very small bed, but certainly not 'room to swing a cat'! For the three days of the examination the candidates occupied these rooms. But there was not sufficient accommodation for all, and Father told me that at examination times most of the small inns in the neighbourhood used to be full of candidates. They were allowed to bring a few reference books with them and they had to be ready at midnight. At 5 a.m. the official fire-gun was sounded three times from the residence of the examiner, and the candidates went to their cells. Then the main gate of the *kao-peng* was shut and nobody, not even the examiner, could go in or out for three days. The cells had no doors but the candidates were prevented from talking to one another by wooden bars across the front. I murmured to Father that they were worse off than prisoners (although at that time I had no idea what a prison was like)! But Father said that though they were very uncomfortable, they were respected by every one and, if they passed, had a higher position in society. I quite forget now how Father answered my questions about how the candidates ate, drank, slept, &c., but I remember re-marking finally that no one could write good essays under such conditions, and his giving in reply the proverb: ' If one can endure the bitterness of all bitternesses, one will become the man above all men.' I knew that he had himself never entered for the examination and that he was only encouraging me to endure the 'bitterness'!

From my grandmother I heard how busy my second great-aunt used to be when the examination period drew near each year, for at these times her husband would be diving deeper than ever into his books. As this elderly 'undergraduate' saw his thick beard growing longer and whiter, he may have wondered when people would cease to call him *Tung-sheng*, which means 'boy-student'. Those who sat for and failed to pass the district examination were called *Tung-sheng* because this first examination could be taken from the age of twelve! Having passed it, one was called *Hsiu-Ch'ai*. After passing the provincial examination one was called *Chu-Jen*, and after the palace examination, *Han-lin*. A Chinese proverb says, 'Age does not count in knowledge,' and certainly there were always great differences in the ages of the candidates for these examinations. Stories tell of fathers carrying their sons on their shoulders to the *kao-peng* to sit for the examination together. Sometimes a grandfather's name would appear on the honours list immediately after his grandson's. If a candidate failed twice he could change his career, but a number of people persisted in trying over and over again because a notable scholar always ranked before anybody else in society. My second great-uncle was one of those who persisted. But after his own failures he made up his mind not to encourage his sons to attempt the same course, and they all went into commerce. His fifth son, however—my seventh uncle—entered on one occasion with great-uncle. But he too failed.

Every time my great-uncle set out for the *kao-peng* the elder members of the family and their friends wished him success. And every time he came home having failed he confessed sadly that he was still a *Tung-sheng*. Only a few days before his death he wrote:

What secret of the Classics do I not know?
I, still a boy-student at sixty-two!

—which lines have been handed down in the family and are
familiar to all of us. I am glad that I was born too late
to sit for that type of examination!

FRESH DATES SELLER

6

A CURE FOR TOOTHACHE

My mother was so ill after I was born that she could not feed me, and I must have been a great worry to her during my babyhood. Cows' milk was at that time just known in Kiu-kiang as a possible food, but I always cried hard when a bowl of hot milk appeared. For this reason from my earliest days I came much under the eye of my third great-uncle.

I remember him well. A bearded man with a kind and smiling face, he was not married. Being a doctor, he was the health-warden of our family and of many other families in the district, and whenever I was not well I was taken to his quarters by my nurse. Sometimes Grandmother would come too, for after my mother's death, which took place when I was only five, Grandmother looked after me.

I was a very sensitive child and felt keenly the difference between my cousins and myself. They had the constant care and affection of a mother.

My father painted pictures most of the morning and went out in the afternoon. My grandmother had always plenty to do in the house, and I could not wear out my privilege of going to Grandfather's room to play. Before I was old enough to go to the family school I was given every morning by my sister four simple Chinese characters, printed on small squares of white paper, with pictures of the things they represented on the back, in case I could not remember the meanings. When I had learned the four characters my sister would say, ' Run away and find something to play with.' Usually I found something amusing to do, but occasionally I was very unhappy. Circumstances often forcibly reminded me of my orphanhood.

I remember one summer day playing ' shop ' with several cousins. It was the idea of my ' fifth Kê ', who was ten and had enjoyed the privilege of being taken outside the house to see the high street of the city. With his superior knowledge he ordered us younger ones to gather the chairs and stools at the corner of the second hall and arrange them in a line to look something like a Chinese shop. He then cut a big piece of thick paper into small pieces, some of which were to represent different types of cakes and sweets and some to represent money. He, as manager, sat in the middle of the shop, and I was the assistant who looked after the cakes and sweets. Some of the other cousins acted as customers and some dealt with the money paid. All went well until one of my youngest cousins, a very naughty girl, tried to get two sweets for too little money. In my endeavour to be an efficient salesman I prevented her from doing so, whereupon she burst into tears and cried so noisily that the sound reached the ears of my aunts, who all came out to call in their respective children. Naturally no mother would scold her own child very harshly if she could find some excuse, so I was held to have been responsible for the trouble. I could not understand why my sister or grandmother had not come out to stand up for me, and feeling in the depths of misery I went to the front garden and leaning on the trunk of the old willow tree silently let the tears stream down my face.

Presently my third great-uncle appeared. Lifting me up he said with a smile : ' Why are your eyes so red ? Who has been unkind to you ? Come and help me attend to the flowers.' At once I felt cheerful again and forgot to tell him what the trouble was. He only did a few cuttings on a small pomegranate tree, which was in full blossom, and said that I could have a large number of fruits from it afterwards. Then he took me to his room and

examined my health as usual.   After giving me a piece of
fresh lotus-stem to eat, he remarked that my health was
as good as that of any of the others of my generation, but
that it was a pity my teeth were not sound.   He advised
me not to eat many sweets.   Sweets . . . !   I did not feel
friendly towards sweets at that moment, and the prospect
of following my great-uncle's advice did not seem difficult,
though I did not grasp his meaning.

But in reality toothache did announce itself many a time.
One spring night when I was about nine years old such
a penetrating pain circulated round my whole face that I
could not sleep, and cried continuously.   The third great-
uncle came to my room and examined my tooth by the
light of an oil-lamp, but he did not agree with other members of the family that the aching tooth should be pulled
out.   He said he would find something to cure the pain
the next day.   He arrived at about seven o'clock to find
my face swollen like a big ball and gave me a small paper
parcel containing a handful of wiry fibrous rootlets of a
herb called in Chinese *Hsi-hsin*, and in English Birthwort
(*Heteropa asaroides*).   He told me to put a few of the rootlets
on the painful spot and to keep my head down so that
saliva could flow out of my mouth.   He warned me not
to swallow even the tiniest bit of the herb.   At first I
refused to use it because it looked like a mass of sharp
needles which would hurt me more than ever.   But ultimately I gave in.   The herb had a pungent taste.   Soon,
however, I felt no pain and my saliva flowed very freely.
This treatment continued for three days, the herb being
renewed four or five times a day.   It was an uncomfortable
business, but my swollen face gradually became normal,
and when I began to chew my food again the painful tooth
suddenly came out.   The lost tooth did not grow again,
and I have never since then had toothache.

A small part of the front garden was reserved for the
third great-uncle's herbs.   He liked to cultivate his own
herbs, though he also bought many dried ones from people

who dug them in the mountains and dried them for sale. Looking after the health of members of our family kept him busy, but he had also a large number of patients outside, especially poor people in the city, whom he generously treated free of charge. He would go out at any time in answer to an urgent call—in the middle of his lunch or dinner, or at midnight. He was obliged to have separate quarters on account of the many patients who came every morning to wait for his treatment. As he could keep to no regular times for meals or other things, he had a special man-servant to do everything for him. I very seldom saw him at our dinner-table except on New Year's Eve.

He once said that to be a doctor one must be generous, philanthropic and self-sacrificing, because this calling was a divine service to human beings, like a charity. He spoke slightingly of doctors who kept their patients waiting while they had their clothes beautifully brushed, or let a patient go on suffering until a bill was paid. A doctor should not consider his personal comfort. I have never forgotten these words. How many times I have met the opposite ! Not unnaturally, perhaps, my third great-uncle was not very friendly with the fashionable doctors in the city, some of whom had never in their lives seen a really desperate and pitiful patient !

So far as I know, my third great-uncle never earned any money. Certainly the members of our family did not pay him for his services to them, and I do not see how his ' outside ' patients could have afforded to do so. But often grateful patients sent him flowers in pots, because they knew that his hobby was gardening. He had charge of all our gardens. All his spare time was spent in tending the flowers and trees. He was particularly fond of the winter-plum, the almond, the peach, the pear, the pomegranate, the sweet laurel, the *p'i-p'a* (*Eriotrya japonica*), the *hai-t'ang* (*Begonia discolor*). Though rhododendron and magnolia, too, were favourites of his, he did not keep them in our garden, but we had, of course, jasmine, peony, chrysanthemum, and rose. I should have learned a lot about gardening had I been old enough to understand, for my third great-uncle always explained what he was doing. My sister and girl-cousins were as fond of him as I was, and I remember that he used to give them flowers for their hair.

Besides medicine and gardening, my third great-uncle was an amateur singer in the local type of opera. In his later days he did not sing much himself, but I remember that among his friends he was considered a very good judge of intonation and rhyme. Occasionally he would gather his friends in the courtyard of our family school, where, playing different musical instruments, they would sing the different parts of an ' opera '. This was generally regarded as a great treat for some of the youngsters ; it did not appeal to me particularly.

The thing I remember best about my third great-uncle is the sound of his voice saying : ' A cure for toothache, *Hsi-hsin*.' It rings in my ears now !

VEGETABLE SELLER

7

'DEATH-AFFAIRS'

MANY TIMES during my childhood I watched my grandmother busily directing the workmen who came to repaint
the family's reserve of coffins. Six of these were kept in
readiness. They were made of *Tzu Tung* wood brought
by one of our relatives from Szechuen province. This
must have been no easy task, for Szechuen lies several
hundred miles to the west of Kiu-kiang, and the means of
transport in those days were rudimentary. It took about
four months to get the wood to Kiu-kiang, but time was
then no consideration.

Szechuen is a mountainous province, rich in many kinds
of valuable wood. *Tzu Tung* is valued for coffin-making
because it is said to possess the property of resisting decay
for hundreds of years even when buried in the earth. The
Chinese have always desired to preserve the bodies and
bones of their dead, probably for similar reasons to those
of the ancient Egyptians; but we have never practised
embalming. I often heard my elders say, however, that
such-and-such a wood could prevent human flesh from
decaying for a thousand years, or that a certain precious
stone would have the same effect if put into the mouth of
the deceased before the coffin was closed.

A filial son does everything possible to satisfy his parents'
feelings on this subject. When my father and my father's
brothers sat together to discuss the procuring of wood
from Szechuen, since their elders were all getting on in
years, my grandparents disapproved very strongly, declaring that *Tzu Tung* was too much of a luxury. But when

the wood arrived and had been fashioned into six coffins, a process which took place in our garden, they changed their minds. Grandfather was delighted, and Grandmother expressed her absolute contentment with life. Their satisfaction was of course occasioned by the proof which this fetching of *Tzu Tung* afforded of the filial regard of their children.

I do not think that I myself ever saw the six coffins, but I remember three, kept together in a locked shelter only a few yards from the school. They were beautifully varnished with the finest quality of red pigment, composed of an important ore of mercury (a sulphide of the metal, known in the West as Chinese red or vermilion). It was said that one varnishing was not enough ; the oftener the coffin was varnished with the pigment, the better it would preserve the corpse. This was the reason why Grandmother attended to the coffins so carefully every summer.

As a rule the early summer in Kiu-kiang is not intolerably hot, though one can always be sure of long sunny days at the height of the season. It would be in these cooler days that my grandmother would ask one of the uncles to buy some *Wu-tung* oil and a large quantity of the red pigment ore, and would summon workmen to varnish the coffins. Sometimes two came, sometimes three. The door of the shelter would be taken off, so that the sun could shine directly on to the coffins, and the work would begin. Chinese coffins are huge, heavy contrivances made like a box with walls about a foot thick. Two men could scarcely move one. Accordingly the revarnishing always took a long time. Once a day Grandmother would come to the spot to examine the work and discuss this and that point of detail with the workmen.

As far as I remember the process of making the varnish, the workmen first pound the pigment ore in an iron mortar and then grind it as finely as possible. The finest grindings are then mixed with pure water and poured through a silk sieve, the coarser part being left to be ground again. This is repeated several times. Then the finest part is collected, dried, and mixed with *Wu-tung* oil. The workmen seemed to know by experience exactly how much of each component was required. They would stir the mixture incessantly until the final state was reached. I always took an interest in this process, for I had noticed that my father mixed the red pigment for his painting in the same way, except that he used gums instead of *Wu-tung* oil. The red pigment on the silk should be so fine that no single particle can be seen ; and this it must undoubtedly have been for

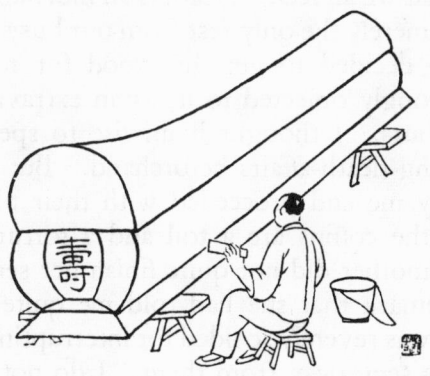

VARNISHING THE COFFIN

the result on the surface of the coffins to have been what it was. I think that our workmen were deserving of admiration for their splendid craftsmanship. My grandmother used herself to make the silk sieves.

I remember overhearing a curious discussion about death and ' death-affairs ' one afternoon when a relative of the family called on Grandmother while she was busy with the workmen. I led the way to the courtyard of the school, where the coffin-shelter stood. Grandmother and the relative exchanged the usual greetings and began to talk generalities. While the workmen under Grandmother's direction polished this and that part of the coffins, the relative sang the praises of the work being done, constantly repeating the compliment ' *Hao Fu-Chi ! Hao Fu-Chi !* ' (' What felicity ! '). Then she sighed deeply. Grandmother thanked her for her kind words and said : ' It is good to know that death-affairs are going forward before one's death. But actually who knows what will happen after death and who really cares ? We have so much to do in our life that we should not be bothered about death-affairs. When Confucius was asked about death he replied that he did not know life yet, so how could he know death ? It is exactly what we all feel. Death is an inevitable event and perhaps it is merely the only rest from our busy life. When my children decided to get the wood for making these coffins, I strongly objected to it, as an extravagance for a family like ours. I thought it unwise to spend precious time preparing death-affairs beforehand. But my children did not obey me and proceeded with their plans. Now, every year, the coffins are a toil and a torture. . . .'

As Grandmother did not quite finish her sentence, I cut in with a remark that she had told me quite differently ! Of course, I was severely scolded for interrupting my elders' talk and was sent away from them. I do not know what conclusion they came to, but I was told afterwards that the relative wept and left the house feeling very sad. I learned that she (whom I called Ku-P'o-P'o, a daughter of my grandmother's uncle) was a widow whose only filial and capable son had died the year before. Grandmother had been anxious not to revive Ku-P'o-P'o's grief for her lost son, and had tried to divert her attention from the coffins, which she spoke of as being of no importance. But human nature is always easily touched by small coincidences. Ku-P'o-P'o was no exception. She must have reflected that she might have had the same or even a better coffin prepared for her if her son had been alive. Although very rich, she was discontented with her life. She could have afforded to have had her death-affairs prepared in the best possible manner, but she would not arrange them herself because they are supposed to be done by a person's children in return for the kindness of the parents. She could have had everything that money could buy, but it would not have had the same significance; and she would have preferred a bad coffin of poor wood if it had been made by her devoted son, rather than a good one made commercially. It is a curious feeling of our race, far from practical sense, that anything done by a person of one's own blood has a peculiar value. We nourish a mysterious affection for the works of our own kin. To us, this is nature, and in spite of some appearances to the contrary I have seen signs of the same belief in the West.

Though I was wrong to break into my elders' conversation, I had, of course, spoken the truth when I said that Grandmother had previously expressed anything but regret that her children should have procured such fine coffins for their parents. Indeed, she was fond of speaking of the great goodness of my father and uncles in insisting on obtaining the wood from Szechuen. She would cite this to me as a model of proper filial regard, and urge me to follow their example. She told me that at my age I could not realize the sufferings and difficulties with which the parents of every child had to contend. ' Children sometimes object,' said Grandmother, ' to the orders given them and the restrictions placed upon them by their parents; but later in life they realize that it was for their own good that these things were done, and then they are grateful and should seek to return the kindness. It is the parents' responsibility to care for the child through his early years: it is the grown-up sons' responsibility to tend the old age of his parents and their death. That is how life goes on.' And she went on to praise once more the pains which my father and uncles had taken to provide suitable coffins for their parents. She smiled proudly when I said that I would do the same for my parents.

But alas! my mother was already dead, and my father died at the age of fifty-two, when I was still very young, and I have no longer the opportunity of fulfilling my promise. Possibly, in the changing times which have followed, my father and mother would not have attached the same importance as my grandmother to 'death-affairs'; but though customs change, human affection does not, and I should like to have tended my parents' last days in the old Chinese way.

PALM-FAN SELLER

8

TROUBLESOME HAIR

My hair was a perpetual botheration to me as a small boy. Every morning I had to go to my mother or nurse to have it done. My mother, though she was paralysed and spent all her time in bed, did not care for the way the nurse did it and preferred to do it herself whenever she could. She had up-to-date ideas on the subject. Whereas my nurse, who came from the district of Hsin-tzu on the other side of Lu mountain, where Fashion held less sway than in Kiu-kiang (which, as the gateway of the Kiangsi province, has been a communication centre for centuries), adhered to the old styles. New fashions from Peking (now called Peip'ing), Nanking, Shanghai, or other big cities reached the people of Kiu-kiang early, especially new fashions in hairdressing and clothes. From Kiu-kiang the fashions spread slowly to the hinterland of Kiangsi province.

Hsin-tzu is not a big district, nor a rich one. Most of the inhabitants are farmers or porcelain workers, simple honest folk who do not bother about such frivolities as fashion. Many of the women have always been employed by families in Kiu-kiang. My nurse was typical of them. Although she had been with us for more than twenty years and had had, both in our house and outside in the city, the closest contact with contemporary fashions, she still stuck to her own style of hairdressing. It served to distinguish her from the women of Kiu-kiang; and although we youngsters may have thought it funny, we dared not laugh at one who had earned respect through such long service in our household.

When a Chinese baby was a few months old, the original soft, spare, dark-brownish hair was shaved off. The object of this was to make the real crop of hair grow thick and black, and also to prevent it falling out in later life. At the second shaving a bunch of hair was left just above the forehead, or at the back over the nape of the neck. Sometimes a bunch was left above each ear, or one in front and another at the back; sometimes three or four bunches were left; occasionally a whole ring of hair was left and just the top of the head shaved. Generally boys had one or two bunches, while for girls there was more variety.

For some reason I had three bunches, one over each ear and one at the back. Every morning I had to stand

HSIN-TZU HAIRDRESSING

very still and endure a horrible strained feeling as my mother plaited my hair into three tight little plaits. They may have looked pretty, for they were tied with different-coloured ribbons, but what was that to me? Sometimes I tried to elude my mother, and the only really clear memory I have of her is of one morning when she managed to catch me as I tried to escape, and slapped my face. Now, sometimes when I brush my hair, I think of her and wish that I had been less disobedient. But long before I was old enough to want to show filial piety towards her and to work hard for her happiness, as a means of repaying her suffering when bringing me into this amazing world, she was dead. I cannot even remember what she looked like.

Another memory of my troublesome hair is connected with our childhood games. We boys and girls learnt many games from our elders. Sometimes girls played with girls and boys with boys, sometimes we all played together. Some of the games did not need any paraphernalia, but were just played with hands and feet to the accompaniment of local folk-songs. These games our elders did not encourage, but the elder boys of my generation learnt them from boys of other families in the city and showed them to us. As there was plenty of space in our house to run about in, the game I liked best was riding on a bamboo horse. Some imagination was necessary, since the horse was no more than a bamboo stick about three centimetres in diameter and two or three metres long. Being very thin and small compared with other boys of the same age, I had a shorter stick. I would put the stick between my legs, holding the upper end of it with my right hand, and then, raising my left hand as if wielding a whip, I made a sound to urge my steed forward. Three or four of us on our bamboo 'horses' could make as much noise in this way as a cavalcade of real horsemen at full gallop. Anybody in the way had to look out. Our elders could have bought paper horses' heads for us to fasten to our bamboo sticks, but my father asked a carpenter to make ten wooden ones instead. They did not look exactly 'horsey', but near enough.

From this game sprang another—and more realistic—riding game. It was the notion of my fifth *Kê* (boy-cousin) but not his invention; he must have seen or heard of it somewhere. I, with my three small plaits, was chosen to be the horse's head and fore-legs. Another boy, who happened to be very strong, stood a little distance behind me and bent forward with his head butting into my back and his two hands firmly grasping my shoulders : he was the horse's body. My fifth *Kê* then rode this steed, holding himself on by means of a string tied to my back plait ! My two other plaits were supposed to be the horse's ears. So we went on. No doubt it was pleasant for the rider: it was anything but pleasant for the horse! From time to time rider and hind-quarters changed places, but I always played the same part. I detested it, for no matter who the rider was he always pulled my hair and hurt me if I did not walk fast enough. Fortunately one of my uncles ultimately forbade the game, not on my behalf but in case the rider should slip off and hurt his back. Now, as I write, I can still feel the pain of my hair being pulled and find my hand going involuntarily to the back of my head.

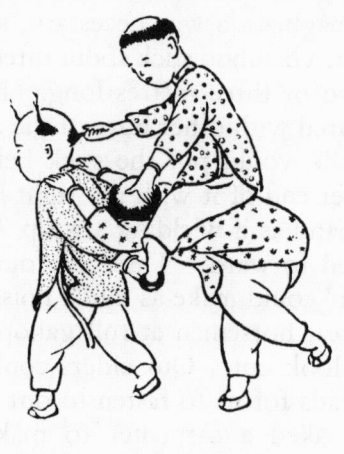

RIDING GAME

After the death of my mother my sister looked after my hair. It was allowed to grow longer, and when I was about seven the three plaits were abandoned for one single one at the back. Only two years later came the Chinese revolution. The movement for the destruction of the Manchu dynasty spread to Kiu-kiang. The elders of my family thought that there might be riots, so they sent the grandparents, the third great-uncle, and all aunts, boys and girls into the country. According to tradition I should not have been taken outside the house and gardens until I was ten, but these special circumstances caused me to be taken out when only nine. We had no house of our own in the country, but a big farm-house was emptied for us by one of the peasant families who cultivated our fields. Some of us went to another neighbourhood where we also owned land. I was with those who stayed at the foot of Lu mountain. It was this occasion which gave me my first taste of life in the country and I have been a friend of Nature ever since.

I had no idea what the Revolution was about, but my boy-cousins and I were delighted when it was decreed that every man and boy must cut off his pigtail. Grandmother arranged for a barber to visit the farm-house and do the deed. At the same time she procured some fireworks with which to celebrate the occasion, and we also had a special dinner. When I first saw my de-pigtailed head in a mirror I thought I looked very funny, but I was most grateful to the Revolution for sparing me half an hour's torture every morning (Frontispiece).

We heard that nearly everybody within the city walls had cut off his hair, or had had it forcibly cut off for him, for Republicans stood ready, scissors in hand, to deal with obstinate pigtail owners. Two men were placed at each gate of the city wall to make sure that all men entering from the country were shorn.

At that time our tenants used to go to the city to sell firewood, so they too lost their pigtails. One of them, Hsun-hsin, a middle-aged farmer, who was proud of being a filial son and was in the habit of entering the city every morning, was most reluctant to go there when he heard of the pigtail shearing. From his first visit under the new régime he came home weeping with his pigtail in his hand, and I regret to say that we all laughed loudly at him. How, I asked, could any one feel sad at the loss of troublesome hair ! He replied that according to what Confucius told his disciple Tseng Tzu, the body and hair received from one's parents should not be damaged or destroyed; not to regard this precept was to show one-self unfilial. Hsun-hsin was quite illiterate, but as the say-ings of Confucius and his disciples were perpetually quoted in our daily conversation, he knew them and strove to obey them. I too had often heard my grandmother quote Confucius' word when I had a bruise or mark on my face or body. My grandfather now explained to Hsun-hsin that the pigtail was introduced to the Chinese by the first emperor of the Manchu dynasty. It was an ugly fashion and indeed was forced on the Chinese as a means of humiliating them. He went on to say that we should all be glad to be rid of our pigtail, or if we insisted on keeping it we should not let it hang down at the back but should roll it round on the top of the head in the Ming dynasty style—the real Chinese fashion. The farmer, having great faith in my grandfather's wisdom, went home smiling.

I do not know what I felt at that time about Grand-father's explanation, but I now know that the Emperor Chien Lung, himself of the Manchu dynasty, did not like the fashion of the pigtail hanging down at the back, because I have seen a number of portraits of him painted by court painters showing the hair done in the Ming style. My father used to declare that no great artist would put a figure with a pigtail into a painting, and that no portraits showing pigtails counted in the first rank of our art. Possibly this is the reason why our ancestral portraits were always done full-face. The artists took this roundabout way of showing their patriotism.

While I thought hairdressing a nuisance, my sister and girl-cousins would cheerfully spend hours on it. I remember I once asked one of them whether it hurt her to have her hair done, and she answered that she did not feel it and liked her hair to be done well and beautifully. My sister used to send me to fetch cold water for her so that each day she could make freshly the jelly-like liquid with which she polished her hair. For this she used very thin shavings of a wood called *Wu-mo* or *Pau-hua-mo*, which, after being steeped in water for a short time, formed a jelly-like liquid. After combing her hair out straight, my sister would brush it with this liquid and then comb it again. She then dressed her hair according to the fashion of the time. As I was a boy and not particularly interested in hairdressing, I cannot recall all the different styles, but here are a few that I do remember :

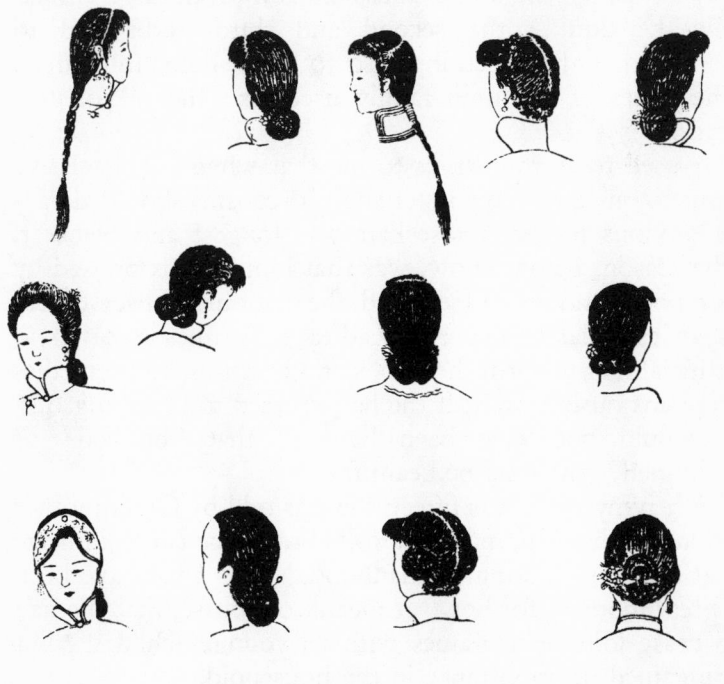

DIFFERENT STYLES OF HAIRDRESSING

Sometimes some of my aunts and elder girl-cousins had their hair done by professional hairdressers, women who travelled about from family to family and introduced the new fashions. For the men and boys in the household a barber called once or twice a month to cut hair. The professional women only came on special occasions.

The liquid dressing made of *Pau-hua-mo* is said to darken the hair as well as make it glossy.   Very dark hair was much praised and women would try every means to make their hair blacker.   I do not remember the names of all the herbs used for the purpose, but I recall *Wu-wei-tzu* (*Kadsura Chinensis*), *Wu-pei-tzu* (*Gallae japonicus*) and *Mu-hsi* (*Osamanthus fragrans*).   The seeds of the first were used in the same way as the shavings of *Pau-hua-mo* and produced a similar jelly-like liquid ; the second and third herbs had to be mixed with something else to have their full effect. The ladies of my own family used also the oil of tea-seeds.

It used to seem curious to me that when a girl relative came to our house, my sister and girl-cousins should always be anxious to see whose hair was longest and blackest. The reason, I now know, was that long hair is praised by our poets, and so had entered the national consciousness as an essential to beauty.   Ladies sometimes resorted to artificial hair to form their rolls and coiffures, and remedies were anxiously sought if the hair seemed to be falling out. It would not have been believed that 'bobbed' or ' shingled' hair *could* be beautiful.

When my sister was fifteen she was told by Grandmother to put her hair up, making a roll above each ear to indicate that she was entering womanhood.   This must have been a great moment for her.   It meant, of course, that she had to cease joining in games with us younger children, but she gained in importance in the household.

Though my sister was the first girl of our family to go to the Girls' School run by the American missionary in Kiu-kiang, she had to stay indoors when she was at home, and we seldom saw her in the courtyard.   I can still remember her self-conscious manner when she first appeared with the two rolls.   She seemed shy of standing before the elders, because their first words were sure to be : ' Now you are a big girl and grown up, you must learn how to become a good wife.'   She tried to talk to me in a grown-up manner, but I just made a face at her. At the same time I did feel that she had more authority over me than before. It must have been the ' troublesome hair ' which made the difference.

CHUN-YA SELLER
(a kind of tree leaves preserved to go with tea)

9

RUSHING IS FRUITLESS

Probably it was my early environment which developed in me a passion for painting and for art in general. Whether heredity also played a part I cannot be sure, for my brother never tried to draw, though he was a poet and loved art ; and my sister's handwriting was very bad, and she seldom wrote.

I began to learn painting in earnest when I was about twelve, but before that I had taken pleasure in going to my father's room when he was at work. I was told that he had always preferred this small study because here he could paint whenever he liked. He was very much attached to mother and grieved deeply when she died. After her death, painting must have been, apart from wine, his only comfort.

He kept his study very neat and clean. On the walls hung one or two good paintings by well-known masters and they were changed from time to time. Very occasionally his own paintings appeared on the walls. On the shelves were a large number of sketches and picture books, all bearing on Father's speciality, bird and flower paintings. The books and pictures were to me like part of nature, and when I was tired I used to slip into the room and walk slowly round imagining that I could hear the song of the oriole on its slender branch and that the flowers were smiling at me. Once, while I was occupied thus, Father watched me through the window. After some time I lifted my head and saw him at the window. He came in, smiling quizzically. I must have been about eight.

After that Father very often called me to stand by his table when he was going to paint (Plate 3). I noticed that he thought a long time before applying his brush to the paper. Sometimes he did not paint a single stroke even after long meditation. When he had finished, I was tempted to try to use the brush. He let me try but told me that it would be better first to take great pains with my handwriting in school. He must have said something about me to the teacher of our family school, for I was told always to show the results of my daily handwriting exercise to my father.

My father, then, did not at that time actually teach me to paint. When he looked over my shoulder at my efforts, he always laughed and said, ' Too young to try.' But he never discouraged me from trying. What he did definitely teach me was how to make pigments. Although nearly all our pigments were minerals, and bought in powder form, we had to grind them again before use. Great care was required to get them fine enough for painting on soft paper, and especially for painting on silk. Father kept a small agate mortar for the purpose. When he had ground the stuff once he would pour in a certain amount of water and separate the finest powder, which would float on the surface, by pouring the liquid through a piece of fine silk. The rest he would grind again and again, each time separating the fine upper layer. The resulting extremely fine powder he used for painting. At first he asked me only to clean his table and put the coloured pigments into the case for him. Later I was allowed to grind the pigments, and thus acquired a good knowledge of pigments before I could really paint at all myself.

Sometimes, if he were going to paint in a very delicate style, Father would make faint rough sketches on the paper or silk first. He told me that ordinary charcoal could not be used for the sketch because it was coarse and hard and easily spoiled our soft paper or silk. Instead he always picked a few long young tender twigs of weeping willow and burned them to very thin black sticks. When the painting was finished the charcoal outlines could be dusted off completely, for they were so soft. My sister used these same burnt willow twigs to paint her eyebrows.

Paintings of butterflies with flowers were a speciality of my father's. He had a special technique for the large black butterfly with a few red spots dotted on its wings. He burned a small strip of a special silk which we called ' Fang-ch'ou ' and used the black ashes of this silk for the wings of the butterflies. They looked dead-black and powdery, just like real wings.

I do not remember that I ever had any proper lessons in painting from my father. He simply told me to watch him as closely as possible. I was allowed to try to paint what I liked, and never given a subject or told which stroke to begin with for a bird or a flower. I remember that after watching my father painting a few times I thought I knew just how to paint, but when I actually began I found I was mistaken ! And the difficulties seemed to increase with each attempt. I asked Father to help, but he only smiled and told me to watch him again. He never pointed out where I was wrong and until I was about twelve did not attempt to correct my efforts. But from then on, when I produced something for him to see, he told me which part I must watch still more carefully. As time went on, I began to know what I was doing and to be able systematically to tackle a subject. Father always quoted Confucius' sayings that ' A gentleman never makes a mistake twice ' and ' One should not be afraid to correct one's fault if one knows of it '. These two sayings made me become more eager to watch carefully and learn thoroughly.

Father's theory was that one could only create a work of art by constantly studying the works of great masters and by carefully watching some one paint. The mind had first to be steeped in the composition and colour of the great masters; nature influenced the artist's mind later on, when he knew how to paint. My father did not approve of talking about art, because as the great masters of the past had not explained how they painted, how could any one else explain it?

Father chose his own tutor, and Grandmother used to tell me stories of the queer ways of this man. His name was Hsü Sheng-hua. Father saw him painting one day in a Buddhist temple and liked the painting so much that he ran home and asked his parents' permission to have this painter as his tutor. Though they agreed, Hsü Sheng-hua would not come to live in our house until he had been granted special terms. Money was not his object, though he was very poor. What he wanted was entire freedom. He was not to be subjected to paying daily respect to the elder members of the house. He was to have his food in his own way at whatever time he liked. After he moved into our house, Father very seldom had meals with the grandparents. Grandmother used to say in a teasing manner that Father had not been so filial and obedient to them as to his tutor. And indeed he would stand beside Hsü Sheng-hua for hours watching him paint, whereas after standing by his parents only a few minutes he would excuse himself and return to his painting.

Hsü Sheng-hua was a good painter. He specialized in portraiture, and our house contained a number of portraits by him of Grandfather, Grandmother, Father and the family in groups. He also painted flowers well.

Father used to describe Hsü Sheng-hua's methods to me. He said that he never dared to question his tutor, because if he did the old man would jump up and hit him, demanding to know why Father was not watching attentively. Fortunately, Father never hit me but only smiled and said gently that I should keep on watching. Sometimes I tried to hurry a painting, and then Father always stopped me, saying that rushing was fruitless, a precept I have never forgotten.

I have not as yet achieved anything in painting, but the fact that I realize this is largely due to the excellent foundation which my father laid, and the sympathetic patience he showed me.

He was a man who believed in getting the best out of life, but he could not get over his grief at the death of my mother, which permanently saddened his outlook, and eventually he died of his irreparable loss. I was told that during the three years of mother's illness he attended her entirely himself. I always noticed that he sighed deeply before her portrait, which he had painted himself. My brother and sister and I could not make him forget his loss, though he loved us all dearly. With the death of my mother his life lost its savour, and he died before I could show him that I had taken his teaching to heart.

BROOM SELLER

10

THE CONFERENCE OF MADMEN

At the age of fifteen my brother had already a reputation as a young poet. To me his poems and learning as yet meant little, though I often heard them spoken of by my grandparents and my father, who told me repeatedly how clever my brother was at my age, and thus made me feel stupid by comparison. At the age of three my brother was taught some of the famous lyrics of the T'ang dynasty and to recognize a few complicated calligraphic characters. He accomplished these tasks after one or two attempts : I needed much more practice. This sometimes gave me a rueful feeling, and at the same time made me determined to follow in his footsteps.

Just as my father was left more or less alone in the household and was highly respected by the elders because of his talent for painting, so did my brother become a distinguished member with certain privileges. We younger ones looked upon him as a sage and none of us dared address him, lest the words of his reply be too difficult for us to understand. Even some of the elders hesitated to talk to him, because they had not at their command such beautiful expressions as he used. So my brother was somewhat isolated. Body and soul he became immersed in study—reading, writing poems, buying books of poetic works by our great masters. In our house the formalities of morning and evening greeting and of the presenting of youngsters to elders every day was practically dispensed with. My brother therefore was very seldom seen by most of the household. He was generally out in the daytime, or if he was in, was sure to be in his own study. At meal-times I was the person sent by Grandmother to call him to table. Sometimes, without saying a word to any one, he would go out just before dinner was ready and come back shortly after it was finished. If he had not eaten anything and our servants were not in, Grandmother would go to the kitchen herself and cook something for him. This consideration was not extended to any other member of the family ; Grandmother always emphasized that both elders and youngsters should be punctual for meals. But no one ever grumbled at her indulgence towards my brother ; all simply wished they were as clever as he.

My brother was not a conceited man and always smiled when he met anybody ; but with members of the family he probably found he had nothing to talk about. With his own friends, on the other hand, he had if anything too much to say. I remember his explaining to me once that his other name, ' Ta-chuan ' (Big Stream), was chosen because he hoped his literary thought would flow through his mind as water flows in a stream, and be as endless. While among his friends his speech must have matched his thought, for when they came to our house there was always a great noise issuing from my brother's study. What they talked about and why they laughed so loudly and were so merry, nobody knew. But the family nicknamed my brother and his friends ' a group of madmen ', and when they were in the house word would go round that a " conference of madmen ' was taking place. This nickname of ' madman ' was not, of course, derogatory. I too was nicknamed ' madman ' when I grew older, and I accepted the name willingly, since it excused eccentricities of be-haviour. Most poets, painters and scholars in my city were called ' madmen '.

Among my brother's several tutors was a famous poet of Kiu-kiang, Hsiung Hsiang-hai. ' Hsiung ' was the family name ; ' Hsiang-hai ' means ' fragrant sea '. He was an old gentleman of over seventy with a tremendous craving for sweets. Whenever my brother had a gathering of friends, Hsiung Hsiang-hai was sure to be there. Most of my brother's friends were his students. It was Grandmother who saw to it that there were egg-cakes, honey dates, almond rolls, dried lichees and dried dragon's eyes, melon seeds, &c., for the occasion. My brother's study was a simple square room. It contained a big rectangular table used as a writing-desk, a small round 'occasional' table, various chairs, and a sofa which could be made into a bed. On the wall hung one of Father's paintings and several transcriptions of Hsiung Hsiang-hai's poems. A few bookshelves completed the furniture. In front of the study was a small sky-well with a palm-tree and some bamboos near the window. My father, who was devoted to my brother, generally himself prepared the room for the guests, bringing more chairs and laying paper, ink and brushes on the table. No servant was allowed to do this. But Father never bothered my brother to bring his friends to see him or the grandparents, but let them come and go as they liked. They always stayed a long time, and the supply of cakes and sweets usually had to be replenished. A kettle of water was kept boiling under the palm-tree and a boy-servant sat outside serving tea continuously. Sometimes the guests stayed on to dinner and went away very late at night. This, however, did not mean they had dinner with the rest of the family. Fortunately, perhaps! For their manner of eating, as I remember it from stealthy glances, was indescribable. Well might Confucius suggest that men who considered themselves superior should eat separately from women on important occasions!

The old tutor used to bring a grandson with him for support as he walked. The boy was older than me, but I was nevertheless jealous that he should be allowed inside the study with the madmen. On one occasion there were seven in the gathering, as I saw through a crack of the doors. The noise inside was tremendous. The guests were reciting poems and laughing at each other's efforts. I could see the old tutor sitting by the round table with the sweets and cakes. He was looking at the poems which my brother and his friends gave him for criticism and was correcting the lines one by one as he ate the sweets. Some of them were still writing at the rectangular table. Sometimes the old man threw his head up and exclaimed : ' That is a good line,' or ' That is a beautifully chosen word.' Although I was too young to understand what they were talking about, I enjoyed listening to the sound of their reciting. Some of my brother's books were consulted for quotations. Everything was in confusion— books on the tables and the outer skins of the melon seeds on the floor. Standing at the door I was practically holding my breath, lest my brother should discover I was there. Suddenly I overbalanced and my hand struck the doors, which fell open. I promptly bolted. Later my brother asked me smilingly why I was standing there when I could not understand what was being said. I made up my mind to join them some day, but unfortunately by the time I was able to compose a few lines myself the ' conferences of madmen ' no longer took place ; and now all its members but one are dead.

We had nicknames for each of the company of seven as well as the generic name, ' madmen ', for them all. The tutor was ' old mad Hsiung '. His eldest son was ' big mad Hsiung '. He it was who could produce a poem on any subject at a moment's notice. Although he had passed the provincial examination and gained the title Chu-Jen he had not been lucky enough to be appointed to an official position, chiefly, I believe, because he was so mad about his poetry. Another, one of our own relations, was nicknamed ' mad Chen '. A native of the Feng-hsin district of Kiangsi province, he was the only member of the party who came from outside Kiu-kiang. He married the daughter of my mother's brother. Being extremely shortsighted he walked with his head flung high, in a lordly manner (as we thought), and we used to laugh gleefully when he bumped into the palm-tree or the bamboos. He could sing as well as recite. I say ' could ' sing : but in fact when he was in the party he insisted on singing, whether anybody listened to him or not. Another of the madmen was ' mad Hwang ', whose name was Fu-chi, which means ' not strange '. Actually he was a very strange man. He talked incessantly and unintelligibly, rolling his words on his tongue. Having been brought up in another province his dialect was different from ours. He was famous in Kiu-kiang as a great reader, and was said to be able to check references and quotations without looking at the original books. When he wrote he preferred to use difficult and ancient characters for his poems, so that ordinary people could not understand them. He never thought about dress and sometimes appeared in a fur gown on a hot summer day, because it happened to be handy. I do not think he ever took a job in his life. The old tutor's nephew, Hsiung Hsieh-tzu, also patronized the gatherings. He was a careful, sensible person and did not deserve to be called ' madman '. He was my teacher for a year and took his appointment very seriously. I regret to say that his poems were always placed last when ' old mad Hsiung ' had finished criticizing. Wang Shih-lien, the last of the group, was the son of a well-known scholar and shared the respect paid to his father. He was the silent member of the group. I never heard him recite.

My brother was married during our stay in the country at the time of the Revolution. He married one of the noted beauties of the city who came from the highly placed family of a court official. She was a skilful embroiderer and widely read, but she never wrote. She met of course my brother's friends, but never mixed with them except for one occasion just after we returned from the country. The ' conference of madmen ' assembled and demanded that my brother should induce his wife to join them, and, although much embarrassed, he could not but obey his tutor's wish. She did not stay long, and when she left the room all she would say was : ' There is too much madness in there.' Unexpectedly I poked my head from under the arm of one of the listening girl-cousins and remarked : ' Brother is a madman too ! ' (Plate 4).

SELLER OF ALL SORTS OF THINGS FOR DAILY USE

'WHAT A BUSINESS!'

WHEN I RECALL our preparations for the New Year
Festival I realize now how elaborate they really were. The
old Chinese New Year was about a little more than a month
later than that of the Gregorian calendar, which was
adopted only after the Revolution of 1912. By the end
of the eleventh or the beginning of the twelfth month
every family was busy preserving food. The quantity
depended on the size of the family and its income, but even
the poorest, and families consisting only of husband and
wife, made what preparations they could, for it was a very
old custom to rest and enjoy oneself at the New Year.
Throughout the rest of the year we did not have ' weekends '
or Bank Holidays, but the New Year Festival could last a
month.

Whether or not the preserved foods could be bought,
every family preferred to preserve its own, and at spring
dinner-parties ladies were fond of comparing methods and
results. Each family had its own recipes. I often heard
my grandmother and aunts instructing my sister and girl-
cousins in the preparation of New Year delicacies, urging
them to pay careful attention to what was being said, so
that the family's good name should be maintained. I do not
think the girls of modern China would take such trouble!

The preserved foods were of two kinds : vegetables and
meats. Among the former were preserved ginger roots,
turnips, turnip leaves and cabbages ; also cheese made from
fermented beancurd. Each was prepared in season and kept
in small earthen jars in the ladies' chambers, one or two in

each. They could be eaten at any time, but some of them, such as the ginger roots and the turnips, were always included in the New Year fare. Apart from this Festival, the preserved turnip leaves and cabbages would only be used when we were short of fresh vegetables in winter.

I did not eat any of them ! My elders declared that my father ' spoilt ' me because he did not force me to eat them. I only liked fresh vegetables. I have never tasted ginger roots for I cannot take hot things. My cousins adored these preserved vegetables. I confess, however, that I had a special liking for a dish—or rather part of a dish—consisting of small pieces of pork cooked with smoked preserved cabbage. The cabbage was smoked by cutting the fresh leaves into small pieces and pressing them in an earthen jar with salt ; after a month or two it was smoked and turned black. I used to pick out the pork and leave the cabbage ; the others ate both, as they were supposed to, and I was always scolded. But I would even now put up with a scolding in order to enjoy the delicious taste of pork cooked in this way !

The preserved meats were chiefly pork, fish, chicken and duck. A few families in Kiu-kiang preserved beef and mutton as well. As my family had so many members the quantity of meat to be preserved was enormous. One of my uncles used to be responsible for getting a couple of big pigs from our farmer-tenants. These, of course, counted as part of the rent due at the beginning of the eleventh month. The whole carcass of the pig was cut into pieces of from five to ten pounds each and washed thoroughly by men-servants. Then my grandmother decided how much salt should be rubbed into each piece before it was pressed with heavy stones in a huge, open-mouthed earthen jar and left for ten days or more. The weather was very cold in winter, but my sister and girl-cousins, though they did not take part in the proceedings, had to be present and watch what was being done. We boys only waited for the time to eat. After ten days or so my grandmother asked the servants to take the pork out and look at it. If it was still as red or redder than originally, it would be very good. The pieces were then hung on the wall near the kitchen, where the winter sun could shine on them, for although we had a very cold winter it was always dry and sunny. After a month's exposure in the sun, the ham was ready to be cooked. Some of the pieces were smoked for a few days, too, and I must say they formed one of my favourite dishes at the New Year Festival. Each big piece was cut again into very small pieces about one inch square, and steamed. I liked it still better when fried with small pieces of condensed beancurd and garlic leaves. This dish I considered heavenly. It is important that the preserved pork should not be too salt. The right amount is only discovered by experience.

The method of preserving fish was more or less the same. The fish we used was always carp from the Yangtse River, but actually that from the Yellow River is better. Each fish weighs from ten to thirty pounds or even more. I remember that at the end of the first stage of preserving the pork my uncle would buy about twenty fish for preserving. All the young girls in the house helped to wash them. Then the men-servants cut each fish into two pieces, salted it, and continued as with the pork. The best fish looked reddish pink after being steamed, and, like the pork, had to be not too salt. I was particularly addicted to this preserved fish, which I liked cut into half-inch cubes and cooked with small pieces of pork of the same size which had previously been lightly boiled with Chinese soya sauce; a few leaves of garlic should be added too. My grandmother made this dish herself sometimes and it tasted extremely good. My fondness for the dish earned me the nickname 'Carp-eater' when each New Year came round. Chicken and ducks were also preserved in much the same way, but in my family not in great quantities. If all these preserved foods turned out well it meant that the next year would be comfortable for us, so every care was taken.

While the preserved meats were being exposed to the sun, the elder ladies of the household were busy making all kinds of rice-cakes, sweets made with dried laurel flowers, baked glutinous rice-grains, &c. The older girls helped to put these foods in jars and jugs and to distribute them round the chambers. By the twenty-third day of the twelfth month the preparations had to be finished.

On that very night, seven days before the New Year, Grandmother always prepared some small dishes of candy and other sweets and placed them in front of a paper Kitchen God. We boys were ordered to kneel down three times to pay him the family's respects. Then the paper god was burned and we were told that he was going to heaven to report what had happened in our family throughout the year of his duty. If his report was favourable we should have a good time in the coming year ; otherwise we should need to be more careful in our behaviour and daily dealings. This, however, did not worry us youngsters. Incidentally, this was the only occasion in the year when I saw our kitchen.

The next day, the twenty-fourth of the last month, was considered a prelude to the New Year, and we had a better dinner than usual. From that moment we youngsters were warned not to cry, or mention ghosts, spirits or death, because our minds should be filled with expressions and compliments suitable to the coming festival. The whole house had to be dusted, and every one's help was required. Boys and girls were not allowed to handle delicate things, such as porcelain, but we enjoyed being in the midst of the busy scene. At any other time we should have been told to get out of the way, but at the New Year every one was tolerant and good-humoured.

This must have been the only time my brother was to be seen taking part in family affairs. He composed Chun-lien (spring-couplets) and wrote them on strips of red paper for us to paste on the doors of every room. In some houses in Kiu-kiang paper Door Gods were pasted up instead of couplets. We never did this, probably because my brother and two older boy-cousins had such beautiful handwriting. We could have bought ready-made spring-couplets, but my brother preferred to compose special ones ; and they must have been good, for we noticed that people often came and copied down the couplet on the entrance-gate. These couplets varied according to the type of door and the nature of the room. One of the couplets on the entrance-gate would welcome the spring, the other record the prosperity of the house. On a side door, the couplet would be concerned with the things which came in and out by that door. For the guest-hall there was a couplet referring to the entertaining of guests from different parts of the land ; for the study, one suggesting that the thought from the pen grew as the spring, and that the sound of recitation was as continual as that of the rain. My brother had a busy time writing couplets for every door. It was our rule that all the couplets should be firmly pasted up before the twenty-ninth day of the month. My father's task was to change the important pictures in the three halls for some of happy omen, probably showing spring flowers.

Towards the end of autumn my grandmother always ordered tailors to come and make new clothes for us all. New clothes were essential for the New Year. The tailors stayed in our house for a couple of weeks or more. My aunts and older cousins chose the silks and other materials and discussed the styles with the tailors. I never liked wearing new clothes at other times, because they made me feel self-conscious and less free in my actions, but at the New Year, when everybody, including elders, appeared in new clothes, I did not mind.

On the last morning of the last month of the passing year we youngsters had our hair done with great care and put on our new clothes. Some of the youngest babies had a round red spot painted just a little above the middle of the eyebrows. The whole atmosphere of the house was changed and everybody was in good spirits. We knew we were safe from scoldings—but then we never felt mischievous on this occasion! When every member of the household was assembled the ceremony of paying respect to the ancestral shrine, to indicate the passing of the old year, began.

First of all one of the servants placed a big square table in the middle of the third hall in front of the ancestral shrine, and on the side which faced the entrance-gate we youngsters could help to tie an embroidered curtain which had on it a sign of happy omen and four characters: *Nien-Nien-Yu-I* (year after year at will). Then all the chairs in the halls were covered with embroidered covers and thin cushions. On the outer side of each hall, the side facing the sky-well, was hung a long and beautifully embroidered curtain; no two of these were alike in design. A pair of huge red candles about three inches in diameter and three feet long were hung by iron wires from the beams of each sky-well too. A round red paper lantern hung in the middle of the entrance-gate and two big cylindrical red lanterns stood on each side of the gate. In each hall there were four silk lanterns, one in each corner and a big lantern in the middle.

When the sacrificial dishes and wine and rice were all arranged on the square table, the lanterns and red candles were lighted. The scene was very gay. No one could be sad in such an atmosphere. Then incense was burned. Two of my older boy-cousins looked after the firing of the fireworks, and as I was tall enough to reach the big round bronze bell on the table, I was given the job of beating it while the male head of the family knelt down and paid respect before the ancestral shrine. This duty should have been performed by my grandfather, but at the time I recall he was getting very old, so my first uncle took his place. Every male member followed him in order of age and generation. Sometimes my father and uncles did not take their turn as they thought the first uncle represented them well enough. We boys from fifteen downwards simply loved this part of

the ceremony. We stood around the third hall and waited
for the first uncle to call us one by one. Some of my aunts
and all the girls were standing there too. They could have
taken part if they had liked, but the older girls were afraid
they might not kneel properly, and the younger ones were
not interested. We received no lessons on how to kneel and
bow for this ceremony ; we just observed how our elders
did it and followed suit. My task of beating the bell was
not negligible. I had to beat it regularly and continuously,
keeping the intervals neither too short nor too long. The
ceremony lasted a good half-hour and I beat the bell from
beginning to end except during my own turn to kneel,
when one of my boy-cousins beat it for me. Being known
as the patient boy among the youngsters of the house I had
this job at every New Year Festival from the age of six
until past fifteen.

After the ceremony we had a really good feast. This
was the only time in the year when all the members of the
house, including the servants, ate together. On ordinary
days, or on other festive occasions, my grandfather did not
join us and some other elders might be missing. The New
Year Festival was different. There were five or six square
tables arranged in three of the halls. At each table sat
eight persons, two at each side, or perhaps three if they were
youngsters. Grandfather, very pleased to see all his household gathered together, did not say much beyond wishing
happiness to all. Grandmother was always in excellent
spirits, congratulating herself that she had finished her task
for the year and could rest. She sat beside Grandfather
at the middle table of the third hall facing the entrance-
gate. The other people at this table were their grand-
daughter-in-law and great-grandson and all the youngest
grandchildren. I was always among them. Nobody else
had any special place, although elders had the better seats.
There were always some spare pairs of chopsticks, extra
bowls and vacant seats among the tables, indicating the
hope that new members would be born in the coming year.

This gathering we called *Tuan Nien* (yearly reunion). There was no class distinction in our house and every one could joke together.

I cannot describe how good the dishes were. There were generally nine or ten different ones, all set together in the middle of each table. Each table also bore a *Huo-kuo* (a small boiler made of bronze with a hollow dish on the top).

During the dinner my father would give the first toast to Grandmother by filling up her cup and his own and drinking with her *Kan-pei* (Drain the cup). Everybody followed suit. As our wine-cups are very small, a few dozen cups did not worry Grandmother in the least. She was a good drinker and so was my father, but Grandfather did not take any wine. After the toasts to Grandmother people could *kan-pei* to each other, strolling from table to table. Those who did not drink had the advantage of enjoying more food. Youngsters under fifteen were not encouraged to taste wine at all, but we could eat as much as we liked, which was not the rule on ordinary days. At our daily meals we were not allowed to leave a single grain of rice in the bowl, whereas on this occasion we were told to leave something in the bowl as a symbol of our hope that we should have something left after balancing expenditure and income in the coming year.

After dinner the tables were cleared, and Grandmother would tell the servants to leave everything in the kitchen, and let us play together. Before the morning ceremony, a big brass basin of burning charcoal had been placed in front of the table to keep the hall warm. After dinner the burnt charcoals were put into the small basins and distributed through the rooms. This signified the distribution of treasure and warmth from our ancestors. Then we all began to play games—mah-jong, dice, cards, chess. I joined some of my young cousins in firing different fireworks in the second sky-well, and then we played noisy musical instruments without regard for rhythm or harmony. We had great fun and could make as much noise as we liked.

It was then time for the elders to show the family clan book to the youngsters of suitable age, as I have described in an earlier chapter. By six or seven o'clock on ordinary days we were tired and not sorry to go to bed : on New Year's Eve we stayed up to enjoy the last hours of the old year, a custom which was called *Shou-sui* (' Keeping the year ', or ' Seeing the Old Year out ' as English people call it). We Chinese always seem to celebrate things passing. My father would paint a small picture to mark the occasion and my brother write a new poem for it too. I remember how thrilled we used to be at the idea of not going to bed all night. We were told that this would prevent our having bad dreams and nightmares which might bring us bad luck in the coming year. But as a matter of fact we often fell asleep in spite of ourselves.

About midnight the next ceremony took place. It was similar to the burning of incense and the fireworks earlier. The first uncle led the male members to the entrance-gate and performed the rite of turning the key to keep happiness and treasures inside the house. After that everybody bowed and knelt to greet each other at the passing of the old year. The younger generation knelt on the ground before the older generation, while people of the same generation bowed to each other once with both hands folded on the chest. This was called *Tzu-sui* (' Fare-well to the Old Year '). My aunts and older girl-cousins then gave each other presents, such as embroidered shoes, handkerchiefs, perfume bags, &c., which they had made for the occasion. Grandmother always got enough shoes to last her the whole year. I do not know why we boys were not in the habit of exchanging presents.

Presently boys and girls from fifteen downwards were divided into two groups to pay respect to the elders who had not been present at the ceremony of locking the entrance-gate. The boy group set out first. Grandfather having gone to bed at the usual time, we did not disturb him, so Grandmother's chamber was our first call. She was always ready for us and had even put a red silk cushion on the floor before her for us to kneel on. At one time we boys were eight in number, including the youngest cousin aged three and my nephew of one, who was in his nurse's arms. The eldest of us knelt first and the rest followed in order. When it came to the three-year-old's turn, he became shy of kneeling by himself, though he had knelt each time anybody else had and thought it a great joke. He had not learnt to put his left knee down first and then the right, and just bumped down on both together, making us all jump. My nephew struggled to get down on the floor too and his nurse had to hold him tightly. Grandmother gave us each her best wishes for the coming year, and in addition a small parcel of copper coins with which to buy fireworks and lanterns. By the time we had visited all the other elders we were quite rich, though it was only aunts who gave us money. There was never any question of saving the money, for we had no use for it since we did not go outside the house and garden; hence the coins usually found their way into the pockets of our nurses, who, incidentally, also received gifts of money on their own account.

When we left Grandmother's chamber the girls set out on their round. The only difference in the procedure was that in kneeling to pay respect they did not fold their hands together, but just moved their hands up and down a few times in front of their chest before kneeling.

Between four and five next morning the first uncle led us out again to perform the ceremony of unlocking the gate. We would go a few steps from the gate and greet each other with *Kung-ho-hsin-hsi* (' Happy New Year '). Then we made another tour to greet the elders with *Kung-ho-hsin-hsi*. This time we got no parcels, and on the particular occasion I am thinking of the youngest cousin did not join in because he was sound asleep. (I must admit I had had a few hours' sleep in between.)

In the crack of the gate or underneath it we usually found a number of greeting cards. We did not send them by post in those days, and those of us who wished to avoid the trouble of performing the ceremonies of etiquette in person preferred to go round their relatives and friends very early and leave greeting cards. This early greeting showed the importance of the friendship. All our elders were in their own rooms by then, probably asleep and anxious to avoid all the formality of greeting early visitors. Two youngsters who were not too sleepy were chosen to stand in the first hall to answer the callers. I was given this job for the first time when I was about twelve. I could not have done

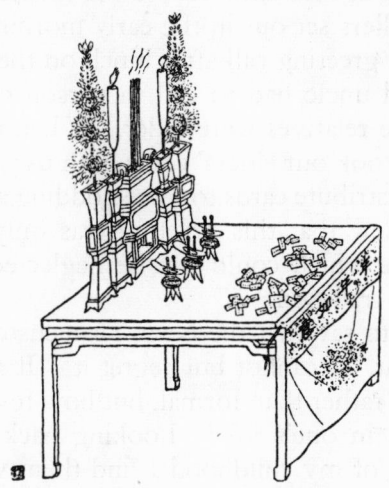

TABLE WITH GREETING CARDS LEFT BY CALLERS

it earlier, for there was much to learn about the formalities of answering callers. For instance, if the caller was a friend of my third uncle, he would ask me first to request my grandparents to come out, then my third uncle and aunt. I would answer respectfully that I thanked him on their behalf, but that they were all engaged and would be informed of his call later. Then the caller left his greeting card and he and I would bow to each other ceremoniously and I would escort him to the entrance-gate and say good-bye with another bow. The expressions used in this conver-sation were extremely formal, but very figurative, and so evasive in meaning that they can hardly be translated. I remember I managed quite well the first time, in spite of some embarrassment when three or four callers came at once, including some of our closest relatives who insisted on seeing the elders and could not be sent away with complimentary words.

My elders also sent greetings and the older boys conveyed them. The list of houses to be visited was divided up and two boys were sent in each direction. It was not necessary to do them all in one day because the festival lasted three days. The callers set out in the early morning, and it was rare to make a greeting call after lunch on these three days. My father and uncle had to call in person on our closest relatives, if the relatives were older. When we set out on these calls we took our elders' cards with us. The servants were sent to distribute cards to mere nodding acquaintances. Everybody knew that this greeting was only a formality, but it was one which could not be neglected. Such was the power of tradition.

I am sorry to say that the New Year customs are gradually dying out. I cannot but regret it. It may be better to be practical rather than formal, but how few really joyful times one has in one's life! Looking back on the New Year Festivals of my childhood I find them very precious. What a business they were! But what pleasure and good fellowship they gave!

CHERRY SELLER

12

NOT 'MISTER'

Our teacher held a very high position in our family life in my childhood. A Chinese proverb, *I-jih-ch'ih-Ssu, Chung-sheng-wei-fu*, states that he who becomes the teacher of a child for one day is the ' father ' of that child's lifetime. This proverb always rang in my ears when I listened to the serious talk of my elders. In the middle of our ancestral shrine we had a big red tablet painted with five golden characters representing Heaven, Earth, Nation, Parents and Teacher. (' Nation ' took the place of ' Emperor ' after the Revolution.) The position of ' Teacher ' was the fifth and last, but it stood next to that of ' Parents '. Twice a month, on the first day and the fifteenth, one of my elders burned incense in front of the shrine and knelt down to pay respect on behalf of the family. We youngsters followed suit if we happened to be there. I used to fire the fireworks for this homage.

The importance attached to the teacher's position is testified to by the fact that he stood side by side with our parents on these occasions. Confucius taught that children should be filial to their parents and respect their elders. I do not know whether the idea of setting up the tablet to Heaven, Earth, Nation, Parents and Teacher originated with him or not. If it did, he must have been an odd man— afraid, perhaps, that his own disciples might not respect him as highly as he expected !

Theoretically speaking, young people in China have always gone in awe of their elders. In my house I felt there were already enough elders to be respected without a most tyrannical teacher as well. Had I known in those days of the free life of English children I should certainly have wished myself in Europe. But probably English children would tell me that they are not free either.

I do not know why my elders always gave way to the teacher's tyranny. Whenever they saw him look distressed or annoyed they would ask us whether any of us had offended him or had not been working well. Then they would apologize to him for us and endeavour to soothe him. This made us very careful of our behaviour in the family school, and also encouraged the teacher to be more tyrannical than ever. The elders seemed to think that he could not be too tyrannical. They often told us that without strict training in youth, one could not expect to achieve anything in later life. They also said that parents could not train their own children well, being influenced by affection for them : we had, therefore, to have a good teacher ; and they went on to emphasize how fortunate we were to have *this* good teacher. To them ' good ' in connexion with a teacher signified not merely one who possessed much knowledge, but one who would beat his students hard for laziness, thereby showing how seriously he took his responsibilities. A teacher was never blamed for inflicting physical pain on a naughty or lazy student. The parents of a student who had been punished, so far from being able to sue the teacher in the law courts, generally had to apologize in person to him and take back the punished child most humbly to the school. If the child returned to the school by himself, the teacher could, if he thought the parents resented the child's punishment, turn him away and refuse to continue to be his teacher. When this happened, the parents were greatly shamed and felt that they could not hold up their heads in society. Accordingly teachers were always pandered to.

The system sounds a good one for encouraging learning, but in reality how many Chinese families had in the course of centuries found it difficult in practice ! I am not regretting the system : I am only sorry that my own elders did not realize what we youngsters endured at the hands of our teacher. Of course, it might have been worse. He seldom beat any of us, though he kept a number of rods and sticks. But then, it was the custom in my family for parents, when sending a child to the family school, to wrap a new rod in red paper and present it to the teacher for use on their child. My father made a beautiful one when I joined the school at about six years of age.

Our teacher had another method of punishing us. My youngest uncle, who was only a year older than I, was considered the naughtiest boy among us. He always earned bad remarks for his writing and his recitation of passages from Confucius' Analects ; indeed, he was really not interested in learning at all. But he was a very good talker and very mischievous. Sometimes before he produced his work he would whisper to us that he was a good prophet and that he expected the same remark from ' Old Beard ' as last time. We all gave him a smile. ' Old Beard ' was our nickname for the teacher. It was not intended to be flattering, and we warned each other never to mention it in the house. Once when this youngest uncle had, for some reason or other, offended the tutor, ' Old Beard ' made him kneel down in the middle of the courtyard not far from the huge Tseng-tree which I have already described. To make him keep his back straight a huge square inkstone full of water was placed on his head. The teacher's seat being directly opposite him, he could not move for fear of spilling the water. At that time our teacher did not possess a watch, so my uncle had to kneel for the length of time that it took a stick of incense to burn. The stick was about eight inches long and burnt out in a little less than half an hour. My youngest uncle bore his punishment with remarkable patience. Although he was supposed to be a warning to the rest of us to be industrious, we were all much more anxious to see how he was bearing up than to go on with our work. Each of us in turn asked permission to ' leave the room '. The teacher must have realized why, but he could not forbid us to go. When I passed my uncle, he gave me a wink and then pulled a long face. It was difficult not to laugh aloud. The girls could not share in this bit of mischief as they had to ' leave the room ' in another direction. When the incense stick had burnt away uncle was told to get up. He did not seem particularly exhausted. My fifth *Kê*, who was also a naughty boy, insisted on uncle telling us how he had felt while kneeling so long. Uncle said that he

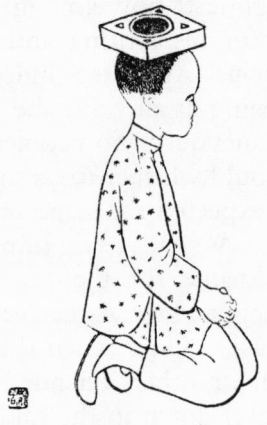

REMARKABLE PATIENCE

felt very strange when the inkstone was first put on his head, but he could not describe the sensation exactly; he wanted to move, but there seemed to be something preventing him from doing so ! Suddenly he remembered a story he had read in some book about a well-trained wrestler, and he went on and on thinking of this until he forgot about himself. Just when he realized that he was very tired, he was ordered to get up. We all laughed and said that he was trying to lure us into tasting the punishment too. Uncle replied that he thought it would be worth practising with the inkstone while ' Old Beard ' was out in case any

of us should be victims on another occasion. Uncle was
eleven years old at this time.

There were in the school eight boys, including the
teacher's son, and four girls. The girls did not study for
as many hours as we did ; when they were old enough they
had to spend a good deal of time inside the house learning
housekeeping and embroidery.

The teacher adopted different methods for each of us,
according to our age and mentality. There were two sets
of simple books, used for both girls and boys, composed
of lines of three characters and lines of four characters with
rhymes. They were universally used in China for teaching
children to recognize the characters. We all learned them
by heart without necessarily knowing their meaning. Then
we began to read the ' Four Books ', with Confucius'
Analects as the first book. We had to be proficient in
each book before we could proceed to the next, so some of
us got on faster than others. At first we were taught only
to read and recite them over and over again. We could
not question the ' by rote ' method and in those days we
did not think of doing so. When we could recite the whole
four books without a mistake the teacher explained the
meaning of them to us passage by passage for an hour or
two every day. Then we began to read the commentaries
on each book by well-known Confucian scholars.

I was not the cleverest boy of my group. My eighth
cousin, who was six months younger than I, could repeat
by heart most of the commentaries as well as the texts.
I could only manage the texts. After the ' Four Books '
came ' The Thirteen Classics ' and the history of China,
all within the framework of Confucian thought. Nothing
else. In the family school we learnt *only* how to read the
classics and how to write well.

Generally we read the classics for two hours in the early
morning ; then we practised handwriting or calligraphy for
another two hours ; after which passages of the classics
were explained to us for perhaps a further hour. If we

could then remember what we had learnt, the day's work was done. Boys of from twelve upwards, however, had to work another hour or two in the evening. The length of time spent in studying was very flexible. Seldom were two or three of us taught the same thing at one time. As soon as we had finished the day's task we could leave the school.

Personally I liked being in the school, because it was near the garden and because there was really nothing to do in the house when the rest of the youngsters were not there. We did not have to go at a definite time and we boys were always there earlier than the teacher. The girls usually arrived later, and did not come at all in the afternoon. I began going at the age of six, and for about a year I only went in the morning, though sometimes I stayed longer from choice.

When I first joined, some of my older cousins, who were practising calligraphy seriously, had reached the stage of suspending their arms in the air while writing. I began to do this when I was about ten. From time to time the teacher praised my efforts and once he came up behind me and tried to snatch my brush out of my hand. He failed and I acquired merit thereby, for it is essential to good writing to hold the brush very tight. In time I began to practise with a weight of books on my suspended arm, and the weight was gradually increased. At first I felt odd writing like that, but I could make no objection, and little by little I got used to it and came scarcely to notice it. When, after long practice, I was allowed to write without it, I found that my strokes were much more sure.

I still cannot make up my mind whether our teacher was really a very terrifying person. He always looked so. Perhaps his invariably serious and unsmiling expression caused this. I suppose he wanted to appear scholarly and dignified. Funnily enough, most of his friends were teachers in other families and looked more or less like him. I have heard Europeans say that the Chinese are emotionless creatures with impassive faces. They must be thinking of our teachers. 'Old Beard' had been in my family for a long time. He had been my brother's teacher; his father had been my father's teacher; his son was going to be my nephew's teacher. Not being a native of Kiu-kiang, he did not know many people in the city and hardly ever left the school. This pleased the elders very much: us, not so much, for it meant we never had a holiday. Sometimes he fell asleep in school. We had special games for these occasions which I have no space to describe here. When we were caught, either the youngest uncle or the fifth cousin was always punished as the ringleader.

The only holiday he took was at the time of the New Year Festival, when he generally went back to his native district for a month and returned to our house about the seventeenth or eighteenth day of the first month. Once I met him at the entrance-gate of our house as he arrived. I gave him a deep bow and the greeting *Kung-ho-hsin-hsi*. Then I shouted towards the inside of the house 'Chou Hsien-sheng is here. Chou Hsien-sheng is here.' The others all came out to greet him. But his face suddenly darkened and he said to me severely: ' Ah, you know my surname is Chou. I am glad that you have not forgotten it. The others can call me Chou Hsien-sheng: not you. You must address me as Hsien-sheng. . . .' I did not know how I had offended him, but my grandfather and father ordered me to kneel down and beg his pardon and I had to obey. Later it was explained to me that Hsien-sheng is a term used in addressing other people besides teachers or professors. It is used after the surname by a person addressing a friend or mere acquaintance of the name of Chou. But for the relationship between teacher and student no surname is needed before Hsien-sheng. Hsien means ' before ' and Sheng means ' born '. Hsien-sheng, therefore, means ' one who was born before ' and so one who knows more than the person who is addressing him. This is merely a polite mode of address. Chou Hsien-sheng can be translated into English as Mr. Chou and Hsien-sheng means ' teacher ' only.   So I learnt that I must not address our teacher as ' Mister ' !

How strict he was ! I do not agree with his way of teaching, but I am glad that I was trained under his tyrannical rule, for otherwise I might not remember Confucius' classics as well as I do.   My nephew and the generation after mine will miss his training !

CHILDREN'S TOY SELLER

13

THE MORNING WALK

THOUGH MY grandfather, at the time that I remember him, was getting on in years, he could still walk perfectly well with the support of a dragon-headed stick, and he rarely missed his morning walk with his birds. He had three caged birds : one *Pai-ling* (lark) and two *Hua-mei* (a species of dark yellow thrush with long white eyes and

GRANDFATHER'S BIRD-CAGES

black-brown eyeballs). Both species sing beautifully and often. In the middle of the *Pai-ling's* cage there was a small round stand on which the bird liked to sing. Occasionally it shook its wings and looked very proud of itself. Its cage had to be much taller than that of the others because it flew higher. There were three sticks across the cages of the *Hua-mei* and the birds hopped from one to the other.

Grandfather took great trouble to prepare food for his

birds and to give them air. He would hang the cages on trees, not only in our garden but in a little wood near a tiny hill called Yen-chih shan (Rouge Hill), so named because of its red soil. He could not carry all three cages himself, so a youngster or a servant always went with him. I often accompanied him.

In the early mornings when we came down the road which led to the wood we met nobody but other bird-lovers. They all knew Grandfather well and at once entered into conversation, mainly about their birds. We were never the first to reach the wood, possibly because Grandfather walked slowly and our house was some distance away. As we approached we would see scores of birds hanging in their cages from the trees and all singing joyously, as if in competition. It was an indescribably charming scene, with the green background of trees and the grass dotted with red flowers. Nobody could have resisted the spell or wished to disturb the songsters.

Once I asked Grandfather in a whisper why our birds did not sing on the way out. Grandfather murmured that they were reserving their strength in order to sing well in the wood. I remember seeing one or two *Hua-mei* belonging to other people being let out of their cages to fly about among the trees. After a while they flew back again and the owners went home. Grandfather never tried this with our birds, however.

Grandfather was always very happy when we got to the wood. After he had hung the bird-cages on trees, he gave little more attention to them and just strolled about with one or two of his old friends, walking very slowly and talking a great deal. I always referred to their talks as 'doctrines of birds'. Occasionally I picked up some scraps of knowledge from them. I might meet one or two young companions who had also been brought by their elders, but in such a peaceful environment I did not mind spending the whole morning alone. If I did not stroll round after Grandfather, I could sit or lie on the ground

and pick the tiny wild flowers, or make different kinds
of knots with long blades of grass. As a matter of fact, I
generally climbed up and down the little hill or sat in the
stone bower. There was nothing to make us hurry back,
unless we felt hungry for lunch.

After birds, Grandfather's greatest passion was chrysanthemums. He never failed to get new specimens each
autumn. Once, after one of our morning walks with the
birds, he suggested taking me to the famous garden of the
Li family, situated at the Yo-ssu gate in the city wall of
Kiu-kiang. It was not far from the wood. As the blue
autumn sky was high and cloudless and it was early for us
to go home, Grandfather thought he might look for some
new specimens of chrysanthemums, as it was the season of
blooming. The garden had long been famous for the
beauty of its structure and the skill with which it was
planted. But the descendants of the Li family had various
troubles and could not maintain it properly, and ultimately
it was taken over by a sort of nurseryman. From time to
time exhibitions of flowers were held there, and any one
could go in to look round and buy. When we arrived I
found that the head gardener knew my Grandfather.
Leading us to a painted bower he served tea and entered
into a discussion with Grandfather on the details of
chrysanthemum culture. After a few minutes my attention
was caught by a tall wooden stand bearing different kinds
of chrysanthemums in pots, arranged in tiers to form a
kind of ' hill ' of flowers. The arrangement is actually
called ' chrysanthemum flower hill '—*Ch'u-hua-shan*. Presently the head gardener conducted us round the garden,
showing us flowers of every shape and colour. Grandfather told me that there were about sixty varieties of
chrysanthemums—more varieties than those of any other
flower. A number of special varieties were pointed out
to us—*Chin-chien-ch'u* (golden coin), *Hsieh-hsin-ch'u* (crab-
shaped), *Han-ch'u*, *Lu-ti-ch'u*, and so on. While we were
slowly promenading the garden Grandfather made, as usual,

some reference to the first Ming emperor. He mentioned that this emperor had written a poem on the chrysanthemum, and that it ran as follows :

While a hundred flowers blossom, I do not.
If I burst into bloom, they are afraid to show themselves.
Tussling with the west wind all night before the doorstep,
The great mass of chrysanthemums waves its golden armour.

Grandfather went on to explain how the poem conveyed the heroic nature of the emperor ; for the chrysanthemum has always been admired by our poets and scholars for the way in which it blooms in spite of frost and sharp weather, as no other flower does. The first Ming emperor was by birth a beggar and an illiterate ; he ascended the throne by driving out the Tartars.

Before leaving the garden of the Li family, Grandfather ordered the gardener to send a few pots of chrysanthemums to our house. How well I remember what care he took of them and of his other chrysanthemums, watering them himself and tenderly pruning them ! It may sound a waste of time, but surely it was a pleasant way for an old man to pass his time ?

Every one in our household liked the flowers ; but I must admit that the birds were not quite so universally accepted. Little quarrels between Grandfather and Grandmother took place over them (Plate 2) ! Not that Grandmother disliked the birds. On the contrary. But often when she wanted a servant for some household job he or she would be occupied in preparing food for the birds. These little ' differences ' were complicated by the fact that Grandmother herself kept pets. She had two cats, one yellowish-brown, the other black and white, and although they never got hold of the birds, whose cages were hung too high for them, they often lurked menacingly beneath. So when Grandfather saw the cats he complained on behalf of his birds : and when Grandmother grumbled about the birds' food she heard about the cats. After each of such little bouts of ' words ' they would part in silence, Grandfather going to the garden or to see the teacher of the family school, and Grandmother to the kitchen. No other member of the family, of course, could break the silence between them.

GOLDFISH SELLER

- 14 -

THE ANIMAL NATURE OF MAN

ONE MORNING one of Mother's cousins rushed into our house and told my father that he had no peace at home and was beside himself. Father took him to his study and calmed him as best he could. I was just going off to school when he arrived and when I returned he was still there. Presently, I heard the elders talking about him. This was not the first time they had done so, but this time it was more serious. The trouble was that he wanted to take another woman into his home. The whole of the previous night his wife had argued with him, so that neither of them had slept. In the morning she had made a terrible mess in the house, destroying anything she found in her way. The floors were strewn with broken porcelain and bits of mirror. She finished up by declaring that she would go and find the woman and fight her. At this point, my mother's cousin had fled to seek help from my father. But my father could not help. It was entirely a matter for the husband and wife to settle between themselves. So they argued.

This cousin of my mother's was very wealthy, and had besides a reputation as a scholar, as well as being a good business man with a number of enterprises in the city. Mother's family was even bigger than ours. Indeed, so big was it that after the death of her parents and uncles, it could not be held together ; quarrels arose nearly every day. At length it was decided to break up the family into smaller units. A family council was called, and every member attended, including the closer relations-in-law, such as my father. The separation was signed and each member took a copy. Since that time this cousin of my mother's had lived by himself with his wife and daughter.

Rumour had it that it was his wife who had caused the break up of the big family. She came of a well-to-do family and was well educated, but she had such an awkward disposition that she could not get on with any one. Her meanness was notorious. She had very few friends, and not even her closest relations cared to see her. People said that her husband owed his wealth to his wife's meanness ; and if this was so it was an ironical fact, for it was certainly his wealth which led him into trouble with other women. If he had had less money he might have been quite content with his wife, and the second woman not have troubled about him. Moreover, his wife was noted as a beauty. They were both older than my father, and their daughter was married, but she and her husband lived with them. They had also an adopted son.

From the time their daughter was ten years old my mother's cousin had been agitating to take another woman into his house, so that he could have a son of his own to carry on the family name 'according to the Confucian principle'. His wife had never let him have his way. She kept the strictest possible watch on him, and he had to stay at home most of his time and even attend to his business indoors. But money has a mysterious power and had caused women to pursue him. Even so, he had not succeeded in introducing one into his house in spite of many attempts. People had begun to think that at the age of sixty he had given up the struggle. But he hadn't. And this was the trouble which made him seek help from my father. He hoped that he was going to have an heir and had told his wife that it would only be proper for the mother to come and live in the house. His wife roared at him with fury, and the disturbance began again.

Just after our dinner, the wife herself came panting to our house to ask for her husband, having heard that he had come to us. My sister-in-law took her into her chamber, she being her niece. The wife was accompanied by her daughter and two maid-servants. Grandmother and the aunts came to listen to her story. She told how she had just visited the place where the prospective mother lived. She had found nobody there but had seen many things which she recognized as having been bought by her husband, and had accordingly destroyed them. Apparently none of her auditors saw any harm in this, though after she had gone, Grandmother did say that perhaps she had acted a little too hastily. Every one fell to discussing what would happen. All seemed agreed that the husband would once more bow to his wife. Divorce was out of the question.

Then one of my aunts mentioned the peculiar methods used by this wife to beautify herself. She still kept her youthful appearance, and though she was mean in general she was not parsimonious over cosmetics. She also expended large sums of money in obtaining good herbs and new medicines for the benefit of her health. Ginseng and bird's-nest soup were her more or less constant tonic. She used to use the white of egg to wash her face, because that was supposed to keep the flesh tender and smooth. And she also had a peculiar way of removing wrinkles by boiling four big fresh pigs' knuckles until they formed a gelatinous paste, which she applied to her face at bedtime. After a fortnight of this treatment there would not be a wrinkle left on her face. That was why she looked about thirty when she was actually the same age as her husband.

Suddenly another aunt asked why it was, if she was still so beautiful, her husband wanted to take another woman? And a third aunt remarked that he must be a very obstinate man to defy his wife so determinedly. Grandmother smiled and said: 'It is the animal nature of man.'

The end of the story is not a pleasant one. The husband, as my elders expected, remained obedient to his wife. How unhappy they must have been together! But two **years** later she died, and he was able to bring the second woman into his home. But only four years after that he died himself.

SWEETS SELLER

THE FIRST SOUP

My GRANDMOTHER and my father were very disappointed that my brother's wedding had to take place while we were in refuge in the country. Had we been at home there would have been a great gathering of relations and friends for the ceremony, and we would all have been very merry for several days. On the other hand, they were quite pleased to have an unusual type of wedding, with all our farmer friends to join in the fun, reminding us that we had once been farmers ourselves. My recollection is that my brother's wedding was more enjoyable than those which took place in the city. I had seen the wedding of my tenth uncle (who was only a year older than my brother), and later I was to see many other weddings, so that the comparison is not without foundation. Frequently we had two weddings in our house in a year, one perhaps for a young Chiang bringing a wife into the family, the other for a girl being sent to her new home. Both required a great deal of preparation, and my elders thought of nothing else for weeks. The whole house was always repainted, and all the closest relatives and some particular friends asked to stay with us for the event ; some of the chambers would have to be equipped with two or three beds to accommodate all the guests. The celebrations lasted two or three days and cost a good deal of money, but the elders believed that the gayer the celebrations the happier would be the future of the young couple. I doubt now whether this always came true. It seems to me that we stressed too much the three events, birth, marriage and death.

Their importance is, of course, undeniable, but elaborate celebrations do not make them more significant, although I must say I thoroughly enjoyed each celebration at the time, and so, I think, did most of the others.

My brother had to be married first because he was Number One in my generation. I saw my sister-in-law quite often before her marriage, for she was the first niece of my mother. I knew there was something afoot in connexion with her, and then one day I was teased by some of my aunts about soon having a new kind of rice cake to eat, and that confirmed it. This was a traditional joke. The ' new rice cake ' was shaped like the palm of a hand, which meant that I would be slapped by my new sister-in-law if I offended her. She could not slap me before her marriage. So after my brother's wedding, I reflected, I should have one more person to control me. What it was to be a small boy in China in those days ! But in reality I did not take the joke seriously, for I knew that my sister-in-law was a kind-hearted person.

The wedding was to take place the following year, seven or eight months ahead, and things were being got ready bit by bit when the Revolution suddenly broke out and we moved to the country. Actually, no disturbance whatever occurred in Kiu-kiang, but for some reason we stayed in the country for a full year, and the wedding was not postponed. Father and two uncles came and made the arrangements. The red invitation cards with big red envelopes, which had been written before we left home, had to be abandoned and new ones prepared for the farmer friends. A good room in the farm-house was redecorated. My sister-in-law's family moved to a village near by, but the girl herself did not come to see us. As the preparations went forward my new companions too, cowherds and farm girls, began to tease me about the ' new rice cake '.

On the day before the wedding there should have been a procession of furniture, curtains, clothes and all kinds of embroidery from the bride's house to the bridegroom's, but this was impossible on this occasion because most of the stuff had not been moved to the country. Everything was simplified. Several good country cooks prepared a banquet in the country fashion. A fine bridal sedan-chair was hired from the city and kept in the middle of our farm-house. Gradually, old and young, boys and girls, gathered round the farm-house, and eventually they all became our guests, though we did not really know them. Grandmother was delighted to have so many people to enjoy the celebrations and so to make the event as impor-

BRIDAL SEDAN-CHAIR

tant and gay as possible. A temporary ancestral shrine was erected in the farm-house.

On the wedding day, after the incense had been burnt and the fireworks let off, the bridegroom knelt down before the shrine three times and then bowed once to the bridal sedan-chair, which was then borne away to fetch the bride. A number of musicians blowing pipes, and two beating brass gongs, led the bearers of the chair. The moment the sound was heard of the pipes and gongs coming back, the musicians in the house began to play their pipes, gongs and drums. When the bride's chair reached the house, a long strip of fireworks was let off and all the lanterns and red candles were lit. Then the chair was set in the centre of the hall and my brother approached it, bowed, and opened it. Two married ladies stood on either side of the chair to help the bride out. As she wore a square veil of red silk over her face she could see nothing except her own feet; so, unlike an English bride with her bridesmaids, she really did need support for the ceremony. The two ladies stood on her right hand and the bridegroom on her left. She and the bridegroom knelt down and stood up at the bidding of the crier, who was responsible for the etiquette of the proceedings. First they paid respect to the front of the house, which stood for the universe, then to the ancestral shrine, and lastly, kneeling face to face, to each other.

After this, two boys, of whom I was one, held a pair of candles decorated with floral designs to guide the bride and bridegroom to their new room. The bride was conducted to the edge of the bed, where she sat down, and then the bridegroom bowed and took off her veil. Then at last I saw my sister-in-law clearly; but she lowered her head and would not notice me. Her red bridal dress was beautifully embroidered with many of the traditional symbols of happy omen, and she wore one of the magnificent headdresses called ' Phoenix hat ' (*Feng-kuan*).

My brother now tried to escape from the crowd in order to avoid the time-honoured jokes, but the merry-making guests stopped him at the door and more and more people came into the room. They felt it was their turn now! The bride was not supposed to laugh or say a word, so the guests vied with one another in attempts to make her do so. The jokes were mingled with quotations from Chinese literature about famous happy couples of ancient times; and of course many figurative expressions were used, such as the wish that the bridal pair would be as happy together that night as a pair of mandarin ducks (the symbol of love) face to face beneath a lotus flower. After a time the guests were asked to retire, and the bride and bridegroom had a short rest.

Later a small formal dinner was held in the bridal room.

Actually there were only four seats, two for the couple and two for the lady supporters; but an exception was made in favour of myself and the other boy who had taken part in the ceremony, as we did not want to leave the room. The lady supporters poured out wine for the bride and bridegroom, mixed it, and then poured it back into the cups, a ceremony called *Ho-chen* (combining the cups), symbolical of the happiness they would share. Finally, the chief cook produced, as an expression of good wishes from himself and his assistants, a stork made of boiled ducks' eggs, the yokes forming the body and the whites the head, wings and feathers; the legs were two thin sticks, and the whole stood on a lotus flower also made of white of egg; green leaves and small red flowers decorated the dish. It was not meant to eat, but it looked very fine in the middle of the table among the other dishes. In presenting it, the chief cook had to speak a carefully prepared greeting, and the couple then gave him a reward. In the end the stork was given to me.

When the private dinner was nearly finished a banquet was given to the guests, ladies and gentlemen sitting in separate halls. My brother had to come out and bow to the gentlemen and his wife to the ladies.

My sister-in-law's nurse had accompanied her and was to stay in our house for a few days to help accustom the bride to her new life. The nurse too had her wedding ritual to perform. The morning after the ceremony she produced a bowl of boiled *Lien-tzu* (lotus seeds), which the couple shared as a symbol of their hope that they would soon have a baby. Later the nurse dressed the bride's hair and helped her to put on the new clothes which took the place of the bridal robe. Then the ceremony of recognizing the family began.

The couple knelt or bowed to each member according to age and generation, the member returning the bow and giving the couple a present called a *Chien-mien-li* (present for making acquaintance). Youngsters gave no present.

Grandmother told the couple that they were getting off lightly : if the wedding had taken place in the city they would have had to stand for two to three hours, so great would have been the number of guests ! Most of them, too, would have stayed in the house, whereas here the majority had left the previous night. Grandmother and Father missed the prolonged merriment.

I could not understand why my sister-in-law never smiled or spoke a word to me these two whole days. I feared the story of the rice cakes might prove true. Suddenly a very young girl-cousin who, with me, had tried to learn some of the hill songs we had heard the cowherds sing when we played with them, sang the following song outside the bridal chamber :

On the mountains there is pure water,
On the plains there are beautiful flowers.
In every family there are charming girls ;
But if you're penniless it's no use thinking of marrying one.

Everybody was enchanted at the sound of this song issuing from such small lips. And my sister-in-law smiled at last. I was sent out to fetch the singer, who at once became full of conceit and sang again :

> Pepper is as hot as ginger ;
> A wife is as dear as a mother.
> But mother is the grass by the roadside ;
> So obviously a wife is better.

There was a great roar of laughter and she was told to repeat this when my brother came in. My sister-in-law kept on smiling. I ran to her and asked her why she had not smiled before. But she excused herself hurriedly and said she would tell me later. I am sure my mother, had she been alive, would have been delighted to hear this last song. As she was dead, sister-in-law was spared all the teasing stories about bad-tempered mothers-in-law which as a rule were the main topic of conversation on such occasions as this. The subject of mothers-in-law was so common that there were even nursery rhymes about it, such as the following :

A mother's praise of her daughter is no praise :
A mother-in-law's praise of her daughter-in-law is like a sprig of flowers.
In every family on earth there is a mother who praises her daughter :
But where is the mother-in-law who praises her daughter-in-law to the skies ?

On the third morning of the wedding my sister-in-law was dressed in more new clothes, this time an ordinary working dress over which an apron was tied, and the nurse led her to the kitchen to make her first soup. Like everything else at the wedding it was a mere formality. My sister-in-law stirred the soup in the pan with a brass spoon and added the seasoning. While she was doing so the nurse murmured some compliment to the effect that the bride would make good soup to please her husband and the household in general. This ceremony accomplished, each of us tasted a little of the soup, and then the whole business of the marriage was at an end.

On the fourth day husband and wife went to spend the day with the bride's family. From then on she lived in her husband's house and shared the kitchen work with the aunts and older girls.

Writing of the ' first soup ' I am reminded of a famous T'ang poem which I think most Chinese, especially girls, know :

> On the third day the bride goes to the kitchen,
> Washes her hands and prepares to make soup.
> Not knowing the taste of her mother-in-law,
> She asks sister-in-law to sample it first.

- 16 -

THE STORY OF A HANDSOME YOUNG MAN

THERE HAD been something in the wind for days. We did not know what it was, but my father kept talking to the grandparents and had many more visitors than usual. One morning my two little boy-cousins and I saw Father at the entrance greeting two friends and a young man about my brother's age with a shining new bicycle. We were most excited at the spectacle of this strange thing, but we had to suppress our feelings out of respect for Father's guests, and could only gaze at the machine from a distance. When the party entered the guest-hall, the young man did not follow immediately, but stayed to adjust something on his bicycle.

I ran into my sister's chamber and told her to come and see this peculiar new object. She came, along with all my girl-cousins ; they stood inside the screen doors, while I and the younger ones went into the first sky-well. The young man turned a curious unsmiling gaze on us. Then the three elders too came to the door of the hall. They looked especially at the group of girls, who at once dispersed in a flurry, causing much laughter, my sister stumbling and almost falling in her anxiety to get inside. Later I heard that the whole thing had been arranged to enable the young man and his father to see my sister before her betrothal. I remember being very puzzled at the time as to why she should have run away from the young man she was going to marry, but habit and custom made Chinese girls shy and nervous when facing any stranger, especially in circumstances which included the possibility of betrothal. Afterwards my sister was constantly discussed and teased by all the elder cousins and by her aunts. It was considered either very bold or very shameless for a girl to retort to or join in the talk about her fiancé-to-be, and any attempt to do so only led to more talk and teasing. So my sister preferred to remain silent. No doubt she was embarrassed, but on the other hand she could pick up a lot of information by just listening.

One summer evening a month or two later we young people were sitting round Grandmother in the garden. It was her habit to tell us legends and stories, about immortals and spirits, or about her own life as a girl and young wife, or about the city and its history. Some of the stories interested me and some did not, but we were all impressed by Grandmother's knowledge. After a cup or two of *kao-liang* (a Chinese strong white wine made of barley) she was always in good humour and ready to entertain us. We all preferred stories about spirits to stories of any other kind; but sometimes I had to hide in my sister's arms if the demon was too frightening. On this particular evening I was drawing close to my sister in case of emergency, when Grandmother said that she wanted to tell us something new.

'It is the story of a handsome young man,' she began. 'Near the lake P'oyang there lived some hundred years ago a family with three charming daughters. The parents were highly cultured and wealthy. Faithful to tradition they wanted a son to carry on the family name and to pay respect to the family ancestors. Having no son they were able, according to custom, to take a son-in-law into the family who would adopt his wife's name. They knew of a suitable man, but unfortunately his family was poor, and he had no social standing. He was, however, very good-looking, with all five organs—eyebrows, eyes, nose, mouth and ears—beautifully formed and placed, hair deep black, and thin hands with long fingers indicating wisdom. In spite of his poor background he behaved in most gentle fashion.   Moreover, he was very clever and had at an early age finished the Four Books and the Five Classics of Confucius.   He wrote charmingly, besides working very hard as a servant.   Being struck by this young man's qualities, the parents of the three daughters made friends with him, although he did not realize why.

'Then they told their eldest daughter that they would like her to marry him.   But she answered that she would starve to death if she married such an unworthy beggar, and asked how he could possibly be good-looking if he wore shabby clothes.

'So they tried the second daughter.   But the second daughter replied that she could not marry him either, because she would be demeaning herself if she married a man from a family of no social standing.

'At last the third daughter was asked to express her opinion.   She made no reply for a long time, except to bow her head, overcome with shyness.   Then she said that she did not consider riches and social standing more important than character.   A young man who had a good character would gain the other things.   Her parents were delighted and the betrothal ceremony was arranged.'

At this point Grandmother emphasized how good, obedient and filial according to Confucius' ideas the third daughter was.

'After the betrothal the third daughter began to dream of her fiancé's cleverness, and imagined him becoming a celebrated man in society, and she thought how happy they would be together.   Everything about him interested her. The young man, for his part, when he heard that he had been rejected by the two elder daughters, fell desperately in love with the third and resolved not to disappoint her. After a time they married and lived in great harmony. They helped each other, worked hard, and made the family more prosperous than before.   Some years later the eldest daughter's husband lost his fortune, and he and his wife had to live on the third sister. And the second sister's husband too was unsuccessful and forced to earn a living by fortune-telling, which is beneath the notice of people of any social standing. Consequently the third daughter was praised by everybody in that city, and her two sisters were condemned as *Hsien-ping-ai-fu* (those who hate to marry into poverty and only love riches).'

There was a long pause when Grandmother reached this point. I did not find the story very interesting, but I listened attentively, hoping for a better one to follow. My sister and girl-cousins, on the other hand, were obviously attracted by it. Presently Grandmother herself said that this story might not be so interesting to boys as to girls, but it did show how wise it was for a boy to work hard and be filial if he wished to have a beautiful wife. 'I want you all to stay and hear the end of the story,' she continued. 'You girls must ponder it and try to get rid of the desire to marry a rich person without good character. Probably Tsui-chen [my sister] is a much luckier girl than the third daughter in the story : she is going to be betrothed to the handsome young man who came to our house with his bicycle the other day, and not only is he clever and good-looking, but his family is well-off.' With these words Grandmother laughed happily. My sister grew very embarrassed as we all looked at her. After that evening she kept away from us. Other girl-cousins explained her absence by saying : 'She has a handsome young man to think about now !'

I did not bother about this gossip. I was a rather easy-going and obedient lad, and easily fooled. One day my cousins and I were given toy figures made of wheat, with a stick attached to each. I had an old sage riding on a dragon ; my cousins had a sage standing on a toad and one holding a huge snake in his hand. After a day or two the wheat became dry and fell off, and we grew tired of these toys. Then my third and fourth girl-cousins told us to pick out the eyes of the animals, as they were really

Hsiang-ssu-tzu or *Hung-tau* (red beans, *Abrus precatorius*). These red beans are small, hard, egg-shaped berries of a bright coral-red, with a black spot round the hilum, making them very suitable for the eyes of dolls. They are also used as beads. We were told to fold our six ' eyes ' up in a small piece of reddish paper. Then I was sent to my fifth *Kê* to ask him to copy a poem about Hung-tau from the *Three Hundred T'ang Poems*, he being the eldest boy in the family school and the best writer at that time. Having copied out the poem on a piece of paper covered with a flowery design, he gave it to my third girl-cousin, who folded it up carefully and put it, together with the red beans, in a tiny embroidered box. Then she whispered to me to lay this box in my sister's toilet-case when my sister was not in her chamber. Knowing now that it was a joke I did not think there could be any harm in acceding to this request, and I did the job. I was then forbidden to mention the matter for a day at least. Nothing particular happened that evening, except that I felt uneasy when talking to my sister. Next morning I found three of my girl-cousins standing under the window of my sister's chamber trying to peep in. I went to the crack of the door and saw my sister opening the small embroidered box and taking out the poem and the red beans. She held the box and the beans in her right hand, read the poem very slowly and then closed her eyes as if her mind were filled with some strange thought. For a long while she did not move to comb her hair. We held our breath. Presently the youngest cousin, who was rather short, fell off her bamboo stool and made a noise. We all precipitately bolted. But later I was sent back to see whether my sister had heard us. I found her still deep in thought, though she had nearly finished her hairdressing. It was strange for a small boy like me to find my sister's manner different from usual, and I was interested in the fun and merrymaking among the cousins. All day they teased her, saying : ' What is a spring day that it makes one uneasy and weary ? ' Or :

'You *must* have found something strange to make you behave so differently.' My sister did not answer, but later in the day she grew very hot when my third girl-cousin came upon the little box.

It was supposed to have been sent by her fiancé-to-be as a first token of love, and I now know what it meant. The Chinese name for the small red beans, *Hsiang-ssu-tzu*, means ' Anxious desire ', and refers to the sorrow of some widow who wept under one of the leguminous shrubs which bear these seeds and died of her grief. Ever since a well-known T'ang poet wrote a poem about it, it has been a symbol of love, especially as applied to girls who long to see their lovers. It is not the Chinese custom for anybody to utter the word ' love ' directly and openly ; this is considered vulgar and may have the opposite effect to that desired. We therefore have many symbols for love, created mostly by our poets. The T'ang poem which my fifth *Kê* had copied runs :

> Red beans grow in the south country,
> In spring they have new branches.
> I should like you to collect more of them,
> Because they are full of anxious desire.

This is supposed to be written by a lady to a lover who was away travelling in the south country. When we were young, we were taught to recite most of the poems from the *Three Hundred T'ang Poems*, but our teacher and elders did not bother whether we understood them or not. We were all used to the sound of many of them because we so often heard our elders reciting them. By this time my sister had of course understood the meaning of the poem. I realized that I had been fooled, and that I had thoughtlessly played a rather heartless joke on her.

There was not much ceremony about my sister's be-trothal, but a great deal of discussion afterwards, for her fiancé asked his father to get her to study in an American

Missionary Girls' High School in Kiu-kiang. My brother-in-law's family was already modern ; the father worked in the Chinese customs house and knew some English through contact with Western officers and advisers. He sent his son to the Missionary Boys' High School, and that was why my brother-in-law rode the first bicycle in the city. The two schools were side by side, and we all knew that a student of the boys' school usually chose his bride from the girls' school, or if he was already betrothed, insisted on his bride attending the girls' school, so that he should not feel ashamed of her. This caused trouble in many families and a good number of engagements were broken off on account of it. I am sorry to say that these two schools were not viewed very favourably by the majority of the elders in the city, who considered that they only taught boys and girls to know each other, to make love, write love-letters, and, in short, to disobey their elders. Besides, the elders themselves knew nothing of Christianity, and could hardly be expected to see much good in it. I seem to remember that the schools were called ' Husband-and-Wife ' schools. In any case, it was natural for my sister's fiancé to want her to study at the girls' school. My father was an open-minded person, trained traditionally as an artist but accepting the inevitable changes, and it was he who finally overcame Grandfather's objections.

After a few days at the school my sister was certainly changed, and lost her shyness in talking about her fiancé. She pleased us youngsters very much by relating her experiences there. We found to our astonishment that the school was entirely different from our family school. My sister was the first of our family to learn the twenty-six letters of the English alphabet. I tried to curl my tongue round the strange sounds, imitating her, thinking she uttered them perfectly. And I also made circles and curves to represent English writing. But after a month or two we were tired of talking about my sister's school. The novelty had worn off, and in any case she was not interested in studying there, as everything was foreign.   A year later she was married and left the school.   And now I doubt whether she still remembers the twenty-six letters.

VEGETABLE SELLER

- 17 -

TWO SPRING DINNER-PARTIES

FOLLOWING THE three-day New Year celebrations my family planned a number of spring dinner-parties to take place during the first and second months of the year. Our relatives and friends did likewise. The catering was generally done by the best-known restaurants in the city, so we had no occasion to keep many dinner-sets. We called these parties *Chun-chiu* (' Spring wine ').

The first of them was always for ladies, possibly because all the planning was in Grandmother's hands. I remember that when I was quite young Grandmother once asked one of my older cousins to write the invitation for her. He used a ready-made red invitation paper which could be folded into four, six or eight sections according to the number of guests to be invited. On the inside my cousin wrote the names and addresses of all the ladies Grandmother wanted to invite, and, at the beginning, the date of the dinner-party and Grandmother's name. On the outside flap he wrote the word ' INVITATION ' in a large character. A servant was sent out with this to make a round of calls. Each of the invited guests saw the complete list of guests and wrote a word of acceptance or refusal under her name. The servant informed those who accepted at what time a sedan-chair would be sent to fetch them. When the servant got back Grandmother at once knew for how many people to prepare. Very few lady guests declined such invitations unless they were ill or otherwise engaged.

On the day of the party the sedan-chairs were sent out early to bring the guests. Dinner usually did not take place until about five o'clock, but the guests arrived soon after lunch. This made it possible for the ladies to bring

their small children with them. There was no question of
the guests arriving just before the meal, which would have
been considered ill-mannered, as signifying that they had
come only to satisfy their appetite. The friendly discourse
which was the object of the party took place before dinner,
and the guests—except those without small children—
departed between six and seven o'clock, as soon as the meal
was over. The hostess, of course, supplied sedan-chairs
again to take them home.

As I could assist with the guest's children I was allowed
to be of the party. When dinner was ready the guests took
their seats in the order indicated in the original invitation.
Those with the more honoured positions made some
deprecatory gesture before sitting down. There were three
tables, each accommodating eight persons. The young
people were seated at separate tables, along with the nurses,
if any. Every one was light-hearted. The guests all wore
their best clothes, and had their hair specially dressed and
ornamented with flowers. I do not remember what they
talked about ; as a matter of fact, I should not have understood even if I had listened. I suppose they discussed
chiefly dresses and fashions and the preserving of food.
The party being on this occasion for ladies only, the male
members of the household generally spent the day elsewhere,
since no servant could be spared to attend to them. It was
entirely a ladies' affair.

The next party I remember was arranged by my father
(of course, after consultation with Grandmother), because
Grandfather was too old to attend to such things, but the
invitation list bore Grandfather's name as the host. This
time the guests were all men. They did not bring their
children and they were not fetched in sedan-chairs. They
should have arrived just a little before dinner, but men-
guests always proved most unpunctual. Only about twelve
guests accepted the invitation, so they were all seated at a
single round table. One of the guests was an old friend
of my father and, like him, a painter and a hearty drinker.

After several rounds of the wines, he suggested a wine-game called *Chi-ku-tsui-hua* (beating the sheepskin drum to urge flowers to blossom). He asked a servant to pick a fresh flower from a flower-pot and to fetch a small drum. I was called in to beat the drum, and told to beat and stop beating just as I liked. While I beat, the flower was passed from hand to hand. When I stopped the person holding

BEATING THE SHEEPSKIN DRUM TO URGE FLOWERS TO BLOSSOM

it had to drink a cup of wine at one draught. Funnily enough the first person to be left with the flower was the very guest who had suggested the game! Father teased him, saying that his suggestion had been a clever device to get more wine to drink, and everybody laughed. At the end of the next round the same thing happened, and again a third time. I was beating the drum in a corner and had no idea who was holding the flower; but the guest unfortunately lost his temper and said it was being done on purpose, so he wouldn't drink the last cup and spoilt the game. As a matter of fact he really had had a little too much wine. I was afraid that he might come and scold me, so I ran away, but the sound of laughter round the table pursued me for some time.

Actually this game arises from a legendary story. One of the empresses of the T'ang dynasty, Wu Tsai-T'ien

(A.D. 690–697), the one who established herself on the throne as the head of the whole empire, thought she could demand any service. Once on a winter day she wanted to hold a celebration in her palace garden and wished all the flowering trees to be in blossom. She ordered the chief eunuch to hang up a board in the garden with the following poem of hers on it:

> To-morrow morning I go to the Palace Gardens:
> Make haste to tell the Spring!
> Flowers must blossom this very night,
> Not wait till the dawn wind blows.

The eunuch could offer no objection, and naturally he and all the members of the court were greatly worried. As a means of getting over the difficulty he ordered a number of people to beat drums in the garden to urge the flowers to blossom. And next morning they were in bloom!

From these two spring dinner-parties I can see now very clearly the different interests of men and women. Probably it was a good plan to entertain them separately so that the guests could enjoy themselves freely and not feel forced to talk of things of which they knew little. The women of the present day refuse to be considered ignorant of things outside the domestic sphere, and so men, to balance matters, are compelled to learn the details of ladies' hats, clothes and jewels! I am afraid I remain behind the march of time.

COOKED-NOODLE SELLER

18

BOATING BY MOONLIGHT

I HAVE MENTIONED before that outside the south gate of the city wall of Kiu-kiang there is a small lake called Kan-t'ang. It is very beautiful, with an artificial bank spanning it and an arched stone bridge dividing the bank one-third of the way across. The bank is artificial in the sense that it was built by man about a thousand years ago, but it looks natural because the sand of which it is formed is covered with green grasses and the edges lined with huge old rugged willows. At the far end, where the bank leads out into the countryside, is a typical small Buddhist temple, embowered in tall trees.

We call Lake Kan-t'ang small because by comparison with other Chinese lakes it is small, but twenty or thirty boats could cruise about on it out of sight of one another. The two parts of the lake have different names. The part surrounded by buildings and houses and of which the water flows under a bridge into the Yangtse River is called *Wai-hu*, ' Outer Lake '; the other part, which is circled by hills, is called *Li-hu*, ' Inner Lake '. In general Wai-hu was noisier than Li-hu, with more boats and more people sitting and playing on its shores. In the daytime, under the scorching sun, people very seldom hired boats to take trips on the lakes, but there were always many people fishing from the stone bridge and along the sides of the willow bank. Occasionally one or two older boys or men might be seen swimming by the bridge or near the shore, but this was *virtually* prohibited—because along the shore near the city wall there were generally a large number of women, old and young, washing clothes, and it was unseemly for naked swimmers to be there at the same time. The coloured dresses of the women as they bent in a row to their work was a picture in itself and the rhythm of their beaters on the washing possessed a poetry of its own. From early spring to late autumn the lake was a playground for the people of Kiu-kiang. Fortunately there were no motor-boats in those days.

Father loved to go boating on Lake Kan-t'ang. He knew the chief monk in the Buddhist temple well, and when he wished to be by the lake at night he often slept in the temple. Most of Father's friends were painters and keen fishermen, and he was sure to come upon some of them round the lake. Father was very fond of gazing at the moon, and to do this would sit under an old willow in front of the little temple drinking wine with the monk. Probably this was why he and the monk were such good friends.

FISHERMAN

One summer afternoon when it was very hot indoors Father suggested taking some of us on the lake for a treat. We were delighted, and after dinner, at about six o'clock, eight of us set out with him. The sun had gone but the heat was still intense. Father told my sister to bring her bamboo-pipe and some small bamboo baskets. At the lakeside we hired a boat and a boatman, for as a rule we did not row ourselves. We sat round a small square table in the covered part of the vessel, while, behind us, the boat-man rowed at the stern. Father gave instructions to row first round Li-hu and then, when some of the crowd had gone home, into Wai-hu.

A mild breeze fanned us as we moved gently along. On reaching the middle of Li-hu our boatman let the boat drift. It was the season of water caltrops, and people who lived near the lake were busy gathering them. Water caltrop (*Trapa bicornis*) is an aquatic member of the Haloragaceae and grows abundantly in Lake Kan-t'ang without either care or culture. I suppose if it grew in Europe or America a big company would possess proprietary rights in it and no one would be allowed to pick it freely. But here, dotted all over the lake, were strange tub-like craft in each of which a girl or fisherwoman in a bright-coloured garment gathered the water caltrops for herself (Plate 5). It was a picturesque sight in the sunset. Father drew my attention to it particularly because I was just then learning seriously to draw and paint. My brother looked as though he were composing poetry. I leant over the edge of the boat and was thrilled by the multitude of water caltrops through which we were drifting. They made a long hissing sound against the sides of the boat. I wanted to pick some but was forbidden to do so. My sister and sister-in-law got some for me. In a short while they had gathered a basketful. While the boat moved peacefully on no one talked.

Occasionally we heard clear gentle singing from the girls in the tubs. Distance prevented our catching what they sang, but the low sound over the water was very sweet. Presently my sister-in-law told us that she had learnt the song from her nurse, who had been a water-caltrop picker in her youth. It was called the ' Song of Gathering Water Caltrops '. We all urged her to sing it to us, and she did so, but I am afraid the great length of it has effaced the words from my memory. Then my brother broke the silence by remarking that there was a similar song about gathering lotus seeds. Father clapped his hands and said that brother should chant it to us when we reached the secluded corner of the lake where, with the hills rising behind, there grew patches of red lotus flowers with huge green leaves. When we reached the spot my sister wanted to pick one of the flowers, but Father dissuaded her, saying that they could only look so beautiful in their natural setting. Then my brother chanted the 'Song of Gathering Lotus Seeds':

> South of the river we gather lotus,
> The lotus leaves are round, how round!
> And the fishes play among the lotus leaves.
>   The fishes play on the east of the lotus leaves.
>   The fishes play on the west of the lotus leaves.
>   The fishes play on the south of the lotus leaves.
>   The fishes play on the north of the lotus leaves.

I always liked to listen to brother chanting poems, though on this occasion he said he could not manage the proper musical arrangement. The poem came from the *Yueh Su Shih*, and brother told me to look it up when we got home.

Darkness came on. Then a bright moon appeared just above our heads and was reflected in the water, making us realize the stillness and coolness of the atmosphere. Our boat glided on under the hill-slopes until we passed beneath the bridge to Wai-hu. Here there was still somebody fishing, his figure silhouetted in the moonlight. In Wai-hu the scene changed. Though the reflections of the lights from the houses were motionless in the water, there was a feeling of noisiness and an impression of urbanism. The lights in the water were red in comparison with the whiteness of the moon. Our boat, keeping away from the shore, skirted the small island in the middle of Wai-hu. Among the willow trees on the island there was a little temple, supposed to be the seat of the god of the lake, but commonly used as a meeting-place for literary men, painters and writers. We made no attempt to land.

Now and then the outline of another boat passed us.

From one came the sound of a *Ti*, a Chinese musical pipe made of bamboo. At once my sister felt impelled to get out her pipe and play a song to us. She was not good at it, but she was the only member of the party who could play it at all. Her repertory, too, was small, consisting mainly of folk-songs and love-songs, unsuitable, Father said, for the occasion. Then brother suggested *Tao-Ch'ing* or ' Say what you like ', a song originating two hundred years ago. The tune was repeated twelve times, twelve different poems being sung to it. While my sister played the pipe, my brother sang in a low voice the song of which the following are the first few lines :

An old fisherman with a fishing rod
By the cliffs or in the bay
Comes and goes in his lonely boat, unconstrained.
Seagulls are dotted on the shore and the light waves fade in
    the distance.
The whispering of the bulrushes makes the sunny day seem cool.
I sing loudly as the sunset indicates the late hour.
Of a sudden a golden shadow trembles in the waves,
Lifting my head I see the moon rising over the eastern hills.

Though my sister's effort was not praised highly—indeed she could only just manage the tune—the effect of the soft tones harmonized perfectly with the evening, and even the boatman was affected and let the boat drift again.

    Each of us contributed a song or a story. When my turn came I said I had written a poem. Everybody was dumbfounded ; then they all burst into loud laughter, thinking it a joke. Only Father understood and urged me to read my poem, which I did :

I drift in the middle of the lake ;
The moonlight is above.
There is also a moon in the bottom of the water.
Surrounded on all sides by flowers I have no sorrow.

My brother at once condemned this as vulgar, on the grounds

that it had neither metre nor rhyme—as of course it had not. But Father comforted me by saying that in spite of these faults I did know how to express my feelings and that my brother should teach me the rest.

The subject might then have been dismissed had it not occurred to some one in the party that in most old Chinese poems a flower symbolizes a girl, and that the last line of my poem therefore offered a splendid chance for teasing. This my first poem, they said, indicated that I should be a 'ladies' man', and they asked me what young ladies I had in mind when I composed it. Tears of mortification came to my eyes. Father, meaning to ease the situation for me, made it worse by saying that if I studied industriously from then on I need not fear not winning a beautiful girl. It was months before I was allowed to forget the poem. My memory of that evening on Lake Kan-t'ang is still associated with it.

CHILDREN'S BOOKS SELLER

PLATE *1*   THREE STAGES OF MY HAIR (at six years old, at fifteen, and in my thirties)

PLATE 2 GRANDPARENTS WITH THEIR FAVOURITE

PLATE 3 MY FATHER AT WORK

PLATE 4 'BROTHER IS ALSO A MADMAN'

PLATE 5 GATHERING WATER CALTROPS

PLATE 6 RIDING ON BUFFALOES

PLATE 7 THE DRAGON-BOAT RACE

PLATE 8 UP THE LU MOUNTAIN

19

THE CH'ING-MING FESTIVAL

CH'ING MEANS clear and *ming* bright, and *Ch'ing-ming* signifies weather suitable for going out into the country-side. Appropriately, the ' Ch'ing-ming Festival', which took place at the middle of the third month (the end of April or the beginning of May in the Gregorian calendar), celebrated the spring. It was the occasion chosen to carry out the annual family pilgrimage to the ancestral tombs. Under the influence of Confucian teaching we Chinese have always set great store upon ancestor worship, and as the time for the festival came round the minds of my elders were no doubt filled with thoughts of their forbears. My own mind, I confess, was full only of longing to see the country-side again. How wise was Confucius to choose this time of the year for the celebration of his most important ritual !

In my family the age at which one was first allowed to join the pilgrimage was about twelve. This was for the practical reason that the family cemetery lay a long way off in the hills and the journey had to be done on foot since there was no other means of transport save sedan-chairs, which were only hired for grandparents and other elderly members. The pilgrimage might, if necessary, take place a few days before the real Ch'ing-ming Festival ; it depended entirely on the convenience of the family.

Preparations began about ten days beforehand. First one of the elders bought many large sheets of coloured paper which the ladies made into *Fen-piao*, ' grave-banners '. They cut the paper into strips and wound the strips round a stick, changing the colour frequently. At the top they fixed a long pennon of paper which waved in the wind when the stick was set up on the tomb, indicating that descendants of the deceased had visited the spot. Fresh flowers were never placed on tombs, and banners were only placed there once a year.

Like the other young people of my family I went on my first pilgrimage at about the age of twelve, and, like them I am sure, my first impressions will always be vivid in my memory. My grandparents being unable to go, my third great-uncle took charge of the party. Not all the elders could leave home, and the aunts could not walk the distance on their small feet. Finally, apart from any

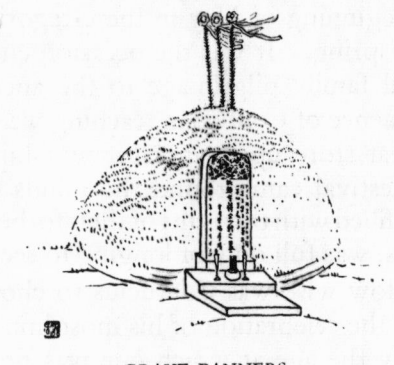

GRAVE-BANNERS

number of my generation, just my father and two uncles supported the third great-uncle. We all set out at the same time but presently split up into three groups to visit our respective cemeteries. I followed my father, who was with the third great-uncle. The two uncles led the other groups. Before separating, the third great-uncle arranged for us all to meet at a village half-way between Kiu-kiang and Lu mountain, where there was a good inn.

It was a lovely day, neither hot nor cold. The sun shone brightly, with intermittent drizzling showers. (I like rain!) All the hills were green. The fields were planted with *yiu-tsai* (*Brassica sinensis*), a plant with a group of tiny yellow flowers at the top of each stem; whole stretches of the countryside were carpeted with yellow. In some fields the young sprouts of wheat and rice were showing. The figures of farmers could be seen here and there; some were still sowing, some leading the buffalo out to plough, some singing *shan-ke* (hill songs) with a long-drawn intonation while they worked. This and the songs of birds were the only sounds to be heard. In the quiet we could even hear the tiny hissing of the mild wind in the leaves and grasses. Nearly every hut or cottage we passed had some apricot- or peach-trees in bloom, and by the streams the willows were all fresh in their new green robes. Petals of apricot or peach blossom floated idly on the surface of the water, and the tiny white feathery flowers of the willows hovered in the air. Two famous lines by one of our best-known poets might have been written to describe the scene:

Touches my clothes as if to make them wet, the apricot rain.
Blows on my face but not cold, the willow wind.

By closing my eyes I can still recall all the colours I saw, yellow, green, pink and white, and sometimes small red spots here and there where country girls in red frocks or trousers emerged from their cottages or walked along the hedges. Most of the people we passed looked very happy and jolly, talking and laughing all the time. We exchanged greetings with them and sometimes had to inquire the direction from farmers. I was always pleased when we mistook our way, because then we could have a good laugh and turn back. This innocent joy, and the whole happy atmosphere, is very difficult to describe. Occasionally, however, we met some pilgrim who, having suffered a recent loss, looked sad.

I was allowed to sit in the third great-uncle's sedan-chair now and then when he wanted to walk for a change. But actually he told us so many stories of the countryside and pointed out so many interesting trees and herbs that I forgot to be tired. Father reminded me of a poem I had learnt from him when I was very small and told me to recite it. I felt a little uneasy at reciting in front of so many people, but finally, with plenty of encouragement, I managed it. It was a poem about the Ch'ing-ming Festival by a well-known T'ang poet :

It was drizzling on the Ch'ing-ming festival day.
The people walking on the road looked heart-broken.
I asked the whereabouts of a wine shop :
A cowherd pointed out the village of Apricot Grove in the
   distance.

THIRD GREAT-UNCLE'S SEDAN-CHAIR

The recitation of this poem pleased everybody, especially my third great-uncle and my father, because they both loved wine. And I myself realized for the first time a little of its meaning.

   The tombs which our group was going to visit were scattered on two hills. One of the tombs held the ancestor who had first moved our family from northern China to Kiu-kiang. We youngsters busily unpacked the banners and dishes. We set a few banners on this tomb first and laid the dishes before it. Then we burnt incense and each of us in order of age knelt before the tomb. On one side was a stone tablet inscribed with the name of the dead and the dates of his birth and death, together with those of his wife ; also a very brief account of how he had moved the family. Then we proceeded to the other tombs. My mother's was on the other hill. Father took my brother and sister and me to it while the rest of the group rested in a cottage. On the way I asked why we had not come to Mother's tomb first. Father explained that the older ancestor had to be honoured first. Though Father spoke the words very seriously, I still felt that my mother was my most important ancestor. But the gravity of Father's face prevented me from asking any further questions. When we reached Mother's tomb Father remarked how well the plants round it were growing. Most of the pines and other trees had been planted by Father himself at the time of Mother's burial. Further down the slope of the hills were masses of wild azaleas, and the contrast of the deep red and green made a beautiful picture. Father seemed very pleased with the scenery but he sighed deeply at times. After burning incense and letting off crackers Father bowed to the tomb three times, but we youngsters, the children of the deceased, knelt down and bowed our heads to the ground three times. Father did not speak except to tell us to read the inscription on the tombstone tablet. We were all silent for a while.

Presently we returned to the cottage. It was the duty of the people who occupied it to tend our tombs. My third great-uncle gave them renewed instructions and Father added a special word about Mother's tomb. Before leaving we picked a few branches of pine, peach and willow as well as a few azaleas to indicate that our ancestors would protect us and keep us as fresh and pure as these branches, which were, at the same time, tokens of spring to take back home.

After a couple of hours we reached the inn, where the other two groups had already arrived. The inn was full. Many other people had picked the same kinds of branches as ourselves. People talked to each other as if they were old acquaintances. Father ordered the dishes for all of us and we had a good meal. I kept very silent, partly because I was rather tired and partly because I liked to watch the jolly reddish faces around me. My third great-uncle teased me for being tired, but I defended myself by saying that I was quite able to walk home. We got back at dusk.

SILK SELLER

20

ON THE BACK OF A BUFFALO

How MANY happy memories of our year in the country stayed with me when we returned home! My grand-parents had hoped that in the country we should just continue the life we had been living in the town; but in practice our habits were modified at every turn. In the country we took no heed for our clothes; indeed, we deliberately wore old ones in order not to excite the envy of the farm children. We would take off our shoes and paddle in the stream and get our feet as muddy as we pleased: behaviour which was forbidden at home lest visitors should arrive unexpectedly. In the country we had only one cook and one maid-servant, and my sister, and later my sister-in-law, washed our clothes. In the town they would not have condescended to do this, but in the open air and amid the beauty of nature it seemed different.

A stream ran not far behind the farm-house. It flowed from Lu mountain, about ten miles away, and its waters were so clear that one could see the small stones at the bottom. Often after breakfast my sister and sister-in-law would bring their baskets of washing to the stream and stay there till lunch-time. Three of us youngsters usually went with them. We had first to walk about two hundred yards along the twisted narrow fences which divided the rice-fields. Then we came to bushes behind which lay a big bamboo grove where we sometimes dug the young shoots. To the left of the grove was a small grassy space, and in front of the grove was the stream. On the far side rose a hill-slope dotted with old pines and other trees. My sister and sister-in-law would set a few big stones by the verge and sit on them while they washed the clothes. We youngsters played on the grass. Sometimes we picked mushrooms and wild flowering grasses, sometimes we played *Cha-tzu* (a game with seven tiny stones), and sometimes we rolled up our trousers, took off our shoes and socks and waded into the water to make sure that the stepping-stones were all in place for passers-by who might come that way. Actually it was very seldom that any one came; the whole place seemed to belong to us. But perhaps it is only in the sunshine of my memory that the weather while we were there was always fine. No sound could be heard except the songs of birds, the running water and the smack of the beaters on the clothes. It did not take us long to discover that a little farther along the hill-slope a number of buffaloes, cows and oxen grazed. We got permission to cross the stream by the stones and to make friends with the cowherds. Two of them turned out to be the sons of our tenant-farmer.

This gave us a new environment and different companions to play with. The cowherds generally rode on the backs of their buffaloes when going out to the pasture and coming back again. For a time we did not venture to ask them to let us ride, but I kept that idea in mind. We followed them on foot. The buffaloes walked very slowly and were extremely tame and amiable. Sometimes other cowherds brought their buffaloes to the same pasture, and occasionally we would see one of them sleeping peacefully on the back of his beast while it grazed. The cowherds amused themselves in all sorts of ways. One, leaning against a tree, would try to make a noise by blowing a piece of fresh rice-stalk. Two others might be having a tug-of-war. We joined in their amusements and learnt much from them. I was particularly interested in watching blackbirds or magpies standing on the backs of the buffaloes as they grazed. Birds and buffaloes seemed good friends and never disturbed one another. Possibly the buffaloes did not notice that the birds were on their backs, but the sight gave me pleasure.

When the sun set it was time for us all to go home. Each cowherd mounted his own buffalo. The first to mount led the procession, and they never quarrelled about precedence. Though the buffaloes could not keep step they moved along steadily and kept together as if joined by a chain. Stepping along a narrow path, with the new green rice-field for background and the red sunset on the

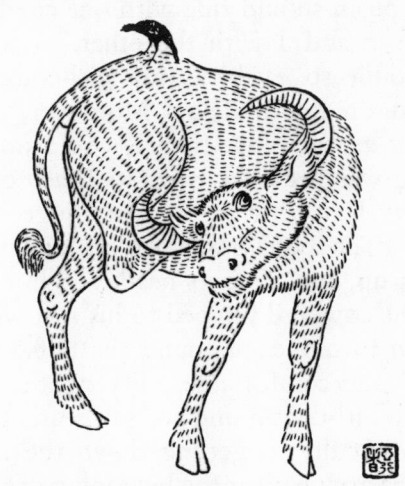

A BLACKBIRD ON THE BACK OF A BUFFALO

horizon, they made a dignified sight. There was no one to hurry them; it seemed as if even the wind were loath to disturb them and blew especially gently. The cowherds generally wore coloured clothes made of red, green or blue cloth. Completely at ease on the backs of their buffaloes, they would enliven the way by singing hill-songs. When they came to the point where their ways parted, there was no formal leave-taking; they just separated, sure of meeting again next day (Plate 6).

At length we suggested tentatively that the two cowherds should let us ride home on the buffaloes. They were surprised that we town-dwellers should want to do such a thing, but they said that they would be very pleased to let us ride, while warning us that there were no saddles and that we must be careful. They also pointed out that there was plenty of room for two people on the back of a buffalo, if we did not mind riding with them. They knew our family owned the land and felt that they ought to show us some deference. We were not worried about formalities and promptly accepted. We decided that my younger cousin should ride with one cowherd, and my older girl-cousin and I with the other. I was short and could not mount so easily as my girl-cousin, who was quickly seated on her buffalo. Moreover, the cowherd, who was only a year older than I, could not lift me up. So the buffalo was made to lower its head so that I could put one of my feet between the two huge curved horns on its head. The buffalo seemed to understand that I wanted to get up, and lifted its head to help me. As soon as I was up the cowherd jumped to his seat with great ease and we began to move. I found the buffalo's back very broad and flat and comfortable. My right arm was linked in that of my girl-cousin and we sat nearly back to back. We had no difficulty in getting down the hill-slope and reaching the narrow path at the beginning of the rice-fields. We three city youngsters were ' as proud as punch ' to be mounted on buffaloes and joyfully joined the cowherds in singing their hill-songs. I could never get the tune right, for I was no good at music as a lad. This kind of hill-song has no accompaniment. The tune is pleasant but very shrill, and there are long intervals between the words; sometimes one sentence takes several minutes to sing. In the distance, however, it falls on the ears intriguingly.

Passing along the rice-fields we saw the farmers collecting their tools and implements preparatory to going home. Some of them too were singing hill-songs :

The sunset is red, so red;
I advise my employer to stop work now.
Other houses are having dinner,
But we are still in the middle of the field!

The sun sets on the western hill with a spot of red;
On my hoe hangs a lantern.
If you, our employer, have candles enough,
We are not afraid to work until the sun rises in the east again.

When they ceased, we applauded with laughter, and the farmers laughed back.

We were still feeling safe and happy when we came to a small drain which carried the water from one field to another. Here the buffaloes had to jump, and I fell off into a morass of mud and water. I could hardly struggle up. When I did manage to get to my feet I was covered with mud from head to foot. There was no possibility of concealing the fact that I had fallen, and the two cow-herds were terrified of being severely scolded by the elders. My two cousins said that it would be my fault if we were forbidden to ride again. I cried and felt very depressed. When we got home, however, the elders proved less difficult than we had expected, though Grandmother did tell us not to ride on buffaloes again.

But we did. We persuaded the herd-boys to let us ride while the beasts were grazing on the hill-slope. And sometimes I was even able to ride alone, with one of the herd-boys walking beside me. This plan worked very well and I thanked them gratefully. What ease and peace we enjoyed in those days!

Though I could not sing the hill-songs well, I learnt the words of many of them. The following are a few fragments I remember:

(1) Plum fruit is good to eat, but the tree is difficult to plant.
    Pure rice is good to eat, but the field is difficult to plough.
    Rice cake is good to eat, but the grinding-stone is difficult to move.
    Fresh fish is good to eat, but opening the net is difficult.

(2) In the fifth and sixth months
    How can any one be idle on the roadside?
    Everybody has a bunch of rice-shoots in his hands,
    Singing the hill-songs without fear for the weather.

(3) Not singing the hill-song makes me feel chilly;
    There will be no oil if the seeds are not pressed;
    There will be no wine if the yeast is not used in the rice;
    One will suffer in old age if one does not learn when one is
        young.

As sung by the local farmers they were very charming to
listen to.   When shall I hear them again?   Possibly never;
for probably the troublous years that have intervened have
effaced the songs from the memory of the young farmers
of to-day.

SMALL-PEAR SELLER

21

A 'SIMILAR-HEART' KNOT

ALTHOUGH MY sister began preparing for her wedding in good time, the wedding day seemed to approach more rapidly than the completion of her embroidery and other preparations, though she had not been to the missionary school for some time. Had my mother been alive to help her she would not have been so pressed; as it was, she had to do most of the work herself.

It was the custom in our city for the bride's embroidery to be displayed to the bridegroom's relations and friends the day before the wedding, and naturally every bride liked her work to be praised. Before my brother's marriage my sister-in-law often came to our house and worked at her embroidery with my sister. Unfortunately, in her case there was in the end no opportunity to display the work; which was a pity, for she was known to be skilful with her needle. Her judgment in the harmonious arrangement of colours was unusually good, and even Father used to give her warm praise!

My sister could embroider well, but slowly, and she often had trouble with the arrangement of the colours. Probably this was not entirely her fault, because Father liked to make new designs for her, instead of letting her buy ready-made ones from shops, and these original designs may not have been easy to follow. For the working of shop designs simple rules governed the arrangement of colours according to the subject, whereas with Father's designs, though the subjects were the same, the patterns were different. However, for the last few months before the wedding my sister-in-law was able to help the bride.

But there was still too much to do. It was the local custom for the bridegroom's family to furnish the bridal room only with a new bed, one or two tables and a few chairs; everything else in it was provided by the bride's

MY SISTER'S BED

A. THREE LITTLE PICTURES	E. EMBROIDERED PILLOW
B. UPPER EMBROIDERED CURTAIN	F. EMBROIDERED SILK BED-SPREAD
C. FLOWER BASKET	G. LOWER EMBROIDERED CURTAIN
D. FOLDED SILK COVERLET	

family. In this case the bridegroom wanted a ' modern ' bronze bedstead, but Father, after consultations with the bridegroom's father, ultimately decided to get a typical old-fashioned bed to match the rest of the furniture. He then painted and had framed three small pictures to be hung on the top of the bed.

My sister's work was much greater. For the bed alone

she had to embroider a sheet, two pillow-cases, the cover of
the eiderdown, and two narrow curtains, one for the top
and the other for the bottom.   She also had to embroider
the door curtains, window curtains, cushion and mirror
covers, and all her own clothes and shoes.   Besides these
big items, she had to embroider a number of silk handkerchiefs, powder-puffs, little cases for visiting-cards, silk
bookmarks and small flower baskets for distribution to the
relations and intimate friends of the bridegroom after the
wedding.   The designs for these embroideries were common subjects such as ' a pair of mandarin ducks with lotus
flowers ', ' a pair of swallows flying round willows ', ' four
magpies and winter-plum blossoms ', ' phoenix and peony ',
' peacock and roses ', ' a pair of butterflies gathering honey
from flowers ', ' ping-ti-lien ' (double lotus on a single stalk),
' tung-hsin-chieh ' (a symbol of a ' similar-heart ' knot), and
so on, all of which stood for love, happiness and joy.   Each
of these subjects could be arranged in many different ways,
and the planning of the variations was what Father loved.
Some of them were very complicated and some quite
simple.   I remember one design, of a door curtain and a
flower basket, which took Father a tremendous time to
work out and naturally took my sister a good deal longer
to embroider.   Only the temperate weather of full spring
and early autumn was suitable for doing embroidery ; that
was why sister had to begin the work two years before her
wedding.

It was most important that all the preparations for a
wedding should, for emotional—or perhaps, rather, superstitious—reasons, be carried out smoothly.   For instance,
I was once given a very simple design to copy for my sister
and I did one line wrong.   Taking the design to Father I
said that I would like to begin again on a fresh sheet of
paper.   But Father would not permit this on the ground
that it might disturb the smooth course of Sister's future
life.   Instead, he took my unfinished design and added a
few lines to weave the wrong line into the design, so that

no mistake was visible. My sister had also been warned that if she ever used the wrong shade of silk she must not unpick it. In these circumstances the preparations naturally went forward slowly. Father would devote much thought to a design before putting it down on paper lest he too should make a mistake.

BRIDAL ROBE FASTENED BY RED SILK RIBBONS

I remember very specially the circumstances which attended the 'similar-heart knot' design. This design appeared several times in various embroideries, but in one case the knot had to be made by the hand of the bride alone. This was a very old custom and not many people bothered about it even in those days, but Father was anxious that Sister should learn it. There were no buttons on the old type of embroidered bridal robe, which was fastened by red silk ribbons. When the robe was put on the two strips of silk ribbon were tied in this special way on the breast as if touching the heart. On the bridal night the knot was undone by the bridegroom as if to open a ' similar heart '. The knot was designed to be both beautiful and simple, so that the bridegroom could easily undo it. If he had any difficulty, either through his own clumsiness or because the bride had tied the knot badly, it portended that the future of the couple would not be as smooth as they had hoped. My sister had to practise the knot assiduously with two strips of silk. The idea, I think, was beautiful, even if fundamentally rather superstitious.

Very little of Sister's dowry was in cash. Apart from her ' trousseau ', it consisted of jade jewels and a few of Father's paintings. It was the custom on the third day after the wedding for the bridegroom's family to invite two ladies to hold a small ceremony for the counting of the bride's new dresses and other belongings. The bigger the number, of course, the more praise would the bride receive. (It was really very difficult to get a daughter married without a handsome dowry !) In the ordinary way clothes for the family were made by tailors summoned to the house for the purpose twice a year. But the clothes for my sister's wedding required four tailors to stay in the house for months. I remember that Father gave Sister a large number of Mother's pieces of new silk which had been part of her own dowry but had not been used before her death.

A few days before the wedding the ceremony of announcing the marriage arrangements took place. On the day before the wedding the display of Sister's embroideries was held. Though my future brother-in-law's house was only two or three hundred yards from ours, a procession, in which each article was carried by one person, made a long detour to reach it in order that as many people as possible could see the embroideries. In front of the procession walked two people holding a pair of big red lanterns and four musicians blowing pipes and beating brass gongs.

The object of this was to attract attention and encourage people to come and look. As the procession approached the bridegroom's house, we, from our own house, could hear the sound of fireworks and could imagine how everything would be arranged in the bridal chamber. Grandmother had secretly sent some one to follow the crowd and listen to the criticisms of Sister's work.

The next morning Sister had to stay in bed until the flowery bridal chair was sent for her by the bridegroom's family. Then she had a bath and put on her bridal robes, all of which were pink and red in colour. A close relation was invited to dress her hair, and the tiny invisible hairs on her temples were plucked for the first time, a process called *Kai-lien*, ' opening the face '. She wore a pair of red soft-soled shoes and was not supposed to walk on the floor of her parent's house on that day. Before she set out, she and four young lady guests had a simple dinner. Sister, not unnaturally, could not eat much, her mind being so preoccupied. Then she was lifted by my brother to the flowery chair. Four young male guests were invited to escort the chair half-way.

After the ceremony a banquet was given to the guests who had come to our house to congratulate and help. They all talked very merrily and were full of compliments. To Grandmother and Father they expressed the hope that Sister would have a very happy life with her husband and that they would be smiling at her baby in a year's time, and so on.

Personally I felt that somehow the atmosphere was not so genuinely cheerful as on the occasion of my brother's wedding in the country. I sensed a big change in my own life, and when all the guests had gone I felt inclined to cry. Grandmother tried to console me by saying that a girl could not go on and on living in her parent's home. Sister would be very happy, she said, in her new life, and would in due course herself become the head of a family.

Next afternoon Grandmother despatched me to the bride

with a round jar of *Hsiang-yu* (oil of sesamum). It was the custom for a younger brother to offer this on the day after his sister's wedding (though actually a servant carried the jar). I saw my sister, but we could not talk on account of the embarrassing number of guests present.

On the fourth day the bride and her husband came to our house. Grandmother arranged a banquet for them, to which a few guests of the bride's age were invited. I was amazed how talkative my sister was. Her voice rang out above everybody's. My brother-in-law, on the other hand, was shy, and was particularly embarrassed by the young ladies who offered him cups of wine. It was not polite to refuse these and he was nearly drunk by the end of the dinner. The formalities were then at an end, and I was left wondering why my sister had become such a chatterbox.

INCENSE SELLER

22

'WISHING FOR SKILL'

In my book *The Silent Traveller in London* I have told the following story : ' A certain weaving-girl, the grand-daughter of the Emperor of Heaven, lived east of the " Silver River ", which is our Chinese name for the Milky Way. She toiled year after year weaving the " cloud-embroidered heavenly dress ". The Emperor of Heaven, seeing that she was diligent and lonely, had pity on her and married her to a herd-boy who lived west of the Silver River. Unfortunately, after she was married she became less diligent in the Emperor's service and gave up her weaving. The Emperor grew very angry, and for punish-ment made her return to her old home on the east of the River. Only once a year, on the seventh night of the seventh month, was she allowed to go and see her herd-boy. And on the same night, on earth, girls hold parties and invite their friends to offer sacrifice to the weaving-girl and to pray to her to grant them skill in weaving and needlework, and especially a good husband. Hence the " Festival of Wishing for Skill ".'

Once the festival dinner was over we boys were not further concerned in the various ceremonies ; but one year we did take part in them, since the occasion was a special one for one of my girl-cousins. She had been learning to embroider for some time, but being very fat, her hands were plump and her fingers so sausage-like that she was inevitably terribly clumsy with her needle. No one could praise her work, though every one tried to encourage her. One of my aunts had apparently suggested that, when the

Festival of Wishing for Skill came round, she should pray to the Star of the Weaving-girl to grant her more skill. Though she was physically incapable, with her podgy hands, of managing the needle and silks, the poor girl innocently believed that the Star would assist her, and she looked forward very seriously to the festival. The other older girls would only have taken part in the festival as a matter of course, but this time they joined in the preparations with a will.

After the dinner it was still light, and some of us boys

WISHING FOR SKILL

followed the girls to the garden in case we were needed to give them a hand. We moved the table to the shelter for them. Then the girls arranged the incense-burner, candlesticks, and some dishes of sweets, cakes and fruits as sacrificial offerings to the Star. Next the fireworks were let off. Then five of the girls, including the ' weaker sister ', knelt down three times facing the open space of the garden, while the rest, together with the boys, stood a little aside. The girls did not murmur any words ; their devoutness was expressed in their posture, and the fat cousin was the most devout of all. When the ritual was finished, each of them, still kneeling on the mats, took a needle in the left hand and tried to thread a silk through the eye. The degree of skill was supposed to be indicated by the speed of threading the needle. The dusk was gathering, but there was light enough for the purpose. I noticed that two of them managed it at once. The fat cousin opened her eyes very wide and compressed her lips even more firmly than usual in her effort to thread the needle. Though it did not come off as smoothly as she hoped, she did manage not to be the last. But then the girl who was actually last was really the most skilful sempstress of them all, and must have feigned clumsiness out of kindness of heart.

Another part of the ritual consisted in each girl placing a white porcelain bowl filled with mountain water on the table with her name underneath and leaving it there all night. In the morning half the water had evaporated, and each of the girls then cut a blade of grass of fixed length and laid it carefully on the surface of the water. This water, which came from a mountain stream, contained minerals, and being of considerable density could support the grass easily, if the blade were placed skilfully. A comparison of the shadows cast by the grass on the bottom of the bowls was supposed to provide another test of skill in needlework. The more complicated the shadow, the better the needlewoman. Unfortunately the fat cousin failed to float her blade of grass flat on the water, her hand was trembling so much, and finally she shook the bowl and the grass sank to the bottom. She was terribly crest-fallen. Her distress was so real that the rest of us could not laugh at her clumsiness, and the older girls told her comfortingly that this was not a serious ceremony and that the Star had not really the power of granting skill. But she was not convinced, and ran away to her chamber.

I have never understood why the Weaving-girl should be asked to grant skill at needlework at all. Her anxiety

was to meet her beloved herd-boy after their long parting.
Surely she should be prayed to by lovers, not needle-
women? Our unmarried girls were, I fear, fooled by the
forefathers who inaugurated this custom.

EGG SELLER

23

A STRANGER'S TOUCH

WITH ONE short interval, Li ma-ma lived in our house continuously for more than forty years. She began her career there as my father's nurse, and when he grew up, stayed on as servant. By my time she had come to be treated with almost as much respect as Grandmother. We youngsters fetched and carried for her, and did her bidding implicitly. Once when I showed unwillingness to perform some errand for her, I found myself being talked to scathingly by Grandmother, while Father threatened me with a stick! It was Li ma-ma who saved me by taking me in her arms—although as a matter of fact Father never did beat me.

When Li ma-ma first came to our house she was only twenty-five. She was married, and her husband, too, worked for our family. Both were illiterate, but both were honest and loyal and devoted to the ideas of Confucius. A few years later they went back to their own district, where my family owned some land, and became our tenants. Thereafter it was always Li ma-ma who arrived first at our house with the newly ripened rice crop. She supplied us all the year round too with many other natural products. She and her husband grew, besides rice, big beans, cabbages, spinach, pearl rice and many kinds of melon. On her visits to us with these foodstuffs Li ma-ma kept us in close touch with farm-life. Her one child died young, and when, not long after, her husband died too, Grandmother invited her to come back to us. Although pleased with the suggestion, Li ma-ma hesitated to leave the land which for her was bound up with memories of her husband; for she had been noted as a model wife, possessing all the matronly virtues advocated by Confucius. To get over the difficulty Grandmother suggested that Li ma-ma could go back to the land whenever she liked, and in addition could take charge of our tenants' vegetable and rice crops now and again, and also look after our own small vegetable garden. The arrangement worked beautifully. Li ma-ma was happy, and we had the benefit of her experience in regard to the country produce which was bought for our household consumption. Grandmother was probably responsible for the fact that we did buy so many things straight from the country, for she held that things grown in the suburbs or within the city suffered from lack of good soil and natural conditions and could not taste as good as those from the country. I think I still feel so. Often Li ma-ma would tell us youngsters about the fresh fruits or new vegetables which were about to arrive, and describe how she would cook them for us. Usually, too, she could remember some legendary story about each of them.

We all liked the newly ripened rice. Just after the harvest our tenants brought us the first lot of unpolished rice. When it was cooked it turned a reddish colour and smelt quite different from the ordinary polished grains: to us it was the smell of the countryside. There was great excitement when the word went round that we were going to have unpolished rice for dinner. Perhaps it was just its rarity that made us imagine that it tasted better than ordinary rice; we had it only for a few days at harvest-time, and then had to wait a whole year before tasting it again. Actually, our elders could have told the tenants always to supply the rice like this, and they must have had some reason for not doing so. But what the reason was I do not know, for although the word 'vitamin' was unknown to them, they knew, and often told us, that unpolished rice had certain good qualities which polished rice lacked.

Another food known to be health-giving was the yellow lily flower, called *Chin-Chen-Tsai* or ' Golden needle food '. As we bought these flowers dried, I suppose they did not grow in our district. By boiling them with small pieces of meat, an excellent sweetish soup very good for the blood can be made. I personally like it very much. This soup has always been given to a mother after giving birth to a baby.

In the middle of a summer day, a couple of hours after lunch, Li ma-ma would make me a small bowl of boiled lily bulb. She would ask the maid-servants to wash the mud off the raw bulbs, select some small young ones, boil them in water, and then, in another pan, boil them again with crystal sugar. When this was stone-cold it tasted heavenly.

I have already spoken of Li ma-ma's virtues as a wife. Our elders used to tell us that after her husband's death she avoided ever speaking to another man. Even the male members of our own household, if they wanted to communicate with her, sent their messages by one of the other maids. The most striking incident exemplifying her loyalty to her husband's memory occurred long before I was born, but I often heard about it. It happened as follows. Li ma-ma had been a widow for over ten years. Sometimes she had to go out to buy things for my grandparents and my father; still she never spoke, all her errands being written down on a piece of paper which she presented to the shopkeeper. All went well until one day when she was buying some pigments at the shop from which Father always got his painting materials, the shopkeeper touched her hand as he passed her the things. She was so upset that she dropped the pigments and ran home with tears streaming down her face. When Grandmother discovered why she was so distressed, Father obtained an apology from the shopkeeper. But this did not console her; she felt as if she had done wrong to her husband. From that time she was never asked to go out of our house and garden.

In her old age Li ma-ma was not always well. She was treated as one of the family and looked after with every care, but she refused to neglect any of her duties. Feeling at last that she was dying, she told Grandmother that she could not have lived so long if she had not been with such a kind family. Then she murmured that she had no relatives or descendants and would like to be buried near the cemetery of our ancestors. Grandmother assured her that she would see to that, and Li ma-ma smiled her thanks and died peacefully. She was in her seventy-ninth year ; I in about my seventh. Her funeral was as elaborate as it could be, and we youngsters all mourned her. She was buried in a small plot we bought for the purpose not far from the cemetery of our ancestors. Every year when we visited our ancestral tombs we visited Li ma-ma's tomb too, knowing that this would please her. Since her death she has been perhaps the most often-quoted person in our family.

In the light of present-day relations between men and women, some may consider Li ma-ma's conduct during her widowhood nothing short of ridiculous. And perhaps she was over-rigid. She practised strictly the principles of Confucius, who instituted certain barriers between man and woman which our people have respected even to extremes. No one of Li ma-ma's generation considered the incident of the shopkeeper ridiculous ; all praised her and despised the man, whether he acted intentionally or not. Scholars have always encouraged women to keep their widowhood until death, and emperors have honoured those who have done so. Conversely, a woman who married again lost her social standing and brought discredit on herself. That is why Li ma-ma was looked upon as a pattern of wifely virtue. I still admire her sincerity and single-mindedness, but I could not encourage any one else to live up to such an ideal—for to be faithful merely because it is virtuous in a married life, and not for love's sake, is false.

I feel, as I look back, that in China the conception of

'love' has been wrapped up in too many embroidered silks for many people to penetrate its meaning. The silks have been embroidered by skilful hands and the designs are as beautiful as all Chinese culture; but one is afraid to spoil them by unfolding; or one wearies of the effort to do so, since there are so many layers. So the bottom of our hearts is never revealed.

I do not, of course, mean to suggest that Li ma-ma did not love her husband dearly. I am sure that she loved him until her death. But I find myself wondering whether the mere fact that he was her husband was not sufficient to make her believe that she *must* love him until her death. If she had had a chance of unfolding those embroidered silks from her heart—of freeing herself from the bonds of public opinion—she might have led a different and perhaps a happier life. But if, alive in some other world, she feels that I am doing her an injustice on this point, then I apologize. I should probably never have thought of criticizing her creed—in which I, too, was brought up— had I not since then faced great changes in my life. But now I cannot avoid the thought that Confucius did not realize that his ideas would be implemented in such unnatural ways. Probably it is rather Confucian scholars who are to blame; and it is noticeable that none of them suggested that it would not be honourable for a *man* to marry again. How wonderful of our ancient genius to work out such a beautiful system without being called selfish!

The system had its practical bearing on morality, for if a woman was expected to rise to such heights of fidelity after her husband's death, how could she be unfaithful to him during his lifetime? Women of any strength of character could withstand any inducement, and those who were weak and easily led astray were always condemned by society and sometimes committed suicide to escape their shame. Only those men who had made big sums of money, usually in undesirable ways, could keep concubines, and their reputation among the public was always bad. Only women of weak character would consent to become concubines, and none of them possessed any standing in society. A woman or girl brought up in the Confucian tradition would fight to the death against concubinage. Money and force have killed thousands of our young women down the centuries. Li ma-ma should be specially praised in this connexion, for I am convinced that even if she had not been in our house, she would have remained faithful, perhaps enduring poverty as well as suffering and unhappiness. Alas! how many people are capable of resisting material comforts merely in order to remain single-minded?

After this digression I want to pay my tribute to Li ma-ma for providing each member of our family with some unforgettable memories. Constantly did we hear our elders referring to her conscientious ways. Li ma-ma would never go to bed until she was sure that everything was in order in the house and garden. It was Li ma-ma who had sufficient patience to prepare bird's-nest soup. ' Bird's nest ' (not an agreeable idea in connexion with soup) is the gelatinous nest of a species of swift or swallow (*Collocalia brevirotris*) found on the sea-coast of Fuhkien, or imported from India. The birds seem to make their nests out of a kind of seaweed or Gelidium. It is a very expensive dish and one which, characteristically, is regarded as a physic for the sick, upon whom it is reputed to have a tonic and invigorating effect. The main thing is that if well made it is very tasty. We had it only on special occasions, such as weddings, but the grandparents were given it from time to time as a token of filial esteem and indulgence. It is made by boiling the nests in water, and is eaten with or without sugar or with chicken broth. The preparing of it is so trying to the patience because the nests in their original state are lined with numberless tiny feathers, and all these have to be removed before the boiling. Young girls are supposed to be good at the job, because they are quiet and have no distracting thoughts in their minds, so my sister and cousins had to learn to do it. But it was only Li ma-ma who could do it perfectly, and we still always think of her in connexion with bird's-nest soup.

We remember her, too, each time we think of our shoes. In China we did not wear leather shoes very often, unless it was raining. Our ordinary shoes were made of silk or cloth. Even the soles were cloth. It will be appreciated that the cloth had to be well sewn, otherwise it would not last. My aunts and sister and girl-cousins used to spend all their spare time making shoes for the male members of the household. The shoes for female members and small boys were usually embroidered with flowers. My sister and cousins were very fond of making shoes, but the stitching of the soles was left to Li ma-ma. How many soles she must have sewn in a year! Alas! the next generation in China will not dream of wearing home-made shoes.

A KIND OF HOT RICE-CAKE SELLER

24

THE FEAST OF LANTERNS

HAD I NOT been born in China I could never have dreamed of the gay and fanciful entertainment known as the Feast of Lanterns. The actual date of the Feast was the fifteenth of the first month, but in Kiu-kiang it usually extended from the thirteenth to the fifteenth. For the

LANTERN SELLER

intervening period, from New Year's Day, most of the shops remained closed, and on all sides one heard people coming and going exchanging greetings in happy phrases. After New Year's Day, as the Feast approached, lantern sellers would be busy in the streets. I remember one who used to pass our house and hold up all kinds of lanterns to tempt us youngsters to buy : lamps in the forms of birds, animals, flowers, reptiles—every conceivable shape.

For the roads and streets there were special dragon-lantern shows. My family, for example, contributed money towards the show for the road on which our house stood. Local committees arranged matters. The dragon lanterns, beautifully constructed of bamboo covered with thin silk, varied in colour : there were red dragons, yellow dragons, green dragons, black dragons and white dragons. Each lantern had to be borne by from thirteen to fifteen people, of whom those at the head and tail needed to be experienced players. The head was usually big and heavy ; it might contain as many as fifty or more candles ; and besides managing these the person who held it had to be skil-ful in the dragon dance. This was performed in each house visited if there were big empty grounds. Four people, each dangling a light red silk ball, pranced in front of the dragon lantern. As a ball moved, the dragon pranced after it in an attempt to catch it. This way and that waved the balls and the whole long dragon swung after them. To enhance the excitement, the men taking part shouted, and the musicians who accompanied the show thumped, blew and twanged their respective instruments as loudly as possible. The greater the noise, the faster the dance. It was the merriest game I saw in my childhood. But once a year was enough. We could see several per-formances of it in one night if we wished ; each company that called did more or less the same thing.

The main item of the show was always a long procession. There might be some performers wearing beautiful period costumes walking on stilts, at the end of the procession. During the daytime, from the thirteenth of the month until the fifteenth, the various show companies went from house to house soliciting invitations for their dragon lantern. One could refuse if one wanted to be quiet, but Grandmother generally invited at least two for each of the three nights. Ahead of the dragon lantern itself came a man acting as 'informer'. He received the presents, such as a number of red candles and a long piece of red silk, on behalf of the whole company. Then the four ball-men entered through the front gate, followed by the head of the dragon. As our house was very deep the ball-men generally penetrated as far as the third hall, so that the entire dragon, including the tail, could be contained in the house.

FLOWER LANTERNS

We were very proud of this fact. Before the dragon entered, all the lanterns in the hall were lit, and we let off a few fireworks by way of welcome. Then one of the ball-men began to chant a song expressing every kind of praise and good wish for the happiness and prosperity of our house. Flattery, perhaps; but, being human, we enjoyed a little flattery.

An additional feature of the dragon-lantern show was the lion game. Two men hid inside a 'property' lion

made of cloth with a lot of Chinese hemp stuck on for hair.
One man played the head and moved the lion's mouth from
time to time; the other, occupying the rear, moved the
tail. A third man held a thick flowered silk ball with which
he lured the lion. The lion pursued him, running and
jumping at the ball. I remember one particularly skilful
lion-game company coming to our house. We put two
big square tables in the centre of the third and second halls.

HORSE LANTERNS

The ball-man led the lion after him from one table to the
other, and from the third hall to the second and back again.
The actors performed their parts beautifully. Very close
co-ordination between the two parts of the lion was necessary, and they gave a brave and energetic exhibition.

These lantern games were played by grown-ups for the
benefit of youngsters. Generally each youngster had a
lantern of his own. In my eleventh year my family happened to have a very good year's business and a good

harvest, so they decided to celebrate even more thoroughly than usual. Father and two uncles suggested that they should make a lantern show for us youngsters to manage ourselves, there being a good number in my generation. They knew that it would be very expensive and probably unsuitable to get the lanterns made by professional artists, so they set about making the whole thing themselves. One of our relations who lived in the country was invited to join in the work. Before the New Year Festival all the necessary materials were bought and after New Year's Day the

DRAGON LANTERN

work began. All the lanterns were finished by the tenth of the first month, but we were not allowed to show them until the thirteenth.

Four of my younger girl-cousins led the show, holding four different flower lanterns. Then came three young boy-cousins, aged from five to seven, with horse lanterns. These were made in two parts, head and rear, each part being attached by a bamboo rod to a string round the waist of the boy who walked between them. Inside each part burned a candle. Five of us took part in a small dragon lantern, and one boy held a red ball lantern. Sometimes

I changed places with the boy who was holding the dragon's head, for as we could not perform the dance it did not matter who held it. In the rear a young boy-cousin pulled after him a string to which was tied a large white hare lantern moving on wheels, with five little hare lanterns on top of it. They were all lit. We could not go out very far, so we displayed our lanterns in our own house for the first two nights. And then on the fifteenth night we were invited to go to my sister's house, which was only about two hundred yards away. On our arrival the four flower lanterns moved in and out in a grand chain.

HARE LANTERN

Then the three horses did more or less the same. Finally, the dragon lantern made a circuit in the house and the hare lantern followed. We all enjoyed the show immensely.

On our return, the ceremony of burning all the lanterns took place. It was the custom for all the lanterns in the Festival, whether carried by adults or children, to be burnt, indicating that the year's work began from the next day. No sooner had we finished the burning of our lanterns than our elders used to tell us to get ready for school. And we felt this was quite fair, as we had had such a good time !

We youngsters were permitted to stay up until about ten o'clock on the last night of the Festival. Dusk fell about five, so the lantern show began early. In the gay atmosphere of the evening, girls and boys went out sightseeing in the most crowded streets, so it was a romantic evening too. I always liked to read the following poem written by a well-known poetess :

Last year on the night of the Lantern Festival,
In the flowery market the lanterns were bright as day.
When the moon rose above the willows,
We planned to meet after dusk fell.

This year on the night of the Lantern Festival
Moon and lanterns are the same as before :
Only I do not see my last-year's love ;
My tears have soaked the sleeves of my blue garment.

The Feast of Lanterns is a very old custom, said to have originated in the Han dynasty some two thousand years ago. It still flourished in my childhood, but, unfortunately, the big dragon-lantern show has not been held in my city for nearly twenty years now. I do not know what has brought the change, or whether it will ever take place again. But who knows ? Perhaps when real peace has fallen on us . . .

CHILDREN'S TOYS SELLER

25

TENDER HEARTS

UNTIL RECENTLY I was always very shy of talking to
girls with whom I was only newly acquainted. Before I
came to Europe I had talked little with girls, even relations,
except of course those in my own home. I wonder now
why I should have been so shy, but the fact that I was so
has made me realize how deeply I was influenced by Confucian thought and the old Chinese tradition. I do not
mean to suggest that I never mixed with any girls outside
my own family, for like almost every other young man, I
recall certain tender hearts which stirred my own when I
was a boy. It is of these I shall write in this chapter.
One died when she was only ten years old; another may
be by now a middle-aged nun; a third I know has two
daughters and a son. I cannot describe what I felt and
wondered then about the mysteries of love; but the
recollection of my childish musings is still sweet.

Hsiao Hung or 'Little Red' was the youngest daughter
of an artist friend of my father's. She came to our house
for the first time at the age of six. I was two years older.
As her house was close to ours, and her father frequently
visited mine, she often played with us and I was soon her
favourite companion. If I happened to be in school when
she arrived, a restless feeling would come over me and I
would try to hurry through my lessons in order to be free
as soon as possible. But no sooner had I managed to escape
than I was overcome with shyness: and it was always she
who rushed to make the greeting. People began to joke
us about our 'forthcoming engagement'. In view of our

tender ages this sounds comical, but actually it would not have been unusual in our tradition. As we became more friendly a strange feeling grew in me towards her. I felt I wanted to be particularly kind and generous. She must, I think, have had the same feeling towards me. Young as we were we knew enough of our tradition to hide what was in our hearts. Kissing was unknown to us in those days, and we did not even try to hold each other's hand ; but something intangible conveyed our thoughts. One must have had a similar experience to appreciate the sweetness of this.

One afternoon my sister and two cousins were sitting with ' Little Red ' and me under the willow-tree in the garden when my sister suggested we should play *Lo-wen*, that is to say compare our fingerprints. Fingerprints are usually in one of two designs : a whirling circle, called a *Lo* ; or a series of loops. Every hand has some *Lo*, but the number varies. Upon examining our various fingerprints my sister found that ' Little Red's ' hand had exactly the same number of *Lo* as mine, and she cried out laughingly : ' How strange ! "Little Red" and my brother must be a heaven-made couple ! ' The two cousins joined in the laugh. I turned scarlet. Having been brought up in a tradition which would have condemned me for accepting this kind of joke and brought further jokes and gossip on my head, I stared hard in the direction of the pond. ' Little Red ' jumped up and ran off. But in doing so she tripped and fell. My impulse was to run to help her, but I hesitated for fear of the overwhelming laughter this would cause. She may have hurt herself but she did not dare to cry. Scrambling to her feet she ran to her father's side. My sister of course went after her, but she had vanished into the house.

The next time ' Little Red ' came to visit us I found an opportunity of asking her in a low voice whether she had hurt herself when she fell. She put her head on one side, and looking at me with her mouth twisted scornfully, asked why I had not tried to help her, and added that obviously I could not like her. Filled with shame, I wanted to explain how much I liked her; but not a word would come. My tender heart was too tender! Neither of us seemed able to say anything more for some time. We were sitting on a low ornamental rock, well apart from one another as we had been taught that boys and girls should sit; our affection did not need to be expressed by blatant proximity. At length I summoned up courage to say that I had not known she was waiting for me to help her and that I would certainly go to her aid another time. Suddenly she poked her finger into my hand and asked me if I would like it if she fell down again? This embarrassed me more than ever. Silently I bemoaned the fact that she was always so much cleverer than I. Then the moon-gate leading to the family school opened and some one came out. 'Little Red' ran off through another door. I was relieved to find that it was only my third great-uncle, come to spend a little time in the garden. Had it been my fourth or fifth aunt, dreadful jokes would soon have spread through the house. I sighed with relief.

A year or so later 'Little Red's' family moved to a house farther away and her father did not come so often to visit us. Then I heard of her illness and death. She was only ten and most of my family had practically forgotten her. But I had not, and I went into the garden and cried for a long time. Nobody disturbed me, and I was glad to be able to think of her in solitude.

Another little girl who touched my heart was dumb and had no father. Her mother, widowed one month before the child's birth, had taken her, at the age of four, to live in a temple. The poor woman had very little money, and in those days no woman in China could easily earn a living for herself; moreover, she was too steeped in traditional thought to want to marry again. So, being a person of very ardent religious faith and friendly with one of the nuns in a Buddhist temple, she presently became a nun herself. Nobody wanted to adopt her little dumb daughter, so the child was taken to live in the temple too.

Chinese Buddhist nuns live an extremely secluded life. They shave off their hair, are vegetarians, and drink no wine or stimulant of any kind. My grandmother was a Buddhist. She used to recite the Buddhist doctrine every morning before a picture of Kuan-Yin (Goddess of Mercy) in her chamber. From time to time she subscribed to the funds of the temple in which the mother and the little dumb girl lived. About once a month she visited the nuns, usually choosing occasions when she was irritated with one or other of my aunts for opposing her ideas, or when she was bored with the endless succession of household trifles. She rarely stayed the night in the temple, lest something should go wrong at home in her absence. As a rule she left home early in the morning and returned about twilight. The nuns always prepared a very good meal for her, entirely composed of vegetables. I used to accompany Grandmother on these excursions, in order to support her on the journey and save the hire of a sedan-chair. The other boys disliked going because there was nothing at the temple to play with; but I always found something to occupy me pleasantly, and, moreover, since my mother's death I had been very attached to Grandmother.

I must have been ten when I made the first of such visits to the temple. The building stood on a small hill by the south gate of the city wall, near the beautiful lake Kan-t'ang; but the lake and the hills beyond could only be seen when the temple gate was open, and it was always kept shut. In the various halls images of Buddha and copies of the doctrines were displayed, and at the back there was a large garden, which supplied vegetables to the nuns, and many flowers and fruit-trees. The whole building stood very high and was surrounded by great walls which ensured absolute quiet within except for the song of birds.

On our arrival it always seemed as if the nuns had put

on new dresses to receive us, a piece of etiquette which they carried out with ceremony. After greetings, the chief nun took Grandmother into each hall to burn incense and pay tribute. I followed, kneeling and kowtowing as they did. When Grandmother went into the inner chamber, where the chief nun slept, a little nun was asked to show me round the temple. I was told not to make a noise or talk loudly while passing through the halls, so I simply did not speak at all. In any case, the atmosphere of the towering halls awed me and the little nun walked with such steadfast calmness that I was afraid to disturb her. At home I had been taught the Confucian Analects and had been constantly trained how to behave like a ' superior man ', so I walked with my eyes looking straight ahead. Even the rustling of my new blue satin gown seemed to disturb the silence and made me walk slower. Having since then visited Western cathedrals I can imagine now what our two figures looked like, the little nun's and mine, moving slowly through the vast halls. I guessed that she was three or four years older than me, but I did not know that she was dumb. When we had been round the garden and she had shown me the young fruit on the trees, I thanked her and said I should like to go back to Grandmother. She smiled and smiled, as if anxious to keep me a little longer, but at length I was taken to the inner chamber. Grandmother asked me if I had enjoyed my tour. Then she said something to the little nun, who smiled again and went away. When lunch was ready the chief nun suggested that I should take my meal with the little nun, and Grandmother agreed. I did not take kindly to the proposal myself, but the little nun was smiling at my side and after some kindly urging I went with her to a small shelter in the garden and we ate together. It was then I discovered that she could not speak. She was, however, extremely clever at reading people's thoughts and hearts, and we got on famously. We had dinner together, too. By the time Grandmother was ready to return home I was having difficulty in keeping my gaze off the little nun, who had not ceased to smile at me. When we left the temple she waved after me for a long time.

The next time I came, she displayed manifest excitement at seeing me again, and the Superior had to warn her to control herself. We spent most of the time playing together in the garden. When I had to get ready to go home she was suddenly overcome and could not stifle her tears. I felt very sad at heart and did not know what to do. I did not even think of offering her my handkerchief, being still bound by the Confucian rule. Running to my Grandmother I asked if she could stay a little longer. But Grandmother was insistent, and I had to explain that the little nun didn't like my going and was crying in the garden. When the Superior and the mother of the little nun heard this they called the poor girl and scolded her. She stood before us most pathetically, and I could not keep back my own tears, although the little nun had managed by that time to control hers. Afterwards Grandmother scolded me too for being so foolish. I knew I ought not to have cried, but I could not understand why the little nun should have to live in the temple with no sisters or brothers to play with. Grandmother replied by telling me the girl's story. I suggested that we should ask her to come and live in our house. But Grandmother said that was impossible. The girl was already a nun, with her hair shaven and the Buddhist marks on her head. In any case, it was not, Grandmother added, a matter for a little boy like me to bother about.

I often went again to the temple and played with the little nun. Once, with Grandmother's permission, I took her some toys and packed a few cakes in the parcel. At first she seemed struck with the toys, but soon she lost interest in them, perhaps because she was really too old for them. Then I gave her the cakes. But she wouldn't eat them, and only smiled. Having no idea of the reason, I felt hurt. She could not explain. This was the first time she had seen me sad, and bending down she smoothed my forehead with her hand and stroked my cheek. She kept smiling, as if to say, ' Do not mind so much '. I ought, I knew, to have drawn back from her immediately ; but I didn't. It was a strange sensation. Afterwards I asked Grandmother why my cakes had been refused and was told that the nuns at the temple all had pure hearts and would not take anything from outside, except rice and salt, lest their hearts should be defiled. Being vegetarians, they could not eat anything made with animal fat, and to avoid breaking this rule they were careful never to eat anything not made by themselves. I understood only vaguely. It seemed to me terribly hard that this beautiful young girl should be cut off from so many of the pleasant things of life. Now I wonder whether perhaps she was not more fortunate than I, in being able to live apart from the tangled web of contemporary life and to keep her heart pure. She must be nearly forty by now. I hope she is safe and happy.

The girls in our house had many privileges as compared with the boys. A group of them could invade a boy's room and turn everything topsy-turvy, but no boy dared intrude upon a girl. Boys were expected to bear the blame when anything went wrong, and we seemed to accept this state of affairs as a matter of course. I, being of a mild disposition and disinclined to retaliate, was perpetually plagued by my girl relatives. I was known to like reading and to be able to tell stories, and my services were therefore often called upon. When I began to learn painting from my father I was expected to draw for them too. After school they would come to my room, and one would ask me to draw a hen, another a flower, a third a tree, a fourth a bird—anything to keep me busy. They did not mind whether or not I drew the things well. Fortunately my patience was longer than theirs and they usually tired first. Sometimes I was asked to make embroidery designs for pillow-cases or handkerchiefs, and this I liked.

There was one girl relative who did not bother me.
She did not live in the house but came to visit us from
time to time. There was some connexion by marriage
between her parents and the elders of my family. Everybody praised her beauty; in my eyes she was beyond praise.
I wanted to talk to her, but she was as silent as myself, and
we got no further than smiles. Since the days when I
knew ' Little Red ' I had come to understand more of the
traditional customs governing these matters: and now I
found it impossible to discover means to bring myself to
her notice. It was difficult in those days for boys and
girls to find topics of mutual interest for discussion. We
read more or less the same books but none of us understood
them. Embroidery, of course, was an exclusively feminine
interest. There were no plays or films to discuss. Luckily
the girl sometimes came to my room with the others. She
would ask me to draw for her, but never insisted on a
definite subject, which I should have liked her to do, so
that I could guess her interests. I confess I painted more
carefully for her than for the other girls.

Once, coming in from school, I found six or seven girls
in my room. They had scattered my books on tables,
chairs and floor, and unearthed all my many small pieces
of paper and drawings. I was furious at the mess, but they
only made faces at me. Then I noticed the girl I admired
so much picking the things up off the floor to tidy the
room and reprimanding her companions. They promptly
told her that she could not speak to them like that until
she was their sister-in-law, and she would have to wait a
few years for that! She did not let this embarrass her, but
went on tidying up; so I had to be bold too. Going to
her I said that I was used to having my things upset and
did not really mind. But she answered in a low voice
that she would like to help me if she could. This gentle
murmur from her small lips echoes still in my mind. The
sound of footsteps coming towards my room made the
girls pick up my drawings and flee. Later I heard that

Father had remarked that the drawing I had done for this girl was much the best, and I was very gratified.

In due course—about the beginning of my fifteenth year —I tired of reading novels about heroes who robbed the rich to help the poor, and began to read love stories. And the more love stories I read the more I thought about this girl relative. New Year's Day arrived and was followed by the usual spring dinner-parties and visits from relatives. She came among them. At such gatherings everybody was occupied in some way—playing cards, mah-jong, talking. I managed to persuade my youngest cousin to ask her if she would care to see my latest drawings. The two of them came to my room and I showed my pictures. Then the girl produced a small embroidered silk visiting-card bag, such as was commonly carried by men and boys in those days, and said that she had made it for me a long time before but had had no chance to give it me. Such a bag was usually a sign of love from a girl to a boy. The design of the embroidery, I found, was my own. Nowadays it is easy for boys and girls to send each other presents—but then it was not easy, and I can still feel the trembling thrill I felt when she handed me the bag. I could not speak for some minutes ; then I murmured that I would keep it carefully. She told me what difficulty she had had in keeping the making of the bag a secret, and we smiled together. I am ashamed to confess that I do not know where the bag is now, and since I went to college at Nanking I have not seen the girl. I hear she has two daughters and a son. She cannot, I know, read English, but I do not feel I can mention her name, and I offer my apologies to her, wherever she is, for being unable to obtain her consent to write this.

A few years of living in Europe has taught me how much environment moulds human life and thought. My European readers may think these three youthful heart-stirrings of mine too trivial to relate, being used to such experiences from their very early days ; I dare say a good many of my modern compatriots will think the same. But to me it seems that an experience too often enjoyed loses in value. In London I have, of course, seen many films and read many modern novels, and am no longer shocked by Western ways. But when, at parties, I see the hostess merrily kissing her husband's friends, or a white-bearded gentleman congratulating a girl on her coming-of-age with a hearty kiss and a joke about being sweethearts, I find it difficult to take this behaviour as natural, though I know it is common enough. If a girl's face were to be photographed under the microscope and every detail of her skin thus revealed to her lover, would he like her the better? Fortunately modern science has not as yet succeeded in revealing why a girl loves a particular man and not another, or why many a young man has taken his life through a disappointment in love.

I even prefer to endure pain in love. Where there is pain there is sweetness too. When love goes smoothly it may end in boredom. People always try to avoid pain, and in so doing frequently involve themselves in further pain. Is not this one of the mysteries of life? Perhaps my over-tender heart endured unnecessary pain in childhood, but the counterbalancing sweetness is still fresh in my memory.

BAMBOO-SCREEN AND MATS SELLER

26

OUT OF BALANCE

In the old Chinese calendar a definite day marked the beginning of summer. A small celebration was held and we had a better dinner than usual, but the festival was not considered an important one. What made it memorable to us youngsters was the fact that it was the only occasion in the year when we might expect a small gift from the teacher of the family school. He himself received presents from the elders of the family on any festival or important occasion ; but he never gave us anything except on this first day of summer, when it was customary for teachers to give presents to their pupils. I do not know why this should have been so. 'Old Beard's' presents seldom failed to take the form of paper fans. It was a practical idea since the time to use fans was beginning. If he happened to be in a cheerful mood he would write poems on the fans and perhaps also give us a half-holiday. Of course, he joined Father and the uncles in partaking of the special dinner.

After the dinner my fourth uncle used to gather the members of the household in the second sky-well and weigh them one by one. This uncle had the reputation of being the most light-hearted and jovial of the elders, but he could be very rude when in a bad temper, and we were always cautious in our dealings with him. We were supposed to be weighed twice a year, on the first day of summer and the first day of autumn. A sensible arrangement, surely, for on the first occasion we would be taking off our fur gowns and putting on light silks, and on the second we would be taking to the heavier garments again.

We were supposed to notice how much weight we had gained at each weighing, but though the figures were written down at the time I do not think they could have been kept, for no one seemed to remember his or her weight from one half-year to the next. In any case it was of no importance whether one had gained or lost weight; the weighing was a matter of custom and a means of entertainment. You may ask why we should take the trouble to weigh ourselves at all if we attached no significance to the result, but I reply: 'Why should not the weighing give significance to the occasion?' I find I never nowadays feel tempted to use the handy modern machines I see in so many shops, because it would seem so dull compared with our ceremonial weighings.

My fourth uncle would begin the proceedings by going to the kitchen himself to fetch the largest steelyard we had. Two servants helped him to bring a strong ladder, lean it against a beam in the sky-well, and suspend the steelyard from one of the rungs. Then they spread under it two or three thick red rugs. The fourth uncle then chanted songs of his own composition, just as a street pedlar might sing the praises of his wares. His songs in themselves entertained us and tempted us to approach and ask to be weighed. Father and the other uncles generally gave him a smile and went away, and some of the aunts did not join in the fun, but Grandmother loved to watch the fourth uncle perform his amusing ritual. We youngsters always scrambled to be weighed first, but he made it a rule that the youngest should come first and then the others in ascending order of age—an arrangement which was, of course, quite contrary to the usual rule which invariably gave precedence to the eldest.

Once my nephew, when only three months old, was the first to be weighed. Wrapped in a large sheet of red silk, he was hung on the hook of the steelyard. Most of the younger boys and girls were weighed in this manner, because it was rather difficult for them to hold the hook tightly enough. I could just manage it, but I had to curl my legs up in order not to touch the ground. It was great fun hanging on and swinging round and round until my weight was taken down by one of my older cousins. It took quite a time to weigh all the members of my generation. Then came the turn of the elders.

The few aunts willing to be weighed were so bad at handling the hook that they could not get their bodies off the ground, and it often took even longer to weigh them than it did the children. The fourth uncle kept making jokes which made the aunts laugh and loosen their grip

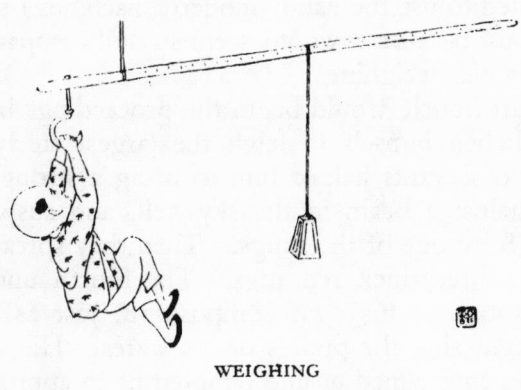

WEIGHING

on the hook. At last it was my seventh aunt's turn. A jolly person, always good-humoured and smiling, she was very fat. On this occasion she joined in the laugh at her own expense. The fourth uncle suggested removing the ladder and getting two servants to hold a strong bamboo pole on their shoulders and hanging the steelyard from that. This was done; but when the seventh aunt tried to get on the hook she found herself sitting on the red rugs with one end of the steelyard pointing to the sky! Apparently her weight was too much for it. There was a roar of laughter and the weighing came to an end, for there was no bigger steelyard in the house. The fourth uncle declared that he was an unsuccessful pedlar and would have to find a new means of earning his living. The laughter continued for some time, but the seventh aunt was not in the least offended. This was notable on account of her seniority, not because fatness was a source of humiliation. As a matter of fact most of us rather welcomed growing fat. 'You are fatter' was a compliment often passed when friends met after a lapse of time. It was thought that one could not become fat without possessing an open mind and taking life easily. My seventh aunt must have been over two hundred pounds in those days, and the degree of her geniality must therefore have been considerable !

DUCKLINGS SELLER

- 27 -

TWO NOTABLE PERSONALITIES

I REMEMBER THEM well, those two curious figures, and
I think any other citizen of Kiu-kiang of my age would
remember them too. Not that they were either rich or
highly placed; indeed, they were actually beggars : but
they were so unusual and led such strange lives that they
could not fail to fix themselves on my mind. One was
an old woman of over seventy, the other a man of middle
age. I can hardly hope to do justice to them in a short
description, but I want at any rate to mention them because
I do not think one could find such types nowadays, after
all the changes which have recently taken place in China.

The old woman was called Chu Ta-chiao. Chu was her
family name, Ta-chiao, meaning ' big foot ', her nickname.
In those days Chinese society was in good order, and house-
holders, having nothing to fear, seldom shut their gates ;
so she just walked in. Once a month she came to our
house supporting herself on a good polished stick held in
her right hand. She was bad-tempered, even in old age.
Whenever she entered a house and was not given anything,
or if she found the gate closed to her, she would abuse
the head of the family in the foulest language she could
muster and continue until placated with some trifle.
Actually, however, she was seldom kept out or allowed to
go away emptyhanded, for on the score of age alone she
could command respect. Generally she was very gay and
amusing, despite her age, though her eyes had lost their
lustre. Her hair was always decorated with fresh flowers
and she used to dress in bright colours, which was unusual

for an old woman and made her very conspicuous. She knew many interesting stories and could even sing songs. When she came to a house and was satisfied with its donation she would express her gratitude in those figurative compliments of which our language is so full.

My grandmother always kept something ready for her, so the compliments she showered on us youngsters, when we crowded round her in the first hall, were couched in language of unimaginable flattery. And she never repeated herself! My girl-cousins were moved by these compliments; I was not interested, but I was very impressed by the old woman's wonderful manners. I felt sure she could be no ordinary beggar : and, sure enough, I learned later that she was the daughter of a Manchurian prince.

In her younger days it had been the custom for the Emperor, at the opening of his reign, to select a number of girls of good family to live in the palace and do court service. It was impossible to refuse this service, although it meant the complete severance of the girl's connexion with her family. Of course if she were fortunate enough to find favour with the Emperor, things might go very well with her. If in addition to being fortunate she was clever, she might turn the Emperor's head and become Empress, as did the late notorious Empress-Dowager Tzu-hsi. But as a rule if one in a thousand girls in the court received a single glance from the Emperor she was considered lucky. Most of them lived, decked in beautiful garments, as if they were dead. Indeed, many of them actually died of boredom and grief. In spite of this, some families longed to have a daughter called to court, hoping thus to become a relative of the Emperor. But most families disapproved and tried to get their daughters married before the date of selection. Occasionally girls would run away from home to escape the imperial tyranny ; others even took their lives. Our poets and scholars have for centuries depicted the sorrows of these girls. Luckily, under the Manchurian dynasty, Chinese girls largely escaped selection for court, for the Manchurians decreed that there should be no inter-marriage between the Chinese and themselves, and this decree was strictly observed by the royal family. Manchurian girls, therefore, rather than Chinese, were summoned to the palace.

Chu Ta-chiao was one of the thousands who, appalled at tne prospect of a life of virtual incarceration, ran away from home during the selection. Rumour said that she had been very beautiful and that her name had certainly been on the list; but how she had got away from her family nobody knew. It was still more difficult to imagine how she came to marry a native of Kiu-kiang and to live in the city. Her big feet established her Manchurian ancestry, as also did her facility in compliment, an accomplishment on which Manchurians prided themselves, and her good singing voice. We never mentioned Manchuria to her— we never, as I have already described, mentioned Manchuria at all—and probably in her old age she had forgotten that she was not Chinese. Grandmother told us that her husband had been a shopkeeper in the city and that the pair had had two sons and a daughter and had been very happy together. Unfortunately the husband and all the children died, and Chu Ta-chiao was left without any means of livelihood except begging. This distressing situation seemed even more shameful and hard when one knew her sad story. Grandmother impressed upon us that we should realize how sorrowful the old lady's heart must be, although she was usually so gay, and she said that we must forgive her occasional fits of temper. These words always come back to me when I think of Chu Ta-chiao. She must be dead by now, but her story will live.

The second of my ' two notable persons ' was ' old third Hsiao ', so called because he was the third son of a Hsiao family. He was in his early forties, and spent his days wandering about the city, very seldom speaking to any one. He could not be made to utter a proper sentence, although he was certainly not dumb. He could not even be bribed to do so. He begged from house to house, standing at the gate until some one gave him something, or going quietly away if nobody took any notice. Many a time I saw him standing at our gate with a rice bowl and a small basket in his hand, his lips murmuring unintelligibly. Not one of his garments was whole, his hair was always uncombed, and he had a bushy black beard. I heard that he painted his face with different coloured pigments and jumped about on some empty piece of ground playing the part of a solo actor in a play of his own invention. People called the play 'Ghosts Fighting', because nobody had any idea what it was about. He also shouted and sang incomprehensible songs.

Grown-ups of course thought him mad, but children, especially boys, loved him for his peculiar gestures. The news would go round that he was at the gate, and some of my elder cousins would come out and urge him to play 'Ghosts Fighting', but this he would always ignore. Later, when I was allowed outside the garden, I saw him on several occasions performing his fantastic antics. He could make every one roar with laughter while himself maintaining, like all good comedians, a perfectly straight face. There was no time-limit to his performances. He just played on and on till he was exhausted, and then moved quietly away without even asking for any reward. His name was used, as was Chu Ta-chiao's, to threaten children who would not go to sleep; but it could not have been very effective, for he frightened no one, least of all a child.

And in reality he was not mad. His heart was broken. This trite phrase really describes his condition. He had been a very learned man who could write poetry and paint pictures. His family being poor, he obtained a post in the family of a high official, where his writing and painting were so much admired that he was asked to give lessons to the official's children. He accepted. But he was only twenty and very handsome: and by the end of a year he had fallen in love with the official's daughter and she with him. Marriage was out of the question for them, owing to the old Chinese ideas of prestige, so their love was never made known to the girl's parents. In due course the parents arranged for the girl to marry the son of an official of the same standing as her father ; but before the wedding day she took her life. This was what broke old third Hsiao's heart. When he heard of his beloved's death his health broke down and he was sent home. And from that day he spoke to no one. When his two brothers died and there was nobody left to look after him he took to begging.

I have often wished that old third Hsiao had written his own life-story. But perhaps he was wise not to do so, for it is no use wasting tears to amuse others. And, after all, how many girls and boys in the long history of China have been deprived of their freedom to love, and have taken their lives rather than submit to our all-too-fallible human laws ! Probably young people in the West have suffered in like manner, in spite of their apparent freedom. With us, venerable custom was the stumbling-block. In the West I think *money* has more often served the same unhappy end !

FLOWER SELLER

28

BEATING THE FLOWERY DRUM

Among the many folk-song singers whom I heard in my youth none made a greater impression upon me than the children who came to our house to sing *Feng-yang hua-ku-ke*, the 'Flowery-drum song of Feng-yang'. They were natives of the Feng-yang district of Anhui, which was not very far from Kiu-kiang. Their native folk-song was distinctive in character and accompanied by the beating of a flowery drum and a gong. They went round Kiu-kiang in springtime, about the third and fourth months.

Feng-yang was a small northerly district. Its soil was poor and its people could hardly grow enough to live on. To supplement their incomes the inhabitants devised the practice of visiting houses in other cities to sing songs. Strangely enough, the first emperor of the Ming dynasty (1368–1643) was born in Feng-yang. The son of a very poor farmer, he had a miserable childhood. During a famine his parents died and he, having no means of livelihood, became, simply for the sake of food and shelter, a monk in a monastery. Later, for some reason or other, he became a beggar. The people of Feng-yang were very proud of having produced an emperor and felt no shame in begging for their living by singing songs, since the emperor had himself done the same.

Several groups of these Feng-yang singers came to our city, but one group made a particularly vivid impression on my mind. The principal member of it was a young girl of nine or ten with five or six bunches of hair tied in plaits round her head. She was dressed in a flowered

red jacket and green trousers. Her face was painted, and a small round drum varnished with flower designs hung on her chest ; she held three wooden rods of equal length, two in one hand and one in the other. A boy of about the same age or a little older held a small bronze gong and a beater. An old couple, perhaps the parents, stood behind and helped with the singing.

When they reached our house the girl struck the edge of the drum three times with the rod and the boy beat the gong three times. We agreed to pay for the song, and the girl then again struck the drum three times and began to

BEATING THE FLOWERY DRUM

throw each of the rods in the air in turn, holding the other two one in either hand. Each time she caught the tossed rod in her right hand she struck the drum with it once. She must have been well trained, for as well as all this she sang her part of the song. When she had finished, the boy sang his part while beating his gong, the girl continuing to juggle with the rods. All four of them joined in the chorus. It was a most delightful entertainment, made more charming by the beauty of the girl.

The song could be long or short according to the wishes of the audience. I do not remember all the verses, and, as a matter of fact, they could hardly be translated if I did, for the manner of singing was essential to the effect of the song.   But the following lines give the sense of a small part of it :

> Let us talk of Feng-yang, speak of Feng-yang.
> Feng-yang was once a decent place,
> Since the Emperor Chu was born there.
> Nine years out of ten it has suffered famine.
> The gong is in the left hand and the drum is in the right ;
> With gong and drum in hand we come to sing our song.
> We have no other song,
> Only the Feng-yang song.

Chorus :
> Feng Feng Yang song ay, ay, ay, ay . . .
> Drr dlungdung p'iao-i-p'iao,
> Drr dlungdung p'iao-i-p'iao,
> Drr p'iao, drr p'iao,
> Drr p'iao, drr p'iao-p'iao,
> Drr p'iao-p'iao p'iao-i-p'iao.

Girl sings :
> My wretched life, my terrible fate,
> I have not married a decent mate.
> Others' husbands become officials,
> But mine plays the drum day in, day out.
> Beat, beat the flowery drum ay, ay, ay, ay . . .

Chorus.

Boy sings :
> It's just my luck, my terrible luck,
> I have not married an attractive girl.
> Others' wives are skilful in embroidery,
> But mine has a pair of enormous feet.
> Measure, measure about a foot long ay, ay, ay, ay . . .

Chorus.

The women of Feng-yang never bound their feet.   How fortunate they were !   It was interesting that this kind of grumbling, common enough in my country, should have been sung by two little children who probably did not understand what it was about. Certainly I did not trouble about the meaning, but just enjoyed the song as a song, and liked it all the better because it was sung by youngsters like myself.

My grandfather never minded these singers coming to our house, for he had a great admiration for the first emperor of the Ming dynasty and therefore respected people who came from this emperor's birthplace. He welcomed also young girl folk-singers between the ages

YOUNG GIRL FOLK-SINGERS

of sixteen and twenty-five. These came mostly from the same Kiu-kiang district on the north bank of the river in which our ancestral temple was situated; a large number of people with the same family name as ourselves lived there. Some, however, came from the adjoining district of Huangmei, in Hupeh province. They always came in pairs and were never accompanied by a man. They wore new clothes, their faces were beautifully painted, and they had fresh flowers in their hair. Each held a fairly thick bamboo stick with several holes in it. An iron wire strung with old Chinese coins was passed through each hole. When the girls struck the stick against their bodies, as Spaniards strike a tambourine, the coins clinked pleasantly. The performance was like a dance, for the singers struck each shoulder and leg in turn with the jingling stick, singing the folk-songs at the same time. The songs were usually about love and were unquestionably meant for grown-ups! But at that time I did not bother about love stories.

FIREWOOD SELLER

29

DOUBLE SEVENTIETH BIRTHDAY

On any ordinary birthday there was only a small celebration. Incense was burnt before the ancestral shrine, as if to inform the ancestors that one of their descendants had grown a year older, and on the evening before the birthday a special bowl of noodles with chicken broth was given to each member of the family after dinner. That was all. Not much more was really feasible, for with so many people in the house there could be four or five birthdays in a single month.

The celebration of my grandparents' ' Double Seventieth' birthday was quite a different affair. It was customary for a grandfather at seventy and a grandmother at sixty to have particular notice taken of their birthday. In the case of my own grandparents, all I knew was that I was to wear new clothes and to have special things to eat. It was only later that I discovered that my grandfather was seventy-four and my grandmother sixty-six in that year, and that accordingly they had combined to celebrate a ' Double Seventieth' birthday. The celebration actually took place on Grandmother's birthday, which was about a month later than Grandfather's.

Three halls were repainted and a huge Chinese character signifying ' longevity', made of gold paper sewn on a large piece of red satin, was hung on the back wall of the third hall under the ancestral shrine. The pictures on the side walls were changed for others whose subjects had some connexion with long life. Actually most of them were scrolls bearing congratulatory poems presented by friends of the elders and of my brother. All the chairs in the halls were given embroidered covers and cushions, and in the third hall a thick red carpet was spread on the floor. From the beam in the first sky-well was hung a pair of large red candles, each of which bore four golden characters, one side saying ' Happiness as large as the Eastern Sea ' and the other ' Longevity as old as the Southern Mountain '. A beautifully embroidered curtain with a Taoist legendary story was hung in the second hall. In each hall there were four silk lanterns and a big round one in the middle. On some of the pillars were pasted strips of red paper with couplets in Chinese calligraphy. All this presented a gay picture from the entrance-gate.

Printed red invitation cards were sent out, and about two days before the birthday presents began to arrive in a continuous stream. Besides scrolls of Chinese writing and painting, the most common present was two large dishes of uncooked food : one of Chinese noodles, symbolizing a life as long as the endless noodle, and the other a large number of hand-made wheat peaches as in the Taoist legendary story, also symbolizing longevity. They were beautifully made and well arranged in the dishes. During the two days before the birthday a quantity of these pairs of dishes were showered on Grandmother and Grandfather. One of each kind was set on the square table in front of the golden character ' Longevity '.

In the afternoon of the day before the birthday there arrived a special present consisting of a huge wooden board, perfectly varnished and bearing four big characters : *Ku-hsi-hsieh-lao*, ' living together from seventy on '. On the right-hand side were the names of my grandparents and on the left the names of the senders. The characters were all engraved in gold, and the senders were the six fiancés of the older girls of my generation. My sister's fiancé's name came in the second place. This board was hung at the top of the back wall of the second hall. After this the celebration really began ; but of this first part of it I remember little, for, being tired with all the excitement, I went to bed early.

Next day, about noon, the guests began to arrive. By the entrance-gate sat professional musicians who blew pipes and beat a gong as each guest arrived, thus summoning the elders out to perform the ceremony of welcome. My older cousins and my brother were posted about the house to entertain the guests in the various halls and studies.

When all the expected guests had arrived, a puppet or 'shadow' (*Ying-tzu-hsi*) play was given in the second hall. A wooden frame was erected on a table and a piece of thin cloth nailed across it. An operator sat behind the frame and made thick paper figures move to act parts in a story. As each figure moved, some one in the company sang its part. There had to be as many singers as figures. The operator was extremely skilful and the show amused us all very much. The first scene had some connexion with the birthday, for it was the story of *Ma-ku-hsien-shou* (Lady Ma-ku represents longevity). The singers were friends of my third great-uncle, and were at particular pains to give a good performance ; my third great-uncle even took a small part himself as a sign of congratulation to the grandparents.

After the puppet shows babel broke loose, all the guests striving at the same time to offer their personal congratulations. Father and my uncles begged them to desist and just enjoy themselves as much as they could, but they insisted on going to the grandparents' rooms. So, to avoid confusion, two big chairs were placed in the third hall before the golden character of 'Longevity', and Grandfather took the left-hand one and Grandmother the right, facing the entrance-gate. The family friends then approached to pay their respects, bowing or kneeling once according to age and generation. The friends of my grandparents and of the third great-uncle bowed, only, to the 'Two Old Stars of Longevity '—as, for the occasion, my grandparents were called. Next, the friends of my father and brother knelt. Then came the group of relations with different family names. After them, those with the same family name but resident in different houses. Finally my great-uncle took the lead for the direct descendants, and we all followed, down to the youngest of my generation.

Father had chosen eight younger members of my generation, including myself, to be dressed up as the eight Taoist immortals of the legend. In the story these eight immortals attended the celebration of the birthday of the Western

EIGHT 'YOUNG' TAOIST IMMORTALS

Queen-Mother in the Palace of Heaven. Only one of them was a female, but as there were three girls in the group selected by my father, two of them had to play male parts. We wore paper hats and our dresses were sheets of many-coloured silk. I had a long black moustache on my upper lip, and I remember that it was roughly made and hurt my lip, but the duster that I held in my right hand soon made me forget the discomfort. To carry out the story, one immortal had to be lame and support himself on a stick. The lady immortal was obliged to wear a long, old-fashioned skirt, and the girl-cousin who took the part was not used to it. When we appeared in the hall there was a burst of laughter, and we all, forgetting our parts, ran forward. The female immortal tripped over her long skirt and fell flat on the red carpet. None of us carried out our instructions, but at any rate we all knelt before our grandparents and everybody enjoyed the scene. By the time we got up, I had lost my moustache, some one else had no hat, a third had broken his flower basket, and the dress of a fourth had fallen off.

The whole birthday proceedings lasted two or three hours. At the conclusion the grandparents were very tired and withdrew. A banquet was then held for all the guests and every one joked and made merry with wine games. At the end of the banquet a bowl of noodles—not rice—was served to each guest as a reminder of the occasion of the feast.

FORTUNE-TELLER

30

STONE-BELL MOUNTAIN

IT WAS very difficult to persuade Grandmother to let me take a trip outside Kiu-kiang ; but when the school authorities assured her that I would be quite safe with them, she consented to my going ; and thereafter I joined almost every trip arranged by the Third Middle School of Kiangsi. The trip to Stone-bell Mountain was one of them.

Shih-chung Shan, or Stone-bell Mountain, was a very famous spot on the south bank of the Yangtse River, just at the mouth of Lake P'oyang, one of the five biggest lakes in China. Though it was only thirty miles from Kiu-kiang, the only satisfactory way to get there was by a small steamer which ran once a day from Kiu-kiang. The steamer was too small to hold forty children besides its other passengers, so we were accommodated in two big junks towed by the steamer. I was most excited. It was my first time down the river, my first time in a junk, the first time I had spent a night outside my home, and the first time I had mixed with so many people none of whom was a member of my family. It was different from any previous experience in my thirteen years of life and I was tremendously impressed.

Grandmother and Father had always said : ' At home you will find things go smoothly for a thousand days, but once you go out you will quickly come across difficulties.' And they were right. I had to wrap myself up in a small thin rug in a corner of the junk, where I could not move an inch on account of the crush of my schoolmates. When we were told we could have a meal I had to find a pair of chopsticks and a rice-bowl for myself, instead of, as at home, having servants to set the table and prepare every-thing.   And I had to look after my belongings, which made me realize for the first time that I *had* belongings of my own, for at home everything was common property.   However, these minor bothers only added to my enjoyment.

While the junks moved steadily along under the river-bank, we could hear the hissing sound of the high weeds brushing against the hull.   There were two small windows on each side of the junk I was in, and I was fortunate enough to be sitting near one of them and could therefore look out most of the time.   Occasionally I saw fishermen casting their nets into the water and waiting for fish ; but there were very few people to be seen on the shores in these parts. Green hills showed here and there dotted with trees covered with red blossom.   Lucky birds flew in the distance, enjoy-ing the tranquil countryside.   I supposed that our farmers must be busy where I could not see them, for it was just the season for them to be in the fields as much as possible. The chugging of the steamer at the other end of the very long thick towing-rope only reached me faintly.   Some-times I could not see the steamer at all for the tall weeds. The river was wide, so that other boats did not disturb us. Some of my schoolmates joked with each other and told fanciful stories, some of which made the two teachers with us laugh.   I found our teachers much more cheerful than in the classrooms.   As I lay in the junk, leaning my head against the corner of the window to watch the river scene and with my ears catching the jokes, I felt completely happy. Grandmother and Father, I thought, could never guess how happy I was.

Presently one of the teachers informed us that we should soon be at our destination.   We got our things ready and I noticed that our junk turned to the right where there was a huge gap leading to wide open space.   The hills along the shore stopped abruptly at this gap.   In the far, far dis-tance I could see a group of faint blue mountains.   We all gazed at the water with interest, for at this point a clear-cut line marked the junction of the yellow muddy water of the Yangtse with the deep, clear, blue of the lake. This was the mouth of Lake P'oyang. The sharp division between river and lake was due to the fact that the river water ran very fast and the lake water was still. Presently the small steamer cast the towing-rope and my junk had to be rowed to shore. There were only two oars, and two of our four boatmen applied themselves to each. They sang, while they rowed, a boatman's song which none of us could understand. On the huge oars there was plenty of room

A CHINESE JUNK

for us to lend a hand with the rowing, and we were all anxious to help. We joined in the boatmen's song—though, not knowing either the words or the tune, the best we could do was to try to keep the rhythm. The junk moved very slowly in spite of our united efforts ; it took half as long to reach the shore as it had taken to cover the whole distance from Kiu-kiang. But we did not worry.

I could now see the mountains clearly. The first rocky mass stretching along the shore was Shih-chung Shan, the one we were going to visit. Its foot was half in the water and its rocks were stiff and steep. I wondered how we could climb them, and on asking, was told that there was a way on the far side. It was not a very big mountain, and there appeared to be plenty of trees on the top. The typical curved roofs of many bowers, pavilions and temples and of two small pagodas could be discerned. . . . Behind the mountain lay the city and district of Hu-kou (Mouth of the Lake). In spite of the thin, greyish evening mist I could see the city clearly, for it was built on the hill-tops and a high city wall encircled the buildings and houses. At the back the hills rose higher and higher. It suddenly struck me that the scene resembled a painting in our collection.

It was dark by the time we reached the shore and we were all tired with the rowing. The boatmen would have liked us to stay in their junk for the two nights; they would have taken us back to Kiu-kiang in the way we came. This would have been cheaper, but our teachers had already made arrangements for us to put up at a small inn in Hu-kou, and thither we went. The food, to our sharpened appetites, was delicious. It had been intended that after dinner we should hire a small boat and row round the bottom of the Stone-bell Mountain, but there was no moon and the wind was too strong. Unfortunately, early next morning, when two schoolmates and I went to the shore of the lake, the wind was as strong as ever. We could hardly fight our way along, and its howling frightened us. We could not see the other shore. Leaning against the blast, we stared at the vast lake, and were filled with a sense of our own insignificance.

In due course the party set off for the mountain, and came to a building which looked like a temple but which contained no priests or monks. By entering this building we reached the ' Stone-bell Mountain '. ' Mountain ' was not perhaps the right word to describe it, for it was like a beautifully arranged Chinese rock garden. The trees were abundant; some were in bloom, others were ancient and grotesque in shape. Here and there stone steps led to a bower, pavilion or halls, and to the small pagodas. One of the pagodas and a bower were built on the edge of the huge rock which jutted out into the water, and looked very dangerous. I did not go there myself. At one point the stone walls of a long corridor were engraved with many poems and winter-plum paintings by the late Commander-in-Chief Peng Yu-ling. The teachers told us how this officer commanded all the Chinese sailors fighting against the Tai-p'ing Rebellion (1850–6). He had his headquarters on this mountain. I have never been interested in stories of fighting and I did not listen ; but I was greatly impressed by the stone engravings of the poems and paintings of this warrior who was also a great scholar and painter. He loved a beautiful girl whose name had some connexion with the winter-plum flower, and as he could not get into touch with her and marry her, he devoted his leisure to painting this flower and writing poems about it. I liked his constancy and loyalty.

Then we came to the middle of the mountain. Many huge rocks, with big holes in them due to the washing of the lake water, formed a circle. One of our guides threw a small stone into the middle of the circle, and a sound like that of a huge bronze bell being struck was emitted. This was the origin of the name Stone-bell Mountain. We were thrilled and all threw small stones into the circle and listened for the ringing sound from the bottom.

There must be a myriad small stones in this stone bell, for it has been known to visitors for thousands of years. It is mentioned in a well-known essay by the famous poet, Su Tung-p'o of Sung dynasty (A.D. 960–1276). Su Tung-p'o said he had heard of the spot and wondered why it was called Stone-bell. He had been told that it was because any stone found on this mountain could produce a sound like that of a bronze bell, but he did not believe it and took his elder son with him to find out the truth. On arrival, they hired a boat and had a moonlight trip on the water. Su Tung-p'o heard the loud sound from the holes in the huge rocks standing in the water and decided that the ringing was due to the rapid expulsion of air by the lapping of the lake water into the holes. Before we had set out on our own trip, our teachers had told us to read this essay and learn it by heart. It was considered a beautiful piece of Chinese literature.

We spent a few hours looking round, and then, as the weather did not promise a moonlit night, the teachers arranged for us to take the same trip by water round the foot of the mountain as the one Su Tung-p'o described. We saw huge rocks full of holes and heard loud sounds, and wondered whether they were exactly the same as the poet heard a thousand years before. How many generations had listened to those ringing tones since Sung times—and passed away! Our human life is so brief: what possible reason can there be why we should not enjoy ourselves to the utmost of our power?

When we got back home again, we had to write a description of our trip. I remember I received a good mark for my essay, but I have no recollection of what I wrote. Nearly twenty-four years have passed, and I have been much occupied in other cities and have had no time to visit this beautiful spot again, but the image of the mountain remains in my mind and the hollow sound of the stone bell rings to me through the years.

PEAR SELLER

THE BIRTH OF MY NEPHEW

I WAS A BOY of fourteen, supposed to have some knowledge of manners and regulations and not, as in the days before I was seven, to wander in and out of any room in the house. No doors were ever shut in the daytime, but over each hung some sort of curtain made of cloth, silk or bamboo according to the weather. The regulations were so scrupulously observed that nothing more than this was necessary. Indeed, there were many rooms in the house which I only saw for a few minutes on New Year's Eve. Doors could be left open, because no violation of recognized privacy ever occurred. We youngsters chiefly used the garden, corridors, halls and school.

When I was twelve, my brother suggested to Father that I should go and study in the school of which he was principal. This school was founded by a local authority and run like a modern elementary school. After becoming a pupil there I talked to the members of the house differently, and they were not the same either. These differences were even more marked when, at the beginning of my fourteenth year, I entered the Kiu-kiang Third Middle School (equivalent to a Western secondary school) of Kiangsi province. I state this to show that during those years I was more or less separated from the female part of the household. Boys and girls were by no means forbidden to mix, but the separation seemed to arise naturally. So I did not see my sister-in-law every day during the first few years of her marriage. But I knew that she delighted my elders, as she had been brought up in all the old traditions.

Each New Year's Day my grandmother and aunts greeted
her with the hope that she would have a beautiful baby
during the year. But nobody seemed greatly concerned
when four years passed and still she had no baby.

Then one day she did not dine with us, and later I heard
some one say that she was not feeling well and that the
third great-uncle would have to be consulted.   During the
following days she was frequently missing from our dinner
table, and I heard that she was having hot and bitter things
to eat such as preserved ginger roots, *ku-kua* (bitter melon
or *Momordica charantia*) and *La-chiao* (capsicum) and *Yan-mei*
(*Myrica rubra*, very sour).   Then my third great-uncle told
Grandmother that   sister-in-law was *Yu-hsi*, 'having
happiness'

The news spread rapidly through the house and everybody was pleased, although there was no excitement.   My
younger cousins were warned not to make any peculiar
noise near sister-in-law's chamber.   Grandmother, I noticed,
went in and out of the room very frequently. Under
normal circumstances sister-in-law had to look after her
own room, with the help of a maid shared with two or
three girl-cousins : now she was given a maid to herself
and was forbidden to do any housework.   She was not to
sit in draughty spots, nor on part of a chair ; she was not
to stand crookedly or lie on her side : but she was to walk
slowly to and fro in front of or inside her chamber for
some time every day.   Two older girl-cousins kept her
company and took their meals with her in case she should
want anything.   They were warned not to discuss unusual
matters which might over-excite sister-in-law, and on no
account to mention funerals, ghosts or spirits, as these
would affect the baby.   Above all, they were not to tire
her.

I heard of these injunctions and they seemed to me rather
hard to carry out, but the two girls made no objection.
My sister, now the wife of a member of the Kuo family,
came on a visit and stayed in sister-in-law's chamber longer

than usual. My aunts went there in turn from time to time. All were busy making something for the baby. Each of the older girl-cousins was embroidering a small bonnet, a pair of shoes or a bib. Funnily enough, I was busy too, the girl-cousins having asked me to copy this or that old design of flowers or symbols for them. They could have bought designs from the professional woman or man who visited our house with them every two or three months, but they preferred to bother me.

My sister-in-law's mother was dead, otherwise she would have come to live in our house during her daughter's pregnancy; instead, her only sister came for several months. Other relatives called on us regularly and brought many presents, such as barley sugar, coarse red sugar, dragon's eye (*Nephelium longan*), lichih, *Shan-yueh* (*Diosciorea sativa*), &c., all of which were supposed to be good for the health of the expectant mother. My sister-in-law's father, who had a good post in another province, sent her a large quantity of ginseng and pure white bird's nest, both of which were esteemed to have excellent tonic value. Once I was called in to see my sister-in-law when I was passing her room. There were a number of people in the chamber. She smiled at me and I did not know what to say. One of my older cousins said that my sister-in-law was now an empress and everybody there was at her service. At once I answered : ' Then brother must be an emperor ! ' Everybody laughed heartily, including my sister-in-law, and then I was sent away lest I should excite her too much. This was about two months before the birth of my nephew.

My brother seemed completely left out of all this. He went out to his school as usual and behaved in no way differently except that he slept in his study. But my father was very active. He kept consulting Grandmother about preparations and the third great-uncle about food and medicine. He also had a special duty. He had to execute some paintings to hang on the walls of sister-in-law's chamber. I was allowed to help with the less-important parts of these. Father told me that according to the old teachings our ancient sages set up a system of *Tai-chiao* (pregnant education—that is, education of the baby before birth). They said that the baby would be good and clever if the mother had the right environment. What she saw, heard, said and felt would affect the baby in her body ; so the mother-to-be must be very careful. She must look at beautiful things, hear virtuous talk and think of Confucius' teachings. It was said that if the mother-to-be looked at carps and peacocks the baby would have wisdom ; pearls and jades would give it beauty ; flying eagles and running dogs would give it strength and health. As these things could not actually be brought into the house, Father painted them. I never doubted or questioned the power of these influences. It was said that my sister-in-law's chamber looked very beautiful, but I had no chance to see it before the birth.

At last everything was ready. Even a wet-nurse had been procured in case the mother should prove unable to feed the baby herself. We very seldom used cows' milk for infants, and there was no artificial food at all in those days.

For a couple of days the house was full of cheerful anxiety. Then one morning about the end of the first month my old nurse told me when I came home from school that I had a baby nephew. The words ' I have a nephew ! I have a nephew ! ' sounded in my mind for some time.

The entire household was happy, especially the grandparents, who were delighted to have lived to see the fourth generation. The father of a new baby had, I knew, to burn incense and to pay respect at the ancestral shrine, as if to inform his ancestors of the addition to the family. But my brother was at his school when the baby was born, so Father performed the duty for him. I, having heard the news, went to see Father in his room. He was looking at my mother's portrait, and, catching my right hand, he said how happy Mother would be if she were still alive.

There were tears in his eyes and we did not speak for a long time.

After that it seemed as if the household grew busier and busier. A messenger was sent to my sister-in-law's family with a large number of red-coloured eggs. The symbolic meaning of this I do not know, but I suppose the red colour signified happiness, for the ritual was called *Pao-hsi*— 'Reporting Happiness'. When the messenger returned, my father had to be ready to receive a representative of my sister-in-law's family who would come followed by a pro-

A SERVANT HELD A LONG CHAIN OF FIREWORKS

cession of servants bearing presents for the child. There were no wheelbarrows in my city in those days, so everything had to be carried by hand. My father stood in the first hall and a servant held a long chain of fireworks at the entrance. As soon as the representative was sighted the fireworks were let off and Father stepped forward to the entrance to meet him. The two bowed to one another, and the representative delivered to Father a message of congratulation from the head of sister-in-law's family. Then followed two servants carrying a case with four shelves on a bamboo pole, and two women carrying small baskets in their hands. They all wore new clothes and

were taken on into the third hall to deposit the gifts.
Grandmother and the aunts were already assembled there.

Father and an uncle removed the cover of the case and
took out from the first shelf a long envelope. It contained
a folded sheet of red paper bearing expressions of congratulation—of the wish that the family would increase in
prosperity, and of the hope that the new baby would be
clever and add splendour to the family name, &c. I forget
the wording—it was formal and could be copied from
books. (The expressions were different for a girl, con-
veying instead the hope that she would be very beautiful
and would bring splendour from the family into which she

TWO SERVANTS CARRYING A CASE

was born to the family into which she married, and so on.)
The name of the head of my sister-in-law's family was ap-
pended, together with that of her father, though he was not
in the city at the time. Then the second shelf was opened.
It contained a whole set of things for study : the *Four
Treasures of a Literary Room* (inks, inkstones, brushes and
paper) and some simple books. On the third shelf were
hats, trousers, jackets, shirts, gowns, shoes, and some
gold and silver jewels for the child to wear in babyhood.
On the fourth shelf were a number of pieces of cloth and
silk with which the mother could make new clothes for the
baby from time to time. (For a baby girl the first shelf
would contain things for a boudoir—mirrors, powders,
needles and coloured silks for embroidery, a pair of ear-

rings and a bracelet—the number and choice of articles depending entirely upon the decision of the head of the family.) Then there were the baskets carried by the women to be unpacked. One contained a pair of live chickens and some ducks with red spots on their heads and wings ; another contained freshwater fish. One of the men brought a big loaf of fine vermicelli-like noodles. All these were supposed to be good food for a mother in the immediate post-natal period.

When everything had been unpacked, Father presented the representative with a large red envelope containing a message of thanks in most figurative language and signed with Grandfather's, Father's and Brother's names in succession. The inside of the shelves of the case was pasted all over with red paper, and on one shelf Grandmother placed several red-coloured eggs. Finally Father thanked and bowed to the representative and the present-bearers, who then took their leave.

From then on presents for the baby and the mother from relatives and friends poured into the house, and Grandmother and the aunts were kept busy dealing with them all. Although the present-bearers were generally the servants of the sender, they were welcomed with a cup of good tea or a bowl of chicken-broth soup with fine noodles in it so that they could join in the rejoicings. When they were ready to leave, the present-bearers always took back with them a number of red-coloured eggs to the senders, and were themselves well tipped. I simply cannot remember how many hundreds of eggs had to be coloured for the purpose. The house was full of the sounds ' *Kung-hsi, kung-hsi* ' (Congratulations, congratulations !). Though I was only a boy of fourteen, I was congratulated by any number of people on my good fortune in having a nephew. Yes, indeed ! Every member of the household was involved ; some of the servants felt even prouder than we youngsters. The maid-servants themselves gave presents for the baby.

For about a month presents continued to arrive, then the lady relatives and friends of the family began to come to congratulate Grandmother and sister-in-law in person. They usually stayed for at least one meal. So Grandmother and the aunts were genuinely overworked. I, a male and therefore immune from these disturbances, felt very sorry for our ladies, although I doubt if they appreciated my sympathy for they seemed all to enjoy it thoroughly. I wish I could penetrate into my grandmother's heart and describe all the happiness she must have felt during those days.

For three days after the baby's birth nobody except those who had been present at the birth was allowed to enter sister-in-law's chamber. Then a washing ceremony took place. The baby was carefully washed by the midwife in warm water which had been boiled with some leaves of a herb called *Ai (Artemisia moxa)*, because this plant was supposed to be good for the skin and prevent disease. Then the baby was well wrapped in new clothes and the midwife took him out to the third hall where incense had been burnt in front of the ancestral shrine. Holding the baby in her arms the midwife bowed three times to the shrine, thus as it were causing the baby himself to bow. This was called *Hsi-san*—the 'washing-after-three-days' ceremony. On the same day the whole family held a special celebration dinner to which some of our closest relatives were invited.

After the ceremony sister-in-law's chamber was open to any member of the house who wanted to congratulate her personally. I, being the only brother of the baby's father, was called in particularly. Sister-in-law, propped up on cushions, was smiling and happy. She showed me the baby lying beside her, and I stroked his little face with my finger but did not say anything. The thought was in my mind that I must be more attached to this baby than any other cousin in the house because I was his direct uncle. There were five people, all grown-ups, sitting in the chamber talking to sister-in-law, and they all asked me what I would do for the baby nephew and waited for me to say a few words. As I had not been accustomed to talk in front of several elders, I did not know what to say and just murmured that I would do everything for him. They all cheered. I felt an impulse to leave the chamber at once, but was obliged first to drink a large cup of hot barley-sugar water with a few dried dragon's eyes in it. This was the customary drink for the occasion. I liked it, but found difficulty in swallowing with so many people watching.

Sister-in-law kept to her chamber for about a month. She got up, of course, and was able to walk in the sky-well before her window, but otherwise her only thought was of getting stronger and of providing food for the baby. Fortunately this she was able to do. Before the birth, she was advised not to take any meat but only vegetables cooked in vegetable oils such as *Ch'a-yiu* (oil of camellia), *Ma-yiu* (oil of sesamum) and *Tsai-yiu* (oil of cabbage or a kind of colza oil), because the hard part of meat and fat were held to be harmful to one in her condition. She was not encouraged, either, to eat any hot or strong-smelling things. After the birth she was given a bowl of chicken-broth and fine noodle soup. Later she was given soup made by boiling pork and dried lily flowers (*Chin-chen-tsai*, in Chinese, the flowers of *Hemerocallis graminea* and of *Lilium bulbiferum*, used as remedies in affections of the lungs). But the pork itself was not given to her. Sometimes she was given a boiled freshwater fish called *Chi* (a species of bream), because this fish was supposed to help in the production of a mother's milk. She had also a special chicken dish, cooked so as to make it extremely tender and sliced into very tiny pieces. As a matter of fact, all her food had to be very soft and was generally well-boiled. She was advised not to resume eating dried cooked rice for some time, and was given instead *Ch'u* (rice congee) or noodles. Presents other than clothes for the baby were mostly the ingredients of special dishes for mothers. Grandmother consulted the third great-uncle about sister-in-law's food nearly every day. They thought that her appetite would probably be capricious, and always tried to make something new for her. For a time food seemed the only concern.

One of the presents was a kind of chicken with black feathers, a black tongue and even black bones, which we called *wu-ku-chi*. After being washed thoroughly it was roasted and fried with the seeds of *Wu-wei-tzu* (*Kadsura chinensis*), a plant to which tonic, aphrodisiac, pectoral and lenitive properties were attributed, and then steeped in two or three pounds of rice wine for a night. The next day the mother could sip this wine, which was said to be most effective in helping her to recover her health and in making the skin smoother and whiter. My sister-in-law was given three *wu-ku-chi*. Fortunately we had a garden in which to keep them. Eventually one was used for making the wine and the other two were cooked for her to eat.

As my sister was asked to be the child's godmother, my baby nephew was given on the third day the ' milk name ' of Kuo-erh, which means ' a son of the Kuo family '. When he was a month old his mother was able to go about the house as before, and on that day a big feast was prepared to which all relatives and friends who had sent presents were invited. This is called *Man-yueh*—the ' fulfilling the 1st month ' celebration. My sister-in-law's mother would have been the guest of honour had she been alive. As it was, an aunt took her place. The gathering was entirely a ladies' affair. Though men guests were invited, it was taken for granted that they would decline the invitation. At that time I began to feel like a grown-up and did not want to be found in a group of ladies, so I knew very little of what was going on among them. But the roars of laughter and merry sounds which issued from the feast filled the whole house with cheer.

The next celebration in which my nephew was the central figure was his first birthday. It is our custom to give special importance to the first birthday and to those after fifty. On these occasions we hold a special ceremony and give presents. On other birthdays a sort of celebration is held, but no presents are given—at least, certainly not by elders to youngsters—so that children did not develop the habit of looking forward to birthdays. When my baby nephew was approaching his first birthday all aunts and older girl-cousins busied themselves with the making of hats, shoes and clothes. My sister, as godmother, had to make a special effort. Altogether, on that first birthday, as many presents came as at the baby's birth. My sister-in-law's family sent a large number of presents, but this time nothing much in the way of foodstuffs. A large number of guests were invited. My baby nephew was beautifully dressed in red and green embroidered silks. He had a pair of new shoes, embroidered with tiger heads by my sister. The small tuft of hair left in the middle of his forehead was just long enough to be tied with a coloured silk ribbon. After the incense-burning, my sister-in-law held him in her arms and tried to make him bow three times before the ancestral shrine. Then he was set in the centre of a huge round table, in the midst of an assortment of articles representing the various professions he might enter—inks, brushes, an abacus, a sword, scissors, a very small hammer, an official seal, herbs, and so on. He was encouraged to pick up anything he liked. This is called *Cha-chou*, the Grasping Celebration of the first year of age. At first he did not know what was expected of him, and stared round inquiringly at the assembled company. Then, seeming to realize that we were all waiting for him to do something, he stretched out both hands towards the nearest object. But without touching it he drew back again and laughed at us. This made everybody laugh too and impressed me greatly ; I wish I could find expressions to describe his delightful laughter. After a while he picked up a green herb, which was actually not very near him. Grandmother smilingly announced that he would be a medical man when he grew up. My third great-uncle, the medical member of our family, smiled encouragingly.

The child is grown up now, but he has never thought of becoming a doctor, though my brother, before he died last year, advised him to study medicine. The advice, however, did not, I think, arise out of recollection of this incident of the child's first birthday!

I, the boy's uncle, did more for him in his babyhood than I am afraid I did in his boyhood or early manhood. My sister-in-law and the baby's nurse were always very

CHA-CHOU

kind to me, and I tried in return to help them when I could. When I got back from school one or other of them generally asked me to look after the sleeping infant and let them have a little free time. I never refused, and I found that I could read the popular novels, such as *Shui-hu-chuan*, *San-kuo-ch'ih*, *Hsi-yu-chi*, *Feng-sheng-pan*, in which just then I was absorbed, very well at the same time.

I do not remember noticing any difference between the treatment of girls and boys in my home. Until they were more than ten years old both received precisely the same care. My third elder cousin's first baby, for example, was a girl, and she was treated exactly as my baby nephew. The same celebration was held on her first birthday, and the thing she picked up was supposed to show the career of her future husband.

All this was twenty years ago. Since then things have changed too much in China. The girl members of my family now *buy* things for presents to newly born babies instead of making them themselves. And I have heard of a lady relative of mine who, after going into hospital for a week to have her baby, came out and played mah-jong the next day! Maybe I have an old type of mind, for I cannot feel satisfaction or approval at the change. But even if in my time too much was made of birth, marriage and death, it is certain that nowadays often too little is made of them.

FLOWER-DESIGN SELLER

DIFFERENT PATHS

I AM NOT very fond of the word 'fate'. We Chinese are too frequently called 'fatalists'. We believe, it is true, that there are things in life which cannot be striven for, but we believe also, as much as others, that the rest of life is mostly struggle. At the risk, however, of being dubbed a fatalist myself, I must confess that I feel deeply the force of fate. When I review my own short life, the course of which has carried me so unexpectedly from the home of my childhood in old China to my present two small rooms in London, a large element of fate seems necessary to account for such a transition. And the stories I am going to tell of two of my aunts seem to illustrate the hand of fate even more strongly.

My mother had three sisters, two of whom were twins. One of these I called *Pa-I* (eighth aunt) and the other *Chiu-I* (ninth aunt). They were only a year younger than my mother. All the sisters were brought up and educated with care, for they belonged to one of the noble families of the city.

Pa-I married a scholar who had been a high official. He held a position in the Chinese Government equal to that of an M.P. Their only son rose even higher, becoming Minister of Justice in our National Government. Thus Pa-I attained most of the things which are traditionally desired by Chinese wives. Being a good-natured, easy-going person, things usually turned out well for her. As time went on her family grew more prosperous, and she lived out her life to old age very happily.

Chiu-I, on the other hand, never married, and after a wretched life she died in pain without a single close relation to attend her. I think I know more of Chiu-I than of Pa-I. She joined a curious religious Order and lived with a few other ladies in a lonely building which my grandmother sometimes took me to visit.

The Order was neither Buddhist nor Taoist. The members held a service every day and worshipped God, but they had their own teachings to follow. All the members worked hard, for they kept no servants, and only those who could contribute to the common fund were accepted. Everything in the building was kept spotless by the personal efforts of the members. The entrance-gate was always shut and the inmates could only go out at certain times. Invitations from close relations could occasionally be accepted, and the institution was open to visitors about once a month. The diet was strict. Like Buddhist nuns, they ate no meat of any kind, not even fish; only vegetables. But their heads were not shaved and they wore no special clothes. Their main work was among the poor. They devoted their lives—often themselves not happy ones—to helping others, in the belief that they would be rewarded in their next incarnation. They lived austerely, tasting every bitterness, that they might understand the bitterness of life and thus the better render help. My elders always spoke highly of these dedicated lives.

Ever since Buddhism was introduced into China in the fourth or fifth century there have been nuns. But ladies and unmarried girls were never encouraged to join monastic Orders, for any who did so lost their family name and became cut off from their relations, which was directly contrary to the Confucian tradition. Only those rendered desperate by circumstances or by the loss of all who were dear to them ' took the veil '. Chiu-I had not these reasons for joining her Order, and she must have been very unhappy to have taken such a step. But as time went on she became almost as isolated as the other members of the Order, for of her three sisters, my mother died young and the two others both lived away from Kiu-kiang; our family thus became her only close relations.

Grandmother was a professed Buddhist with a passion for philanthropy. She was greatly attached to Chiu-I and would go to see her in the institution on visiting days, taking me with her. I remember that once when we arrived we were shown into a small room, spotlessly clean, where, for some time, we could not see Chiu-I. Then Grandmother spied her. She was on her knees in the hall washing the floor. Grandmother sighed deeply and wept. Chiu-I could not stand such heavy work, she murmured to me; she was far too delicate. Presently Chiu-I finished her work and took us to her own room. She explained that the rule of the Order was that each member should scrub floors on a certain number of days in each month. She talked cheerfully and always smiled at Grandmother's remarks—smiles which, I now realize, were rather forced.

I wonder if any one ever urged Chiu-I to unfold her sorrow? Very few people at any time are able to penetrate the hearts of fellow-beings, and it is my belief that we all have some hidden grief that cannot be shared even with our closest intimates. Perhaps it was better for Chiu-I to follow her vision in silence. To have attempted to explain might have involved misunderstanding; and are there not always enough misunderstandings in the world?

My sister-in-law was Chiu-I's niece, so she too used to visit the institution from time to time. Occasionally Chiu-I was invited to our house for a meal. When she came Grandmother had special foods prepared for her and tried to arrange for the cooking to be done in new utensils. Chiu-I would have a smile for every one and was particularly kind to us youngsters. Throughout the year she made clothes which she would bring with her on these occasions and ask Grandmother to distribute to the poor before the New Year Festival. She also found time to do embroidery for my sister-in-law and make beautiful embroidered presents for Grandmother.

When I heard of Chiu-I's death I was in Hai-chow, in Kiangsu province, and my brother and my sister-in-law were in Canton. No one seemed to know how she died; we knew only that the full page of Chiu-I's life was ended. I hope that in the new incarnation to which she looked forward her life is happier than it was when I knew her.

But when now I reflect upon her life and upon the life of Pa-I, I marvel at the divergence of the paths Fate appointed for these twins who started life together.

BAMBOO-SHOOTS SELLER

THE BIRTHDAY OF THE FLOWERS

THE BIRTHDAY of the Flowers, a festival instituted in the T'ang dynasty, was celebrated in various parts of China on the 2nd, 12th or 15th day of the second month. The original date was the 15th, the most recent the 12th. In Kiu-kiang it was for some reason not the custom to celebrate this festival, probably because the city boasted only a few good gardens. Our own garden, for example, was not in any real sense a Chinese garden, for we did not grow many kinds of flowers nor had we any of the typical arrangements of bowers, pavilions and big grotesque rocks. The people in the surrounding country held a festival of another kind on the same day, but it had no connexion with the Birthday of the Flowers. Once, however, my family did celebrate the festival, when a relation came to visit us from Suchow.

Suchow was famous as the garden city of China. Many of the best-known Chinese gardens were there, and the people of the city were keenly interested in horticulture. Our relative was born there and possessed a wide literary knowledge of flowers. It was her first visit to the upper part of the Yangtse River and she noted every difference of custom and habit between our city and her own. Her parents brought her to stay in our house until the summer, when they could all go up Lu mountain, the great beauty of which they wanted her to see before she was married. She was about my sister's age.

From earliest childhood we had been told that the girls of Suchow were the prettiest in China, and our visitor did not belie this reputation. She attracted us boys with her smiles, and she was always surrounded by our girls, who besieged her with questions about fashions in hairdressing, clothes and flower-ornaments. One afternoon she remarked that that day was the birthday of the Goddess of all Flowers and that we ought to hold a celebration. We thought the idea a splendid one, and I was sent to seek Grandmother's permission to hold it, permission which we were sure she would give out of a desire not to offend the visiting relative. It was too late to prepare anything

A DECORATED TREE

for that day, the twelfth, so the relative suggested that we should hold the celebration on the fifteenth.

The preparations devolved upon us youngsters, especially the girls. Nine of us set to work. The girls contributed disused strips of coloured silk and the boys did the heavy work of climbing the trees and tieing them to the branches. Some of the girls were able to help with the decoration of the lower branches. Our peach-tree was budding and the willows were just opening their tiny green eyes. Soon the garden looked as gay as if all the trees were in full bloom.

We tidied the small garden shelter and put a rectangular table in it. One of the older boys wrote on a strip of red paper: 'The seat of the Goddess of All Flowers.' On twelve smaller strips of red paper were inscribed the names of the gods or goddesses of the flowers for each month in the year. They were: Liu Meng-mei, god of the prunus, for the first month; Yang Yú-huan, goddess of the apricot, for the second month; Tsui Hu, god of the peach, for the third month; Chang Li-hua, goddess of the rose, for the fourth month; Chung Kuei, god of the pomegranate, for the fifth month; Hsi Shi, goddess of the lotus, for the sixth month; Shih Tsung, god of balsam, for the seventh month; Lu Chu, goddess of laurel, for the eighth month; Tao Chien, god of the chrysanthemum, for the ninth month; Hsieh Su-Chiu, goddess of the mimosa, for the tenth month; P'o Ch'u-i, god of the Camellia *oleifera*, for the eleventh month; and Lao-ling-po or Old Madam Yang, goddess of the winter-plum, for the twelfth month. The sex of the various gods and goddesses is interesting. There were, as a matter of fact, three other goddesses in addition to those dedicated to the months: the goddesses of the peony, the magnolia and the rhododendron. Chinese literature records that the twelve flower gods of the months were originally twelve persons each of whom had loved a particular flower so much that he or she had become the god or goddess of it after death.

Our girl relative arranged all the red paper tablets on the table with a small stand made of raw potato, the large tablet for the Goddess of All Flowers being in the middle and the rest ranged on either side and in front. Before the tablets she placed a few small dishes of fresh mandain-orange (of the season), dried lichih, dried dragon's eyes, preserved dates and other sweets. After letting off fireworks and burning incense she knelt down and murmured a few words which we could not catch. The rest of us followed suit though we did not know what to murmur.

Then she led us to each of the trees and flowers in the garden to bow, herself murmuring a few words to each. She spoke the Suchow dialect which some of us did not understand clearly even when she explained afterwards that her words had been laudatory and congratulatory sentences. Nevertheless, we were most sincere in our observance of the ritual and kept very quiet all through the proceedings.

The weather was beginning to grow warm, and after our devotions we scattered through the garden, talking and amusing ourselves. I followed our visitor, who related the following story :

The Goddess of All Flowers, who lived in Heaven, had the power to control the gods and goddesses of all the different flowers. When it was time for the prunus to bloom she would order the god of the prunus to go down to Earth and call forth the prunus blossoms ; and similarly with the others. She had to see that nothing blossomed out of season. If anything went amiss she was responsible and was subjected to punishment from the Palace of Heaven, where the legendary Queen-Mother of the West lived. Once, together with thousands of other fairy goddesses, she attended the birthday celebration of the Queen-Mother of the West. The Queen-Mother of the West was very pleased to see them all and every one was very happy. Then the Goddess of the Moon lifted her cup and toasted the Goddess of All Flowers, saying that for such an occasion as this she should order all her flowers to bloom at once. But the Goddess of All Flowers answered that this was impossible because each flower had its appointed season for blooming from which it could not depart. The Goddess of the Moon was very much displeased and asked what would happen if the lord of men wanted all the flowers to bloom at once. The Flower Goddess answered that no emperor would be so unreasonable. The conversation caused an unpleasant feeling between them. It also reminded the Goddess of All Flowers that she was not only subject to the law of heaven but had to accept orders from time to time from the lord of men, since all her subjects were grown on earth where they needed the protection of the emperor. Strangely enough some time after this the notorious Empress Wu Tsai-t'ien ordered all flowers to bloom in the bitter cold of winter. As the order had to be carried out at once none of the gods and goddesses of single flowers had time to report to the Goddess of All Flowers, and the blooms appeared, without orders, next morning. When the Empress came to the palace garden she was pleased that her order had been carried out so thoroughly, until she found that the peony, alone among the flowers, had not obeyed. She ordered her court people at once to burn all the five thousand peony plants in her garden. When the pile was just half burnt, the Goddess of the Peony could not stand the pain any longer and the remainder of the flowers burst into bloom. This meant that all the flowers were now in bloom at once, most of them out of season, and the Goddess of All Flowers had to be punished. Through the intrigue of the Goddess of the Moon she was turned into a girl in the world of men, a very heavy punishment, for in Heaven no one knew sorrow and suffering such as is the lot of human men and women.

When I grew older I came upon this story again in a famous long Chinese novel called *Ching Hua Yuan*.

As a race we Chinese are devoted to flowers. Though I did not learn how to plant them in my childhood, I cannot remember a time when they were not all round me. Every article of daily use bore some sort of flower design. My father specialized in flower-painting and my third great-uncle was skilled in horticulture. My girl-cousins and female elders liked to buy flowers from the peasants who brought them to the city for sale—orchids, lotus and laurel, and especially jessamine, becho and *Pei-lan-hua*. My sister and girl-cousins always planted orchids, becho, jessamine and balsam in their own quarters and used them, together with *Pei-lan-hua*, for ornaments in the hair and on the dress. Father often made designs for flower-baskets, which the ladies liked to hang inside their bed-curtains.

Balsam flowers were also used for dyeing finger-nails. They took a long time to prepare, but the girls did not seem to mind that. When the flowers were in full bloom they were picked, together with an equal quantity of the leaves, put into a jar and exposed to the sun. After exposure they were cut into very fine pieces and mixed in a bowl with about five per cent of fine yellow tobacco and

PEI-LAN-HUA SELLER

five per cent of burnt alum, the whole being pounded with a pestle for some time. The mixture was then wrapped in a leaf of Pien-tou or *Lablab vulgaris* for a while. On being taken out it was pounded again and put back into the leaf. This would be repeated about seven times. The result was applied to the finger-nails on going to bed. Next morning the nails would be a pinkish red. The depth of colour could be increased by applying the stuff several nights running. The colour was supposed to be 'fast' and the stuff was said to have two remarkable properties: that of preventing skin disease in the fingers, and that of warding off sickness in the stomach. These were good reasons enough for the trouble involved, but if they were true why were we boys not expected to treat our nails in the same way?

MELON SELLER

- 34 -

FEEDING SILKWORMS

THE TITLE of this chapter must not mislead the reader into thinking that I cultivated silkworms methodically during my childhood. Like other young members of my family, particularly girls, I fed silkworms as a hobby. We had no proper silkworm rooms and did not even lessen the work by letting the insects make cocoons. We never had more than a few hundred silkworms altogether, and I rarely tended more than ten or a dozen.

Historically, China has been regarded as the originator of silk. Our records say that Lei-tsu of Hsi-ling, Consort of the Yellow Emperor (2698 B.C.), first introduced the rearing of silkworms and the use of the loom. During the reign of this emperor and empress an annual festival of agriculture and sericulture was instituted. And after that the Emperor was always supposed at this festival to plough a furrow and the Empress to make an offering of cocoons and mulberry leaves at the altar of the ancestral temple. Under such patronage the sericultural industry was widely pursued in China for centuries. The provinces of Kiangsu and Chekiang became the main silk centres. In my own district sericulture was pursued only as a sideline to farming.

One of my aunts, who lived in the country, kept a large number of silkworms, but we in the city learnt how to feed them only because Grandmother considered it good for us to understand country ways. From looking after silkworms we should acquire, it was felt, skilful hands and careful minds for dealing with bigger things. We were, however, under no obligation to feed silkworms ; girls were encouraged to do so more than boys, and some of my boy-cousins, being uninterested, did not do it at all. Personally I found the job of tending them a nice quiet occupation.

The task of keeping new-laid silkworm eggs from one year to the next was extremely difficult. At rearing time —about the middle of spring—my aunt used to bring eggs to us from the country. I always asked for just a few more than ten, lest some should fail to hatch out. She told us to watch for the new leaf-buds on the mulberry tree in our garden and then to place the eggs in a rather warm place. We did not have fires in our rooms after the Lantern Festival, so I used to put my eggs under the mattress of my bed. At first the eggs were yellowish in colour, but after a few days they turned blackish-blue. I looked at mine every day. Soon creatures that looked like small black ants began to hatch out. I put these into a wooden box with some chaff on the top. Then I cut the new mulberry-leaf buds into very fine pieces and put them in the box. Presently the ant-like silkworms climbed up the leaves and ate them. The chaff could then be cleared away. These young leaves only served as food for a few meals and had to be specially prepared. We dried them in the air for a few days in order to reduce the moisture they contained, because too much water could easily make the silkworms develop disease. As the bodies of my ant-like silkworms grew, they turned greyish-white in colour and lost their ant-like appearance.

At first our one small mulberry tree provided enough leaves, but as the silkworms grew the supply became in-sufficient, and a servant and some boy-cousins had to go out in search of more. Mulberry leaves could be bought, too, from farmers. We often heard stories of the mulberry-leaf pickers in Kiangsu and Chekiang provinces, where silk-worms were cultivated systematically and whole fields of mulberry trees had to be grown. The pickers went out to gather the leaves in groups, women and men, girls and boys, singing folk-songs. Romantic stories were woven about them. Some of my cousins had not the patience to do the feeding-work, but they were always ready to go out searching for mulberry leaves. Not that they were concerned in those days, I think, with romance.

At seven days old the silkworms were two-thirds of an inch long and gradually turning a brownish colour; the heads waved to and fro. After that they began to eat less and less and at last refused to eat at all. The head-waving also gradually declined to immobility. This was their period of sleep, during which they changed their skins. The new skin grew beneath the old one. Then a reddish spot appeared near the head and the old skin broke at this point and the silkworms gradually emerged in new skins. After a couple of hours they began to eat fresh food again, much more of it than before. This, of course, resulted in rapid growth. They generally underwent four such periods of sleep and changes of skin, each taking two or three days. Unfortunately not all the silkworms went to sleep at the same time, and this was a serious problem for those who fed them on a large scale. It did not worry me much. I kept a pair of new bamboo chopsticks with which I lifted out the sleeping silkworms and placed them in a bamboo sieve. All this time the silkworms had to be kept in a warm room, free from draughts as well as from flies. On waking from the last period of sleep they developed much larger appetites and ate considerable quantities of leaves. This generally placed us in a difficulty, the mulberry trees being by that time nearly denuded of leaves. We managed somehow. Eight or nine days after the last period of sleep, when the silkworms were as long as three inches, their bodies became transparent. They stopped eating and were ready to spin silk. I used to put a piece of paper on the top of a small bowl and place one or two silkworms on that. They would crawl round and round paying out their silk until the paper was covered. If two could not manage to cover the paper I added another. By the time they had finished, their bodies had changed from being long thin things to barrel-shaped objects with a point at each end. They remained like that for some days, then their eyes came out, they grew wings, and I put them out on the trees.

I used my small pieces of silk for wrapping my ink-stamp. The smooth surface of the silk kept the ink from sticking to the seal. I was always amazed at how beautifully the silk was woven, as though with a mechanical instrument. Some silks were pure white and some golden yellow. My sister used her small pieces to make powder-puffs. She embroidered ordinary silk very well to make the outside

PAYING OUT THE SILK

of the puff and used this raw silk for the fluffy surface with which the powder was applied. Unlike me, she also made large pieces of silk, keeping hundreds of silkworms for the purpose. When the insects were ready to spin she would cover the surface of a table with large sheets of paper and let any number of silkworms spin on that until they had made her a sheet of silk large enough to use for wrapping up her embroidery silks. Coloured unwoven silks were very sticky and clung to the fingers, so it was necessary to use some smooth material to keep them in.

These were the rewards of our careful labour. My sister and girl-cousins used to compete against each other to see who could produce the best piece of silk. My aunt judged the pieces when she visited us. I am sorry to say that among the members of my family belonging to the generation after mine, most have not even had the chance to see what a silkworm looks like!

PRESERVED-DUCK SELLER

- 35 -

AS-IF-WE-HAD-MET-BEFORE SWALLOWS

The what-can-I-do-with-them flowers have fallen,
The as-if-we-had-met-before swallows have returned.

THESE LINES can also be translated : ' The flower falls
which has made me feel sorry, the swallows return which
seem to have met before ' ; but the two expressions, ' what
can I do with them ? ' and ' as if we had met before ', have
become common sayings and it is better to use them in
translating the poem.   Swallows come to us in spring and
stay until autumn, and the lines convey the feelings of a

A PAIR OF SWALLOWS

lovesick person on an enervating spring day.   It is warm
and flower petals fly about, but the beloved is not there
to be whispered to.   The swallows, which have just returned, dart hither and thither busily building new nests :
and they do it in pairs !   It is unbearable.

There are many Chinese stories about the swallows, and
the bird figures largely in our poems.   We love swallows,
but it is a point of honour that they should be left free.   If
they nest in a house they do so unbidden, and if they do not,
no one can force them to come.   And if any one disturbs

a swallow's nest or harms the young, they never come again to that house. To us they symbolize love and happiness, because they always fly in pairs, and we believe that they bring love and happiness to the house in which they stay. They usually nest on the huge roof-beam of the central hall and never go into a small room. As they prefer the large houses of rich people they have become also a symbol of wealth. As a result of symbolic ideas, some Chinese people become sad when no swallows fly into their houses, and methods have been invented to attract them, but with no success.

Like European swallows, our swallows return to the same house year after year. There is a story of a certain Madame Wei whose husband died when she was quite young. She was beautiful and clever, and her parents tried to persuade her to marry again, but she was resolved to maintain her devotion to her dead husband, and even went so far as to cut off one of her ears as a sign of her determination. Every spring a pair of swallows used to come to her house, but one year only one arrived. In the autumn she tied a red string on its leg, and when it came back the next spring with the red silk still on, Madame Wei wrote a poem :

> Last year you went away without your companion,
> This spring you come back single still ;
> Probably your old friend had a deep passion for you,
> So you cannot bear the idea of flying about in a pair again.

That is characteristic of how we Chinese link our lives with the life of Nature.

Two pairs of swallows used to come to our house. One pair built a nest on the roof-beam of the first hall and the other pair in the second hall. When they appeared each year my youngest cousins and my first nephew were taught the nursery rhyme *Yen-tzu, yen-tzu, ni yu lai liao ! Yen-tzu, yen-tzu, ni yu lai liao !* which means ' Swallow, swallow, you come again ! Swallow, swallow, you come again ! '

One of the pairs flew in and out either by the entrance-gate or through the first sky-well, and the other pair always flew through the second sky-well, so there was no confusion and the two pairs never quarrelled. When the spring sunshine grew too strong we used to hang a long bamboo screen in front of each hall, but the swallows knew how to penetrate the screen and get to their nests. As they passed in and out their shadows made a delightful pattern on the curtain. My father was very fond of observing the flight of swallows, for the sake of his painting. He told me to watch them too, but I am afraid I did not follow his example very thoroughly.

It was strange that the swallows liked to build their nests on roof-beams instead of on trees, for they spent the day-time darting in and out among the willows by the little pond. They liked the pond because they found mud for their nests in it. When we redecorated the house for the New Year Festival the two nests were never touched, and when the swallows returned in the spring they simply added some new mud and did up their nests as we did our house.

Unlike most birds, our swallows never wanted us to give them food. I really do not know what they ate.

I remember that one of my boy-cousins had an idea that if he could blow one of the swallow's eggs, fill it with fish eggs and put it back in the nest, the swallow would hatch out small fishes which could immediately be put into water and would then grow into big live fish in a very short time. But he never dared to climb up to the nest, so his theory remained unproved!

The subject of swallows leads me to mention some other birds of which I retain memories from my childhood. The cries of a crow or a raven standing on the roof of a house were considered unlucky if one heard them in the morning on waking or when going out early. In our garden there were in winter-time always a few crows on the trees, and one morning I had been up only a little while when I heard the ominous 'caw-caw' from our roof. Running in to Grandmother's chamber I told her what I had heard, and she at once murmured *O-mei-t'o-fu* (Amitoba in Buddhism) three times. She told me not to worry, and I did not ask her why, though at that time I did not understand the superstition.

The cries of the magpie were considered lucky whatever

MAGPIE

the time of day. When we heard them we youngsters used to chant at once the following nursery rhyme :

> The magpie sings well ;
> Father will get rich,
> Mother will give birth to a younger brother,
> Elder brother will marry a sister-in-law.

The origin of this rhyme must have been the habit of magpies of crying at the same time like several people chattering together cheerfully.

KINGFISHER

I only saw a kingfisher in our garden once. It hung on a long slender branch of a willow by the pond. I was very much attracted by its shape and colour, which I recognized from one of my father's paintings. But it never came again, probably because it found no fish.

Storks and peacocks I never actually saw, but I knew them, too, from my father's paintings. They symbolized many ideas in Chinese thought. Father had one or two fine long peacock's feathers which he arranged in a flower-jar when there were no fresh flowers in bloom.

I met a parrot for the first time when I went to visit my sister-in-law's family.   Their parrot had a red beak and golden green feathers and its frame hung in the middle of the hall.   As soon as we entered it cried out, ' *K'ê lai liao, k'ê lai liao !* ' which means ' Guests have come, guests have come ! '   This made a deep impression on me ; I had not previously realized that any bird could utter human words. I learned that this parrot had been brought from the south

WILD GEESE FORMING CHARACTERS

of China by my sister-in-law's father.   It had been taught to speak a few words when it was a baby.   A big bowl of water was placed under its perch, so that the baby parrot saw itself reflected in the water and thought it was imitating the words of the reflected parrot, while in reality it was imitating a person standing by its side.   It not only pronounced its words very clearly but even spoke our local dialect.   It could not stand the cold days in Kiu-kiang, and when winter came it had to be kept in a warm room.   For those days it was rather an expensive bird to keep.

Unlike the swallows, the wild geese came to my city in autumn and went back north in early spring.   I was amazed how accurately they chose the time to come every year. Flying in a flock high up in the sky, they looked very dignified. They spoke their own language but seemed to understand ours, for when we chanted, ' Wild geese, oh, wild geese, will you arrange the character *I* for us to see ? ' or ' Wild geese, oh, wild geese, will you arrange the character *jen* for us to see ? ' they arranged themselves correctly. The Chinese character *I*, which means ' one ', is a horizontal line, and the character *jen*, which means ' man ', consists of two lines meeting in a V. As they seemed to know only these two characters, perhaps we exaggerated their comprehension ! We would lift our heads to watch them until they were no more than specks in the sky and finally vanished altogether. I was told that wild geese are as faithful as swallows. If one of a pair is shot down or dies, the other does not mate again. So wild geese are a symbol of marriage and order. I remember when my tenth uncle suddenly died at an early age, one of my elders wrote four words to express his sorrow : ' *Yen cheng ching han,*' which means, ' The wild geese group was shocked by the cold.' This conveyed very subtly that his age-group was shocked at the loss of their young brother. The line won praise at the time, and I remembered it vividly when I sustained a similar loss last year at the death of my brother.

PEACH SELLER

- 36 -

THREE POPULAR STORIES

THE THREE stories I am going to tell have always been more popular among our children than any other of our innumerable tales. All over China they are known, though some parts have versions differing slightly in detail. They are known, too, in Malaya, Java, San Francisco and wherever else there are big Chinese colonies.

LIANG SHAN-PAI AND CHU YIN-TAI

The first story I heard one spring day when the garden was full of flowers. Butterflies were flitting hither and thither, dipping their heads between the petals or fluttering through the branches and leaves. Among them were two fine big butterflies with beautifully marked wings which flew about together. One was black with red and blue

228

spots, the other yellow with black and red spots. Their bright colours caught my eye, and I wanted my sister to catch them for me, but she wouldn't. She said that they were called Liang Shan-pai and Chu Yin-tai and that they had a sad story.

Originally Liang Shan-pai and Chu Yin-tai were an unfortunate couple whom Fate prevented from marrying during their lives and who were in consequence buried in one tomb. Like the hero and heroine of all good stories, Liang Shan-pai was handsome and Chu Yin-tai beautiful. They lived in different villages and there was no school in either village. Liang Shan-pai had to go a long way to study. The custom of the time did not allow a girl to go so far, and the parents of Chu Yin-tai, whose only daughter she was, worried very much about her education. To get over the difficulty they dressed her as a boy and sent her to the same school as Liang Shan-pai. On the way Chu Yin-tai met Liang Shan-pai. When they learnt that they were going to the same school they became friends, and soon they were always to be seen together. The other students left them to themselves. It was Chu Yin-tai who made the friendship deepen quickly. Liang Shan-pai, though handsome, was stupid. He seldom spoke a word to his friend. This, however, did not offend Chu Yin-tai, who was in love with him, while he knew nothing about love. She tried by hints to show him that she was a girl, but he was too obtuse to understand. At the school only the teacher knew that Chu Yin-tai was a girl; he had been told by her father. The school was very small and two or three students had to sleep in one room. The old teacher, realizing Liang Shan-pai's stupidity, thought it quite safe to put Chu Yin-tai in the same room with him. He erected, however, a piece of wood down the middle of the bed to separate the boy from the girl, telling them that it must never be moved. And it never was, for Liang Shan-pai invariably went to sleep and snored like a pig the moment he lay down. Time passed, and the three years' course of study came to an end. Both Liang Shan-pai and Chu Yin-tai were coming of age. They set off home together. When they parted Chu Yin-tai told Liang Shan-pai to come and see her as soon as he could. He arrived a few days later to find her dressed as a girl. At first he could not believe his eyes. Then, suddenly awaking from his long dream, he found himself madly in love with her. As both were now grown up, tradition and Confucian teaching prevented him from confessing his love. After speaking only a few dry words to her he went home, where he stayed, feeling very love-sick. After a time his parents sent a go-between to the girl's house to see if a marriage between them could be arranged. But the go-between found that she had just been betrothed to some one else. The news of this made Liang Shan-pai seriously ill. The only cure was marriage to Chu Yin-tai, and it was impossible to cancel her betrothal. Learning of Liang Shan-pai's hopeless illness, Chu Yin-tai asked permission of her parents to visit him, because they had been such good schoolmates. She found him near to death, and before leaving him told him that his body must be buried near the road along which on the wedding day she would be carried to her new home. Liang Shan-pai's dying wish was respected, and on the day of Chu Yin-tai's wedding her sedan-chair was carried past the tomb. A thunderstorm was raging and it became impossible at this point for the procession to go further. Getting down from the chair, Chu Yin-tai went to the tomb and said : ' You have died for me. How can I live for myself ? If you know that I am here, please open the tomb.' Thereupon a queer sound was heard and the tomb opened. Chu Yin-tai jumped in. The people who were escorting her tried to catch her, but only a corner of her long skirt was left in their hands. Presently this turned into a pair of butterflies which fluttered round the tomb. The butterflies were named Chu Yin-tai and Liang Shan-pai after the lovers, and, as butterflies, they have lived together very

happily ever since. After finishing the story my sister
bade me protect the butterflies whenever I saw them and
never to try to catch them.

The second story concerned the Great Wall of China.
I do not think that the importance of this great work in
the history of the world was ever explained to me when
I was a child. But I knew it was built about 214 B.C. by
a most notorious emperor, who spent incalculable sums
of money on it and caused the deaths of millions of human
beings in its construction. No good word for this emperor

BLIND MUSICIANS

can be found in our early history. My conception of the
Great Wall was mainly derived from the story I am about
to tell.

At the end of hot summer days my elders used to summon
blind musicians to play and sing to us while we enjoyed
the coolness of the evening. They liked them to give us
the folk-song ' Meng-Chiangnu cries down a part of the
Great Wall '. Meng-Chiangnu was a charming girl of a
good family. One day she bathed in a pool in her garden
without noticing that a young farmer had climbed a tree
near by and could see her. As a lady should never be

seen naked by any man except her husband, Meng-Chiang-nu decided to marry the farmer. His name was Wan Hsi-liang, and at first they were very happy together. Then a calamity befell them. The farmer was called up by imperial decree to help build the Great Wall. The couple lived in central China, far from the northern area of the Great Wall, and Wan Hsi-liang's summons meant the separation of husband and wife. For days and months Meng-Chiangnu waited vainly for news of Wan Hsi-liang. At last she decided to go and find him. She walked about a thousand miles, but when she reached the Great Wall she could find no trace of her husband. For a whole year she cried and cried along the Wall. The God of Heaven was affected by the great love and loyalty Meng-Chiangnu showed and caused part of the Great Wall to fall down, thus delivering to Meng-Chiangnu her husband's bones. The song of the blind singers was the words she murmured through her weeping. One version comprised twelve songs, one for each month in the year; another contained only four, one for each season. Here are some specimen verses :

The spring comes in the first month ;
Every house lights its red lanterns.
Others' husbands have returned happily,
But mine has gone to build the Great Wall.

We are busy feeding silkworms in the fourth month ;
Sister and sister-in-law hand in hand gather the mulberry leaves.
I hang my basket on a mulberry branch,
And wipe my tears while I gather the leaves.

The laurel tree before my door blooms in the eighth month,
A lonely goose brought a message on its leg :
' Idle people talk idle talk.
Who is going to send me clothes ? '

Snowflakes fly in the eleventh month.
Meng-Chiangnu comes a thousand miles to bring her husband
    clothes.
The flock of crows in front shows the way.
I cry to the Great Wall but find the place lonely and cold.

It was a tragic story but it showed the reaction of people
whose happy married life was broken by war and the
preparations for war. The song had a tune which everybody in the city knew.

The third story, which was about a well-known painter,
was told me by my father while he gave me lessons in
painting. As soon as I could paint even a little he began
to tell me something about the history of Chinese painting,
so the names of famous Chinese painters were already
becoming familiar to me. Father would give a brief
account of each painter's life or of some incidents out of
it, and on this occasion the subject was T'ang Yin of the
Ming dynasty (A.D. 1369–1643). T'ang Yin was a very
famous painter of the period, who specialized in the painting of flowers, ladies' fingers and landscapes. He had won
the title *Chieh Yuan* because he was the first on the list at
the local examination at Suchow, but he did not pursue
the official or academic career thus opened to him. A
thorough bohemian, he was so popular that most of the
notable beauties of the day had heard of him.

One day T'ang Yin and some friends were boating on
Lake Tai at Suchow. T'ang Yin was overwhelmed by
people, old and young, men and women, besieging his boat
with requests that he should paint them fans. He did
not refuse one, but just went on painting and painting.
But finally, looking up for a moment's relaxation, he
noticed a large and beautifully decorated boat passing by.
In it was a young lady wearing a purple dress, who, unknown to him, had for some time been watching him
painting. She smiled, and her boat moved on. T'ang
Yin stopped painting and told his friends that he must

marry that lady. First he found out the name of the family in the boat. He was not dismayed to learn that it was a family from another district. Nor was he discouraged when on visiting the district he found that the family was a very noble one into which outsiders could not penetrate. Even if he could have secured an introduction he would not have seen the lady, for the house in which she lived was a very large one and the ladies lived in the inner court. Still undaunted, he dressed himself like a servant and went there to seek employment. Fortune favoured him. He was given a job as study-servant and told to look after the things of the boys of the house in the family school. At first he seldom had a chance to see the boys, but gradually he became friendly with them by helping them with their essays. Their teacher was very pleased, but their father wondered how it was that his sons should suddenly be able to write so well. Eventually he found out that their servant had helped them, and as a result he began to pay special attention to this new servant. He saw him to be a good worker, very loyal to the house, and he promoted him among the servants. But still T'ang Yin had no chance to see the lady, though he discovered that she was one of the personal maids of the head lady of the house, a circumstance which made it even more difficult for him to meet her. He worked on and on and finally he told the nobleman that he wanted to go home and get married. But his master would not let him go. Somehow the head lady was persuaded to let him see all her maids. The first and second groups did not interest him. At last the four personal maids were called, and the one who had smiled at him from the boat was there. A marriage agreement was made and some sort of celebration held. But the next day, unbeknown to the nobleman, T'ang Yin took his wife away. A few months later the nobleman came to Suchow and paid a visit to T'ang Yin by reason of the artist's fame as a scholar and painter. At once the nobleman was struck by the resemblance between the artist and his former servant; but it would have been an insult to have mentioned such a thing. After a while T'ang Yin asked his wife to come out and see his new friend. The nobleman was so astounded that he thought he must be taking part in a play. But both the lady and the artist were very real, and presently they all laughed heartily.

This story has more literary value than the other two, and in literary circles it is even more popular. For my part I liked all three. Each gave me great pleasure when I heard it, for I was just at the right age to understand the meaning. All three stories are peculiarly full of subtle feeling.

TUNG-KUA (A KIND OF MELON) SELLER

- 37 -

DRAGON-BOAT RACE

'THE OBJECT of this festival,' Father told eight or nine of us youngsters on our way to see the Dragon-Boat Race on Lake Kan-t'ang on the fifth day of the fifth month, ' is to celebrate Ch'u Yuan, the great scholar of the Chu State of the third century before Christ. He was an extraordinarily able man who was ambitious to administer the State in the best possible way. He succeeded in gaining promotion at court, but then he was falsely accused by rivals and lost the favour of the king. He wrote several important works in Chinese literature, but still accusations poured in against him, until finally he saw that the king's eyes were hopelessly blinded by false witnesses, and he drowned himself in the River Mi-lo in a last effort to open the king's eyes. To-day is the anniversary of his death. He was only thirty-three years old. As soon as the king realized his error in the loss of this scholar, he sent out a large number of people to search for Ch'u Yuan's body ; but in vain. So he decreed that each year on the fifth day of the fifth month some memorial ceremony should be celebrated. Thus we have the Dragon-Boat Race, in which all these dragon-boats race up and down the river in pairs as if searching for the body of some one who has been drowned and whom they hope, with the help of the all-powerful dragon, to find.'

Father then warned us not to be surprised if the festival now seemed to have little connexion with the story. We did not mind. We liked to listen to Father talking, though we did wonder why the festival should celebrate a scholar who was not a native of Kiu-kiang and had not drowned himself in Lake Kan-t'ang.

When we reached the shores of the lake, we could hardly find room to stand, there were so many people (Plate 7). I saw five or six dragon-boats. They looked more or less the same as ordinary boats, but narrower and longer and with an ornamental carved dragon's head at the bow and a tail at the stern. Fifteen or twenty people were rowing on each side. In the middle of each boat was a sort of frame-shelter in which were two persons, one beating a drum and the other a gong. A third person stood near the top of the bow with a long bamboo stick in his hand. Here and there among the crowds on the shore a person would hold out a long stick with a strip of red silk fluttering on the end of it like a flag. Two of the boats would race to the spot and try to capture the flag. The one who got it was in a sense the winner, but there was no pause at all : as soon as one flag had been captured the rowers raced away after a second. During each race the drums and gongs were going, and the rowers themselves and the crowds on the shore added their shouts and cries to the general clamour, while fireworks, let off each time two boats approached a flag, added to the merriment. Not always the same two boats raced one another. The crew of one might like a little rest after a race : another would then take its place.

The weather was usually fine at this time of year, and on this particular occasion the sunset, reflected from the blue lake water, threw a purplish light over the scene. All the rowers wore the same style of blue or green or purple clothes, and the boats were beautifully painted in golden red to represent the scales of the dragon, and were decorated with many coloured flags. A great many of the crowd had brought red silk flags and fireworks. We had not forgotten ours. Unfortunately one of my older cousins did not tie the red silk on the top of his stick securely enough, and when two boats raced towards him to capture the flag the silk fell into the water. A sudden silence fell on the crowd in our neighbourhood, for it was considered bad luck for the silk to fall into the water. My cousin blushed with shame. My father had to shout his apologies to the people in the boat. We did not stay long after that.

One of the dishes prepared for the festival was also connected with the sad fate of Ch'u Yuan. It was a special kind of rice cake called *Tsung-tuz*, made of glutinous rice wrapped in triangles in the long wide leaves of a species of weed. The cakes were boiled in hot water and tied with coloured silk ribbons. It was said that people had brought these *Tsung-tuz* to the river-side and thrown them into the water as offerings to the tragic scholar. This was no longer done in my time, but we were still expected to eat *Tsung-tuz* at the Dragon-Boat Festival and did not have it at any other time of the year. It was very tasty, but very rich. In my house we had two kinds of *Tsung-tuz*, one made by mixing the glutinous rice with some black or white sesamum seeds and the other by mixing it with chopped ham. The former was eaten with sugar; the latter was a savoury dish.

Another food peculiar to this festival which I liked very much was called *Feng-cheng-jou*. Fresh pork was cut into small pieces about two inches square and half an inch thick. After each of these had been well seasoned with salt and Chinese soya sauce and covered with baked-rice powder, they were wrapped in fresh lotus leaves tied with straw and steamed for a considerable time. When ready for eating, the wrappers were taken off and they retained the delightful smell of the fresh lotus leaves.

The festival was the sign that it was time to put up summer pictures on the walls of the halls. Lotus and pomegranate paintings predominated. We had a very big and very good painting of a lotus flower with a kingfisher on its stem by my father's tutor. I was always spellbound by the beautiful reddish and green colours in the composition. The picture hung in the third hall from this day until the first day of autumn. As we had no lotus flowers in our garden, we used to buy them from farmers and florists to fill our jars and vases for the festival. The small pomegranate tree in the courtyard of our family school never failed to blossom just in time, and each separate vermilion-coloured flower gave me pleasure. My third great-uncle always allowed the girls of the house to pick the pomegranate flowers to wear in their hair, so that they might look their most charming on the festival day.

I cannot help reflecting how strange it is that a tragic event should have given rise to a joyful anniversary. Ch'u Yuan is a mythical writer but he has a very high position in our literature. His works cannot be understood by many Chinese scholars without great effort. But this reminder of his loyalty to the State to which he belonged has kept his memory green for centuries quite apart from his literary work.

LOTUS-FLOWER SELLER

MY FIRST JOB AS FAMILY REPRESENTATIVE

THE LANDS owned by my family in the Kiu-kiang district were of two kinds. The lands in the valley-plain of the Yangtse we called *shui-tien* (water fields) and the rest, in the hills, we called *shan-tien* (mountain fields). Before the harvest the uncle whose business it was to look after the lands was frequently invited by our tenants to visit the fields, so that he could see for himself if any damage had been done by flood or drought, and if so could, when the harvest was finished, reduce the rent accordingly. Some sort of calamity seemed to occur every year. Grandfather always told us to be kind to our tenant farmers because we were farmers ourselves by origin, and urged reduction of rent whenever there was a reason for it.

I never saw the title deeds of our lands, but I know that the name of the owner on them was not that of my grandfather but 'Hall of Three Footpaths'. This exemplifies better than anything how the land belonged, not to any individual or generation, but to the whole family. The rentals consisted of so much rice-grain per acre. Some of the rentals had not been increased since our ancestors first bought the land in the tenth century. The tenants—or rather their families—very seldom changed either. If any member of our family could afford to buy more land, the name engrossed on the deed would still be 'Hall of Three Footpaths'.

During harvest-time, when the rice-grain was all gathered, our tenant farmers called on us again and invited some elder to go to the country to see the year's crops and settle payment. This was only a formality, since the payment was usually arranged beforehand, but it was a pleasant social occasion. The tenants would prepare a good dinner for whoever was sent to represent the family. My uncle could not go to all the tenant farmers, and as my father and brother were not interested, it once fell to my lot, when I was only thirteen, to act as family representative. I was appointed to visit the farm where we had taken refuge during the Revolution. A relation who lived in the district accompanied me. Before I set out my uncle told me that I had no special duty to perform and was merely to enjoy the good dinner provided; I was to be polite and observe carefully the customary procedure, and if the tenants should mention prices or ask a favour, I was to give no definite answer.

On my arrival an old farmer met me at a little distance from the farm-house with a smile and great courtesy. I gazed at him and wanted to cry out that he was the old man who used to tell us ghost stories, but remembered in time that I was older now and had to behave with dignity. I think he remembered me well, too. I was taken to a room prepared for me, and everything seemed just as it had been four years before.

A couple of hours later the dinner was served in the hall, and about six or seven tenants attended. To me they all seemed very old, but actually their ages varied from forty to seventy. I knew them all, but could not remember their names, because during our stay in the farm-house I had not talked to them much and some of them lived far away. It made me feel odd that they did not address me on this occasion by name but called me *shao-hsien-sheng* (young sir). I had as much vanity, I suppose, as any other lad of my age, and I enjoyed being treated as a grown-up. Standing very upright, I moved slowly, like a scholar, into the seat of honour accorded me. My relation, of course, was also present. Four big dishes were set on the table and a great bowl of soup placed in the very middle. (This was the typical arrangement for country dinners, which were less elaborate than those in the city, but very substantial and delightful all the same, all the ingredients coming from the farm and the stream.) On another table were several big jars of home-made rice-wine. I wondered why the farmers spent so much money on this dinner, for I had never seen them eat and drink like this during my year among them, when their meals had invariably been simple, meat or chicken being included only very occasionally. Here there were two huge chicken besides other meats (chiefly pork), all beautifully cooked and with the flavour of the country-side. The meat and chickens were cut in slices about three inches square, which seemed enormous to me. All the farmers were very merry and talked cheerily. They played the game of guessing-fingers, and I remember that my relation lost a great deal at it, though he won several cups of wine ; but then he did not drink, so the old farmer who had met me drained the cups for him.

My hosts kept pressing me to taste this and that dish and offering me tasty tit-bits. I knew it was not polite to refuse, so I asked for a second bowl and put into that all the food I could not eat. The farmers themselves ate enormously ; further supplies of food were sent for from the kitchen. At the end of the dinner I asked that my extra bowl of food should be given to some of my old play-fellows, who were not present at the dinner because they were too young, a circumstance which, as they were the same age as myself, surprised me until my relation explained that my position as family representative gave me special privileges. One of the old farmers seemed pleased that I should remember my old friends, but another teased me and said he would have put more into his own belly if he had known I was going to give my share away. After the dinner the farmers began to talk business, and I had to evade the issues by saying that it would be better to leave that to my uncle.

BEATING RICE-GRAIN

STACKING STRAWS ON THE ROOF OF THE STABLE

My duty done, I went to find my old playfellows. But they were shy of me, and I too felt embarrassed. How was it, I asked myself, that the short period of four years had brought about such a change in our relations? Perhaps it was the complete difference in environment and thought between the life of the country and the life of the city. My companions, no doubt, thought I would be too sophisticated for them.

I spent the night at the farm, and when, next morning, I was ready to leave, I found my playfellows helping their elders to beat the rice-grain on the open ground in front of the farm. They greeted me, but said nothing more. Some were gathering up the grains, some were taking the straw away and tying it in bundles to pile on the roof of the stables for the cows and buffaloes. One of the elders told me that the rice we had eaten the day before had only been beaten a few days previously. He then expressed his gratitude for the good harvest. I wanted to help with the beating, but they all said it was not suitable work for a long-gown wearer. So, I thought, I was a long-gown wearer! The long-gown is the sign of a scholar in China and its possession a source of pride to a Chinese. But not at my age! I saw now how my long-gown had deprived me of the pleasure of talking with my old playfellows.

When I got home I gave my elders a long account of the dinner and said how surprised I was at the rich food. My uncle roared with laughter. ' It is we, you know,' he said, ' who pay for this great dinner! It will all be put down on the bill which the tenants present to us.' I was astonished. My uncle explained, however, that it was traditional that a good dinner should be prepared for the farmers by the landlord, in order to thank them for their work with the harvest. To save trouble the landlord generally asked his tenants to prepare the meal for themselves and said that he would come and join them when it was ready. For generations this had been the arrangement, and the dinner could not be held without a representative from the landlord's side. So I had been very useful to the farmers. No wonder they had put me in the seat of honour!

LOTUS-STEM SELLER

minister could not be held to afford a representative from the husband's side. So it had been very useful to the Chinas. No wonder they had put the matter to the test of a lawsuit.

- 39 -

RIDING ON A STORK

THE STORK is to us a precious and sacred bird. It figures conspicuously in Taoist legends. The fabulous age to which it is believed to live is responsible for the fact that all immortals are imagined as riding through Heaven

RIDING ON A STORK

on the back of a stork. Once a well-known person, Shao Kanchieh, awoke from a short sleep in the daytime and said that he had just dreamed that a stork came down from Heaven and bore him off into the mountains; his soul having therefore gone, there was no need for him to take any more medicine; and he then died. Stories of this kind are common in our literature. The expression ' riding on a stork to become an immortal ' has come to stand for a happy life hereafter as opposed to the idea of hell.

My grandfather ' rode on a stork ' at the age of eighty-two. He had not been ill, and was in fact feeling so well on the morning of his death that when the servant served him with his lunch of soft food suitable to his age he asked for something harder to eat. He was given a small dish of cooked sweet chestnuts with baby chicken, and he had only tasted a little of this when the servant heard him murmur and, going to him, found he had passed away.

At once Grandmother and all the elders were fetched and messages were sent to those who were out of the house on business. They came to the room weeping loudly. Then a family council was held and each elder was given a special duty. Two aunts were appointed to stay continuously with Grandmother in her chamber, to look after her and try to comfort her. The coffin and funeral clothes had, as I have explained in an earlier chapter, all been ready for a long time, and there now remained only the carrying out of the due ceremonies. The whole house was hung with white cloth curtains—white and not black being with us the colour of mourning. Tailors were summoned to make a white cotton over-garment for each of us. Some aunts and older cousins made white cotton hats for us all too. I and other boys were given big sheets of white paper on which to copy an announcement of Grandfather's death for pasting on the city gates. The death was also announced in the local newspaper.

Grandfather's body was washed, wrapped in several layers of raw silk, and then dressed in the specially made silk clothes. He looked like some old scholar of the Ming dynasty sleeping there in his room, for the specially made clothes were in the Ming style that he loved. An incense burner was put at his head and incense was kept burning all the time.

In the evening a Taoist priest was asked to perform the

ceremony of closing the cover of the coffin. The empty coffin was moved to the middle of the third hall, and every member of the house except Grandmother, who was old and tired, and the very young members like my nephew, knelt in white clothes before it. Four undertakers carried Grandfather's body in a big white blanket from his chamber to the third hall and placed it in the coffin along with his favourite small jades and many other things. Then two long trumpets were blown, producing a very mournful and moving sound ; the Taoist priest murmured a few words ; and the undertakers covered the coffin, nailed it up and repeatedly varnished the joints. The thought that we should never see Grandfather's face again made us all weep.

Next, an altar high enough to reach the roof and enclose the ancestral shrine was built. It was all covered in white and on the upper part a portrait of Grandfather, painted by Father, was hung. Below this was placed a tablet bearing the name of the deceased, and under the tablet a square table with a few small dishes of sweets and cakes as offerings, a pair of big white candles and an incense burner.

Next morning friends and relations of the family began to arrive to pay homage to the dead. Most of them brought presents, such as a sheet of blue satin or other silk bearing the four characters in gold, ' Riding on a stork to become an immortal ' ; or a couplet on white silk or cloth describing how the dead man's character and personality had been admired ; or some paper money. Grandfather's sons were posted behind the curtain of the altar, whence they emerged occasionally to return thanks to the friends and relations ; his nephews were busy dealing with other matters. A few close relations like my brother-in-law were asked to receive and look after the homage-payers. Three boy-cousins and I stood by the altar to conduct the ceremony for the homage-payers. As they arrived at the house the musicians at the entrance-gate blew their pipes to welcome and announce them. They passed straight to the altar. With each arrival I added a pair of incense sticks to the burner, then the homage-payer knelt down once in front of the altar and once to the place where Grandfather's sons were kneeling. On getting up he bowed once to each side, where the four of us were standing, and we returned the bow. Then, saying no word to any of us, he withdrew. On his way to the second hall he was given a sheet of folded white cloth as a token that he was returning from paying homage. In the second hall two members of the family asked him to stay to dinner. If he refused, the invitation was repeated in the first hall. If he could not stay, an announcer instructed the musicians to blow the pipes again as he left. The tune was different this time so that no confusion should arise as to whether the person was coming or going. Unlike ourselves, the homage-payers wore ordinary gowns with a black jacket. The ceremony of paying homage went on all day and nearly all night, for our family had very many friends, and my brother, who was prominent in local society at that time as the head of the local education authority, had an extra number. Some of the intimate friends and closer relations stayed for the dinner, which was different from and simpler than that for wedding occasions.

When we thought that the last homage-payer had been, arrangements were made for the ceremony of *Kao-t'su*, ' Reporting to the Ancestors '. The altar was taken down, incense was burnt at the ancestral shrine, and again every member of the house except the youngest knelt down. An account of the event written by my brother in the old rhythmical style was read aloud by a relation, by way of informing the ancestors that Grandfather had joined them and that the coffin would be taken to the ancestral cemetery the following day.

The preparations for the funeral procession had then to be made, and this was a heavy task. I remember that my elders hardly slept at all that night.

Next morning all the working people who were to take part in the procession, besides friends and relatives, gathered outside the house. Each was given a white-paper flower with a yellow or blue centre to fasten in his jacket. They took their places according to the prearranged list. The Taoist priest spoke, then the coffin was borne out of the house on wooden bars by sixteen undertakers.

The long procession moved very slowly. In front a young workman wheeled a huge paper *Kai-lu-sheng* (' God of Leading-the-Road '). Then came a *ming-chin* of red silk thirty feet long with Grandfather's name and age pasted on it in characters made of gold paper. Four paper animals, a blue lion, a white elephant, a unicorn and a tiger, followed, and after them came my brother-in-law, as one of the closest relations, riding a decorated horse. Next followed, in order, seven Buddhist monks wearing coloured robes, twelve paper figures of the flower gods and goddesses, a decorated wooden bower containing a portrait of Grandfather, eight Taoist priests also in coloured robes, and a green sedan-chair containing Grandfather's tablet held by my brother as the first grandson. After this came the group of guests and then the family, all of whom wore white clothes bound round with a long strip of white cloth. At last the coffin, still supported by the sixteen undertakers, appeared, draped with a silk cover embroidered at the top with a stork and at either end with the head and tail of a dragon. Those ladies of the family who could not walk were carried in sedan-chairs behind the coffin in order of generation and age. My grandmother could not accompany them, so two aunts stayed at home to look after her. The procession passed through the high street watched by a big crowd on both sides. From time to time we stopped so that homage might be paid by the owners of the houses on our route. Progress was inevitably slow. When we passed through the east gate of the city wall, from where the coffin was to be taken to our ancestral cemetery in the hills, the guests were asked to return and my elders knelt

BUDDHIST MONK

TAOIST PRIEST

on the ground as a sign of thanks to them.   After they had gone, all the symbols and images were also sent back. Only the male elders followed the coffin to the hills for the burial service.

At home Grandfather's tablet was put on a table underneath the ancestral shrine.   An oil lamp and incense were kept continuously burning ; any one in the house who happened to be near was expected to help in tending them. The family was in mourning for a year, at the end of which time the tablet was put into the shrine with special rites. According to Confucius, there should be three years of mourning, but in practice the period had been shortened. During mourning the business of the family went on as usual, but no female elder wore jewels or bright-coloured silks ; no sort of entertainment such as a spring party was held ; wedding arrangements were postponed ; and we had to write our couplets for the New Year Festival with white chalk on blue paper instead of in black ink on red paper. We were really in mourning.

All this elaborate ritual and ceremonial implied, of course, a definite belief in an after-life.   Personally I think that no one knows what happens after death ; but I consider it fitting, nevertheless, that members of a younger generation should pay some tribute to one of an older generation who has passed away.   I do not agree with those young Chinese who wish to discard *all* our traditional customs and rites. Particularly I think that those old people who have been brought up and have lived their lives in the traditional ways should have the comfort of knowing that their passing will be marked with the immemorial obsequies in which, in the case of others, they must often themselves have participated.   We younger people who have come to know modern ideas may reasonably elect to have simpler funerals for ourselves ; I myself, for example, would prefer to be cremated ; but let us not ignore the different feelings of our elders.   It was not a desire for show which prompted my father's generation to hold such a ceremonious funeral for

Grandfather. The custom of the time ordained it, and they would have seemed to lack the filial regard for the deceased which they undoubtedly felt if they had not performed all the traditional rites.

A KIND OF RICE-CAKE SELLER

- 40 -

FOXES AND OTHER SPIRITS

From my earliest childhood I heard stories concerning ghosts or spirits and foxes. The belief was, I think, that foxes can turn into spirits, a superstition which possibly arose from the fact that in central and southern China foxes are rare; though fox-spirit stories are not unknown in the north, too. The superstition did not, however, make foxes immune from serving useful purposes. Fox fur was regarded as the finest lining for winter clothes.

I found the fox-spirit stories extremely attractive and even thrilling. The fox-spirit may be either good or bad; there are stories of both kinds. For example, there was a certain female fox-spirit which was said to change its animal body into that of a beautiful young girl and come to visit and comfort, with her mysterious power, any lonely young man who might be in need of her. Only the young man could see her; she was invisible even to his closest relatives. And it was said that so attractive was she that the young man would prefer to keep away from other people and place himself entirely in the hands of the spirit. The result may have been bad, but very many people desired to meet this kind of spirit. There were corresponding stories of a male fox-spirit who visited lonely girls. Probably these were wish-fulfilment stories deriving from the strict Confucian rule prohibiting the mixing of girls and boys, which would result in the desire to seek compensation in mysterious engagements.

But there was not a simple psychological explanation for all our innumerable ghost stories. We believed that every one, on dying, became a ghost and lived again in much the same way as before but in a different world. We had ghost cries, ghost laughs, ghost walks, haunted spots, and, in short, all the ghostly 'box of tricks' with which the superstitious are familiar all over the world. There were even ways of finding out what any particular ghost feared and taking precautionary measures. I propose to mention here only a few stories and incidents with which I had some personal connexion.

One hot summer evening, while we were living in the country during the Revolution, we were all sitting in front of the farm-house enjoying the cool breeze which was swaying the willows by the pond, and waiting for the moon to rise so that we could see the mountains in the distance. At this season we did not usually go to bed until we were all quite cool, and dusk was the time when the old farmer, a tenant of ours, would tell us stories. On the particular evening I have in mind he told us of a Taoist priest who boasted that he feared no ghost. His friends, irritated by his incessant boasting and having suspicions of his vaunted bravery, bet him a good dinner that he would not walk by night through a certain notoriously haunted district full of graves about five miles from the foot of Lu mountain. The priest was in honour bound to accept the challenge. The friends then posted two of their number at either end of the haunted area to check his progress, and managed to tie a big piece of dried lotus leaf to his pigtail. The priest, unaware of the lotus leaf, set off, armed with an old amulet and a copy of *Tao Tê Ching*, the doctrine of Taoism, to ward off evil. He had not of course walked very far before he heard an uncanny noise behind him. Not daring to look round, he clutched his amulet and book closer to him and walked faster. But the faster he walked the louder the lotus leaf rustled behind him. He grew so frightened that he fainted on the way and remained unconscious all night. As he had not reached the second point at dawn his friends went in search of him. They found him conscious but weak from fright. His friends then showed him the lotus leaf and laughed heartily at him. Needless to say, he never again boasted of his fearlessness of ghosts. The story amused us vastly and I still remember the lively gestures of the farmer as he told it.

When we returned home we found that some new cousins had come to live in Kiu-kiang. Their father, my mother's brother, had for some years been a *Tao-tai* (officer of the fifth official rank under the Manchu dynasty) in the provincial government of Anhui, but had lost his post after the Revolution and decided to enter into retirement in Kiu-kiang. Anhui was notorious for its fox-spirits, and nearly every official residence possessed a small shrine at which respect was paid to the fox-spirits once a month as a safeguard against disturbance in the house or in the government proceedings. The exact nature and extent of the belief in these fox-spirits was difficult to ascertain. From the way they were spoken of one would have supposed their existence was regarded as a pure superstition ; but why, then, was religious respect paid to them ?

The eldest daughter told us that she had often seen baby foxes walking along the roof-beam of the *yamen* (official residence). On one occasion she remarked to some visitors that she hoped fox-spirits would not appear and trouble them, and that very night a number of fat babies who were changed from young foxes came to her bed and, drawing nearer and nearer, eventually climbed up and pulled her hair, causing her great pain. She thought she must be dreaming ; but there they were, as clear as daylight. She tried to scream for help, but she found she could not utter a sound. All night long she remained restless, not knowing at what moment her tormentors might return. In the morning the experience seemed so unreal that although she told her parents of it she made no great fuss. They thought it was probably all imagination, but in order to reassure her, told her nurse to stay with her the next night. The extraordinary thing was that the young foxes came again and attacked the nurse too when she tried to pull them away from my cousin. This went on for several nights, and at length my cousin's parents began to worry seriously about it. Then an old servant at the residence, who had lived in Anhui for over thirty years, suggested that my cousin must have offended the fox-spirits in some way and ought to confess her guilt and burn incense at the fox-spirit shrine. The girl did as she was told and was not disturbed again.

A few months later her father, having entirely forgotten the incident, gave a dinner-party to some of his literary friends, and the talk turned on ghosts and spirits. He remarked that he was interested in these superstitions but could not believe in them. At the time, nothing happened. But next morning his official seal was found to have disappeared from its little mahogany case. He was most upset, for the seal was essential to his work. After a day or two he too decided to confess to having been rude to the fox-spirits, and to burn incense at the shrine. At once the seal reappeared in its usual place.

These stories thrilled us, especially as coming from people who had actually experienced them. I no longer knew whether to believe in fox-spirits or not. On the whole, I thought not. In the family I was known as a boy who could not easily be convinced of a thing without concrete evidence; I seldom argued or expressed disagreement with people, but thought a great deal in silence. I now made up my mind to encounter some of these fox-spirits whenever the chance should present itself.

One of the first steps of the Republican Government was to encourage the study of science as a means of killing superstition. We were often told of the cleverness of Westerners in science and urged to abandon our native beliefs and to realize that there was no god or spirit in the world at all. I gradually accepted this idea; and that was why, nine years later, I took my college degree in chemistry. In those days any one who studied physics

or chemistry or any other science was considered a
' modern man', and as such could not believe in gods
or spirits. What a mistake! Our minds are never free
from mystery of some kind. Mine certainly never was ;
for all the time I was absorbing science my interest in
spirit stories never waned, though I was rather sceptical
in some way about them.

There was a shop in the main street of Kiu-kiang which
sold silks and cloth and was owned by a native of Anhui
who, characteristically, kept a small fox-spirit shrine.
When he died his successor, a young man who had been
influenced like myself by science, ordered his staff to
remove the shrine. The staff, apprehensive though they
were of dire results, could not but do as they were bidden.
A few days later all sorts of petty annoyances began to occur
in the day's trade, and some of the staff complained that
stones had been thrown at them. Presently fire broke out
in the shop. But as soon as the fire-engine arrived the
fire went out of its own accord. No sooner, however, had
the engine gone, than the fire broke out again in another
place. The owner had endless trouble, though no great
damage was done, and at last his mother decided to
close the shop. I visited the spot but could see nothing
unusual. Later I heard a very cynical explanation of the
business. The old owner, being heavily in debt at the
time of death, arranged for the shrine to be destroyed
in order that his son should be excused the debts. This
explanation may, however, have been invented by the
creditors !

I still cannot make up my mind about the fox-spirits of
Anhui. When I became myself a district governor in
Anhui I found, while exploring my very big *yamen* (said to
have been built six hundred years before) a fox-spirit shrine,
and I promptly ordered it to be destroyed. Nothing whatever occurred, though I lived in that *yamen* for a year and
a half.

So far I have not referred to the kind of spirits which

in the West are called 'demons'. One such 'demon' I must mention because I myself took part in an attempt to 'catch' it. One of my elders had a friend who had lived in Peking for many years. His wife, a very beautiful northerner, was unfortunately a chronic invalid. Her disease was said to be incurable either by Chinese or Western doctors. She looked normal, but she talked hysterically and disliked her husband to be near her. When alone she appeared always to be talking to some invisible person, and would become frantic if her husband entered the room. Frequently she turned him out. At last somebody suggested that she was possessed of a spirit from which she could not free herself. As her husband was a native of Kiu-kiang he gave up his house in Peking and settled only a few yards from the 'Hall of Three Footpaths'. Soon we heard that he had employed a 'god-pretender' to 'catch' his wife's evil spirit. The process was a long one and I do not know how it began, but I know that the assistance of two small boys was needed, and that was where I came in. The god-pretender stated that he could not approach the gods to obtain the power to catch the spirit if there were grown men present, for grown men have unclean thoughts in their minds and these were an obstruction. My father did not at all care for the idea of letting me take part, and even went so far as to declare that I had a bad character which might upset the proceedings, but in the end he was persuaded to give way. He warned me to be silent and to watch carefully what happened. I did exactly as I was told.

I found the god-pretender sitting in the middle of the hall before a round table, rubbing his hands on a silk towel. Two assistants stood beside him, and the husband knelt down three times and worshipped while I and the other boy burnt incense and lit red candles. Suddenly the god-pretender became possessed. He rushed into the room where the sick lady lay and we heard loud screams. The atmosphere was tense and frightening. We all stood motionless as if in the presence of a god. The god-pretender dashed in and out a number of times. Each time he approached the lady she screamed horrifyingly. Nothing happened, however, and the whole process had to be gone through again the next night. On the third night, at the very last minute, the god-pretender caught something in his right hand and popped it into a jar which was standing ready, and sealed the mouth. We were all convinced he had really caught the spirit and hardly dared to breathe. ' How wonderful ! ' I thought. No one was allowed to address the god-pretender directly, so one of the attendants announced that the jar contained the spirit of a white rat which had lived for over three thousand years and had the power of transforming itself into any human shape it chose. Its capture had prevented untold damage to mankind. Presently the god-pretender came to and behaved quite normally again. He did not know what he had done. The whole story sounds farcical ; but, in fact, after this the lady behaved perfectly normally to her husband, so *something* must have happened to her.

On returning home my father questioned me about the proceedings and inquired if I had seen how the god-pretender actually ' caught the spirit '. I had no idea. He enlightened me a little, and added that he very much wished such methods of extorting money could be prohibited by the Government. The god-pretender, he explained, knew that his client would pay anything to have his wife cured, and approached him accordingly. But I still felt I had had an interesting experience.

41

CREATURES BIG AND LITTLE

PERHAPS NOTHING is more characteristic of our people—and certainly nothing remains more clearly in my memory—than our love of that kind of play which consists in the performances of trained birds and small beasts.

Mice, for example. . . .

In the long, warm, relaxing afternoons of late spring

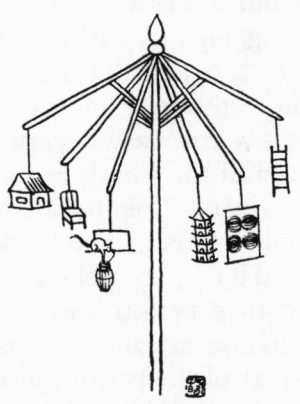

MOUSE GAME

and early summer—but not in winter or high summer—the mouse-trainer and his small charges were to be seen in the streets ready to while away an hour or so for a few coins. I saw them many times in my childhood.

On an occasion which has fixed itself in my memory my sister-in-law sent a servant to find one of them. We all assembled in the first hall and waited. Presently the servant reappeared accompanied by a man carrying a small case in one hand and a long stick wrapped in blue cloth in the other. While he unpacked his apparatus he explained to my sister-in-law that he could present twelve different mice games and that each performance included six. A bargain was struck between them, and the trainer set up his long stick, the upper part of which opened like an umbrella without a cover.

There were six spokes, with a little carved wooden model—a ladder, a frame and water-cask, a house, a pagoda, a wheel and four small wheels, a sedan-chair—hanging by a string from each. The mouse-trainer opened his case and a tiny white mouse came out on his hand. Guiding it to the central stick, the trainer left it to perform while he controlled it by beating a small brass gong and singing a folk-song. The mouse threaded its way through the rungs of the ladder without a mistake. Then it came to the water-cask. Standing on the platform, it hauled up the string attached to the cask as if drawing water from a well. The sight of the little creature's tiny paws performing this very human action was extremely fascinating. The mouse went on to turn each of the wheels and to run in and out of the house and pagoda. Then it mounted to the top of the central stick and stopped. The trainer gave it something to eat and urged it to go on, telling it that the audience would pay for another performance; but it remained motionless. The trainer explained to us that until payment for the next part of the performance had been made he was afraid the mouse would not proceed. He seemed, I noticed, very amused. Naturally we were all eager to see what the mouse would do next and another bargain was struck. The trainer raised his brass gong and beat it louder than before and began to sing another song. At once the mouse continued its performance. We all marvelled at its cunning. There must, of course, have been something in the way the trainer raised and beat his gong that acted as a signal to the mouse. But who would have thought that a mouse could ever have been trained to respond to such signs?

The performance over, the trainer began to pack up his things. He had two more mice in his case, one white and one grey, and he affirmed that they were even cleverer than the one we had seen, but that ' they ' charged more for their performances. We should have liked to see them, but my sister-in-law decided that we had had enough, and the trainer was allowed to go.

He went from house to house in the city with his mice. Past experience had taught him where he was most likely to be welcomed and he seldom pressed reluctant or unwilling audiences. It is remarkable that he should have been able to earn a living with his little charges. I do not know if in Europe mice are ever trained to the same degree, and I fear that now in China the practice has died out, for I do not remember that any mouse-trainers came to our house after about my twelfth year.

Mouse-training in China was not confined to those who earned their living by it. There was once an emperor who was fond of it! His name was Yung Cheng and he belonged to the Manchu dynasty. He was considered the naughtiest and cruellest child in the imperial household, which of course included many children. How and why he came to like mice, no one knows. But, as a boy, he kept hundreds and hundreds of them of two different colours, black and white, and it was his pleasure to train them as soldiers. There was a black regiment and a white regiment, and if a black mouse had the temerity to stray amongst the white regiment or a white mouse amongst the black regiment, it was promptly killed and its place refilled with another mouse. The regiments were made to perform on an elaborate board specially made for the purpose. For days, weeks and months the young emperor trained his mice until they never made a mistake. I can, I am afraid, furnish no historical evidence of the truth of this story; but it is undoubtedly historical that Yung Cheng became in later life the cruellest emperor in the history of China, and the mouse-training story seems at least to be in key with Yung Cheng's nature.

Another of the entertainers who used to come to our house was the Yellow-bird-Fortune-teller, an elderly woman who would call in the restless, stifling afternoons of mid-summer. Some of the older members of the family used to rent a house on Lu mountain for two or three of the hottest months, but we youngsters generally stayed at home, where we frequented the garden. Our favourite spot was a corner where there stood a peculiar kind of shelter, a small pavilion or bower sheltered on either side by a thick leafy tree, called a *Hwai-hsu*, twenty to thirty feet high. After lunch we would carry to this large patch of shade our stools, chairs and beds, all of which were of bamboo at this time of the year, for the sake of coolness, and lounge in them. We were not allowed to lie on the grass or rocks, and this was the only occasion when we could assume any attitude we chose. The boys took off their outer clothes and the girls wore only a very thin silk or Chinese grass-linen garment. From time to time we boys would be sent into the house to fetch cold tea or such cooling eatables as *Hsiang-kua*, *Hsi-kua*, freshwater caltrop or lotus stem. Sometimes the maid-servants sent out soup made from lily-bulbs or small green beans, both of which were refreshing and said to possess the power of warding off heat poisoning. So the long hot afternoons passed.

The garden doors were always kept tightly shut, and in the ordinary way no man could walk straight into our house. Women, on the other hand, even if strangers, could not only enter unhindered but were usually conducted straight to the ladies' chambers. No doubt it was because the Yellow-bird-Fortune-teller was a woman that she was allowed to penetrate to the garden while we were in such an exposed condition.

In the intense heat we could not sleep and we were always glad to see her. She preferred, I think, the girls to the boys, for she always talked more to them—flattering them, joking them about their scanty attire and saying *she* could not wear as little, telling them which kinds of flowers would look best in their hair, and in particular teasing the eldest of them about her being busy with embroidery for her wedding. We boys did not allow ourselves to be ignored. In spite of our strict upbringing with its injunctions as to the treatment of elders, we would play pranks on this elderly woman of sixty. We would hide the little case in which she kept her fortune-telling cards, or pluck the flowers out of her hair. She put up with it good-humouredly.

YELLOW-BIRD-FORTUNE-TELLER

Besides the case of cards, she carried a yellow bird in a cage. It looked like a canary but was probably not one. After talking to us for a while she would deal out a number of cards beside the cage and ask if any of us would like his fortune told. In those days ' fortune ', in the sense of wealth and prosperity, meant nothing to us ; we seldom handled coins, everything we required being provided in the house. We responded to the Yellow-bird-Fortune-teller's inquiry chiefly because we liked her peculiar way of chanting. My sister answered first, and hers was the first ' fortune ' to be told.

The door of the cage was opened and out hopped the yellow bird on to the cards. It turned about once or twice and then picked up a card with its beak. That card signified my sister's 'fortune'. The woman gave the bird a grain of rice as reward, and it hopped back into the cage and the door was closed. The woman then began to 'read' the card. There were no words on it, only a picture of a part of a peach-tree in full bloom with a pair of swallows fluttering round, and in one corner a nest and in another a small box. The 'fortune' consisted of a long poem (of sorts) devoid of any beauty of expression but rhymed. It was to the effect that my sister's face was as lovely as the peach blossom and her hair smooth and black like the swallows who fly in pairs. Peach blossom blooms at the end of March or early in April, so my sister would be married in the following spring. The nest signified her new home and the small box stood for her trousseau of clothes and jewels. The woman chanted on and on without the slightest hesitation, as though she knew it all by heart—as quite possibly she did. When she referred to marriage my sister blushed and tried to stop her, and when she continued, began to move away; but the other girls held her down, and we all laughed.

The fortune-teller went on to chant the 'fortune' of each of us, never saying the same thing twice, though the inter-larded flattery which we all were accorded, girls and boys alike, was inevitably more or less the same. I was very dissatisfied with the card which the yellow bird chose for me, because it bore exactly the same picture as the one chosen for my sister. But the woman explained that it had not the same meaning for me, and went on to chant that I should have a new silk gown in the colour of peach blossom, and next spring would go to a new school (indicating the nest) where I would be as happy playing with my school-mates as the pair of flying swallows, and would keep my books and cakes in a box. The story was entirely different from my sister's, but I was not satisfied and demanded to see all the cards. My boy-cousins supported me, but my sister forbade us to make a fuss. The woman was given her fee and left. I never discovered how she controlled the bird—and she must certainly have controlled it—though I watched her very closely as she opened the door of the cage. Either she was very clever or I very slow.

A more generally popular entertainment than either the mouse-trainer or the fortune-teller was the monkey game. Strictly speaking the monkey was not the only animal performer in it; a dog and a goat also took part. But the monkey played the leading rôle, and the game took its name from him. The trainer, always a Northerner of Shantung province, had assistants and performed in an open space. There was a very suitable empty space not far from our

MONKEY GAME

house, so whenever we heard a gong beating loudly we ran to the spot as hard as we could. We would find the trainer with his monkey on a chain and a circle of spectators, old and young, forming a ring round him.

While the trainer beat his gong, the monkey, dressed in a blue coat and red trousers, went to a small box from which it took out a face-mask for itself. One of the trainer's assistants sat by the box and helped the monkey to find also a suitable hat. Both mask and hat were the traditional insignia of the actors in our local folk-drama theatre. Then the trainer led the monkey forward to play its part. The two faced one another, the trainer chanting and the monkey moving about making simple gestures recognizable as those of the stage character it was impersonating. Presently the monkey went to the box and changed the mask and hat for those of another character in the drama. We did not know the whole play, but we knew enough of it to identify the characters as the monkey performed successive impersonations. Sometimes the assistant by the box gave the monkey additional clothes. The monkey's gestures were adapted in the most life-like way to the part it was playing. When, for example, it put on a long bearded mask it tottered about like an aged man. I never saw it play a female part. The first mask was a round smiling face such as generally appeared on the stage before a play began to greet the audience 'with a thousand blessings'. The monkey held the mask in its teeth and moved its head up and down, as if bowing and smiling to all parts of the audience. Unfortunately on this occasion it nodded its head too vigorously and the mask fell off. The audience roared and the monkey stood crestfallen while the assistant put the mask on again. I was surprised that the monkey could not do this for itself, but I suppose that its imitative little brain could not cope with unforeseen eventualities. We enjoyed the show all the more for such small mishaps.

After performing what was evidently a fixed number of impersonations, the monkey suddenly ran to the trainer, jumped on his hand and snatched away the gong-stick. This was the signal, of course, for a repetition of the mouse-trainer's trick for getting more money. The trainer urged the monkey to proceed, but it simply sat still on the box. There was nothing for it but to pay up. The monkey, holding the gong like a collection-bag, followed the trainer and his assistant round the circle of audience. Generally the monkey got more money than both the men. The performance was then resumed.

The trainer produced some open wooden frames and placed them in the middle of the circle. The dog, a black and white creature shaped like a small Chow, came out, with a string of small brass bells round its neck, and stepped through the frames, moving with the neat accomplishment of an acrobat. The bells tinkled prettily. After passing through the frames once or twice the dog quickened its pace, and the tinkling became quite musical. But as the pace increased, the dog's movements naturally grew less certain, and the monkey was set to hold up the frames. The result was not very successful, but it was amusing.

Then the monkey came on again, still in its blue coat and red trousers, but this time also with a straw hat and carrying a small whip in its left hand. The goat, with a small bell on a silk ribbon round its neck, was led out, and the monkey jumped on its back. The dog ran before them. The monkey brandished the whip and looked exactly like an experienced horseman. The trainer beat the gong very loudly, the crowd cheered, and the dog and the goat ran faster and faster. This was the last act of the show. Sometimes a long pole would be erected in the middle of the circle and the monkey climbed up it. But the imitation horsemanship was what we liked best. I never missed a show if I could help it.

The girls of my generation would have liked to see the monkey game too, but they were not allowed to mix with strangers in the streets. Once an attempt was made to arrange for a performance in our garden, but there was not enough room, and, moreover, we could not have kept the crowds away. I dare say, however, there are not many Chinese of my own age, women or men, who cannot recall seeing the monkey game at some time or other.

The black-bear game, the last of the animal games I propose to describe here, was not often seen in our part of China. I think that I saw it myself only once. Black bears are more difficult to train than mice or monkeys, and they do not inhabit central China. Our elders used to tell us that the performing black bear was originally a small boy who, being poor and homeless, was kidnapped by the trainer and given special food to eat which made his body grow thick, with long coarse hairs upon it, while his head became like a bear's. Not knowing at the time whether or not such a beast as a black bear existed in nature, we believed this story. And it was not discredited when we first saw a performing bear, for the creature stood on its hind-legs and strutted about very like a human being. The trainer, who like the monkey-trainer was always a Northerner, set up in the same open spaces. He would throw the bear a small cake of rice or something similar and the animal would then stand up and walk. It would

YANGCHOW MA-TZU

play a few simple tricks with rods and balls, but the part of the game I loved best was when the trainer dressed the bear in a huge blue Chinese woman's frock and gave it an oiled-paper umbrella to hold and a large bamboo basket to carry. Thus attired, it impersonated a Yangchow *Ma-tzu* to the life. A Yangchow *Ma-tzu* was a maid-servant from the Yangchow district of Kiangsu. These women came in considerable numbers to seek employment in Kiu-kiang. They were noted for their very large feet—much larger than most men's feet. The gait of the bear conveyed the waddle of a Yangchow *Ma-tzu* so comically that I still cannot think of it without laughing.

But though the show made us laugh, we did not forget—bearing in mind the mythical origin of the beast—to take care that the trainer did not catch us and turn *us* into performing bears !

WINE SELLER

42

UP THE LU MOUNTAIN

I FIND IT very difficult to describe in a few pages my beloved Lu mountain. I have for some years looked forward to collecting one day my recollections of it in a small book. Here I can tell only of my first visit, which occurred at the beginning of my fifteenth year.

On a warm day in late spring, Father announced that he would take me up Lu mountain for a few days. Grandmother had no objection, so, very early in the morning, we set out. My brother, who had already visited the mountain many times, did not join us.

Even in those days there was a motor service from the city to the foot of the mountain, and the road was considered fairly good, though I remember that it felt bumpy enough. Father was not disturbed by the bumpiness and I just laughed as we bounced up and down. The drive took half an hour. We found a number of people starting up the mountain, and several farmers gathered round our car soliciting passengers for their sedan-chairs.

As it was still quite early, we did not begin our climb at once but went first to see a tiny old temple called Tung-lin-tzu. It was said to have been built about the fourth century, but it must have been rebuilt again and again, though it gave the impression of being very old and of having preserved its original character, the fallen masonry being covered with herbs and creeping plants and the big peach-tree seeming as if rooted there for centuries. A small stream, coming down the mountain-side, ran in front of the temple. We crossed a dilapidated little wooden bridge, and the young monk from the temple offered us tea.

Father told me that this temple was very famous in Chin times in the fourth century, when a scholar monk called Hui-yuan gathered eighteen other scholars and monks to form a Buddhist institute which bore the name of Pai-lian-shê (White Lotus Society). The best-known poet of the time, Hsieh Ling-yun, was refused admission because his daily conduct was not above reproach. Another well-known poet, Tao Chien, was offered membership but accepted only on condition that he be allowed to drink wine. Buddhist principles severely restricted the drinking of wine, but when Tao Chien arrived at the institute, wine was served freely. The poet was a thoroughly bohemian hermit. Sitting among the other members he would speak not a word, and no sooner was the wine-jar empty than he went away. Nobody minded him. Father went on to tell me that this group of scholars and monks discussed the principles of Buddhism and ultimately Hui-yuan became the head of a new school of Chinese Buddhism. I was greatly amused when Father told me that Hui-yuan made it a rule never to escort his friends over the wooden bridge. Once, however, when Hui-yuan was escorting Tao Chien and another, the three of them, lost in contemplation of the beauty of the evening, inadvertently strolled over the bridge and a long way farther. Then one of them remembered Hui-yuan's rule, and they all had a good laugh.

In the same neighbourhood as the temple was a huge rocky cave called, on account of a big lotus flower found carved in the stone of the cave when it was first discovered, Lien-hua-tung, 'Lotus Flower Cave'. Many big trees, some in blossom, surrounded us as we sat in the cave, and we felt cool and refreshed. A relation of my family lived not very far from the cave, but Father thought there was not time to visit him. Soon we were back again at the spot where the car had dropped us.

Our destination was about two thousand feet above us. The highest peak stood about four thousand feet. The whole mountain was very steep and rocky, but there were good steps forming a path. Father told me that we had plenty of time and need not hurry. We climbed steadily step by step while Father told me stories of the mountain.

Lu mountain was first inhabited by a man called K'uang Yu, in the latter part of the Chou dynasty, about the fourth century B.C. He built the first house on it, and so the mountain was also called K'uang-shan or K'uang mountain. Since then many well-known people in every dynasty had lived on it as hermits. The part called Ku-ling had acquired a snobbish exclusiveness because rich people liked to live there. But the natural beauty spots, Father assured me, had not been spoiled by Western-style buildings with their red-tiled roofs.

At first we climbed easily through big trees, as if playing hide-and-seek with other climbers, who only appeared now and again in front of us. Presently we came out above the trees and drew away from them until, looking back, they appeared quite small. On the left was the steep slope of the mountain with rocks and trees, on the right a deep valley stretching back to our starting-point. I felt giddy when I tried to look down the almost vertical slope at my feet, but the view down the valley, the green slopes stretching as far as the eye could see, was lovely. A thin layer of mist covered the trees and houses, and yet everything shimmered in the sun. As we climbed, the view behind us grew wider and wider. In front I could not now see the peak, being myself so close to the slope. When we reached a resting-bower built beside the steps Father suggested that we should sit down for a while and enjoy the view. He said we had then covered about one-third of the distance.

Then we went on again, and Father told me to walk still, more slowly. Now and again people passed us going up and down, but not so many as there would have been in midsummer. We seemed always to be left behind by those ascending ; but Father would not hurry (Plate 8).

At a turn of the path, lifting my head, I saw some people climbing very slowly much higher up than ourselves, their tiny figures outlined against the sky. Then I saw three men carrying a sedan-chair. The step-track we were climbing ran along the edge of the mountain slope, and as we rounded shoulders of the mountain I could observe the extraordinary control of the bearers as they mounted the steps. I noticed that the chair shook slightly with the motion, and I thought how courageous the occupant was to ascend so high in a chair. Father said that it was not as dangerous as it looked; the bearers were perfectly at ease and the person riding could admire all the views.

After another rest in a bower we began the last third of the journey. My legs were getting stiff and beginning to ache and I was glad that we had not walked faster, though we began now to overtake some of the people who had hurried past us farther down. It was almost evening but still very bright. On the opposite mountains, across the valley, a huge ring of white cloud hung. Father said this was called Shan-tai ('Mountain Belt'). According to the native belief, its presence indicated that there would be rain in three days' time.

As it grew dark the evening mists rose. I thought we ought to hurry, but Father smiled and said it would be lovely to climb in the moonlight, when the scene would be beyond description. I was not sorry; for as a matter of fact, I could no longer control my legs. Suddenly we reached a plain on which were many houses and a great many people; there was even a small street: it was all just like a town. We had dinner at a tiny inn and went early to bed. Father told me that we should have to be up at four o'clock in the morning if we were to go to Hsiao-T'ien-ch'ih to see the sunrise. He also reminded me that if we had hurried up the mountain we should have been too tired to get up as early as that. I realized then how well he had planned everything.

About five o'clock next morning we stood facing the gap between two mountain slopes, with the wide expanse of Lake P'oyan gin the far distance. I could not distinguish where the sky ended and the water began. Everything was wrapped in a white shroud tinged with red by the first glow of the rising sun. Later the whole scene became bright red and sparkling. The great ball of fire rose slowly from the water, and diminished as it climbed above the horizon. Father did not speak, and I could not express my wonder and excitement.

We stayed four days on the mountain. I was taken to as many beautiful spots as there was time to reach : the Yellow Dragon Fall, the White Dragon Fall, the Black Dragon Fall, the Immortal Cave, the Bridge of Heaven, the Ten Thousand Pines Grove, and so on, but unfortunately not to the Three-fold Fall and the Five-Old-Men Peaks. It would perhaps take a year to visit all the beautiful spots on Lu mountain.

The huge bulk of the mountain is situated far from the sea, and there are therefore seldom big storms or typhoons on it. Each rock and peak forms a strange and beautiful shape and changes in colour according to the light. We had perfect weather while we were there. Thick woods and blossoming trees were everywhere. We could hear no sound but that of the waterfalls and the running streams.

Our visit was short, but it made me want to live on Lu mountain all my life. I visited it after that occasionally, but never again with my dear father.

FLOWER SELLER

- 43 -

FIREWORKS IN THE AIR

THOUGH THE city of Kiu-kiang was small, there were two little hills standing side by side within the city walls. One was called Yen-chih-shan (Rouge Hill), near which Grandfather used to air his birds; the other Kuei-shan (Tortoise Hill), because of its shape. On the top of Yen-chih-shan was a bower containing a square table and four stools, all made, like the bower, of stone. On Kuei-shan a wooden terrace was built not long ago. Part of the city wall lay just below one slope of Kuei-shan. From both hills splendid views were obtainable of the junks and other craft on the Yangtse River, which flowed past the wall. Morning and evening there were always a few people to be found on each hill. The best time was the morning, when all the junks and small boats hoisted their sails and set off up or down the river. I often went to these hills, and the views from them are printed on my memory, with the water reflecting the early sunshine so that the whole scene seemed plated with silver.

In late spring and mid-autumn more people than usual were to be seen on Yen-chih-shan and Kuei-shan, the additions being youngsters flying kites. Probably the most popular day was the ninth of the ninth month, a date to which legend had given particular significance. According to this legend a man named Huan Ching, disciple of an immortal called Fei Chang-fang, was told by Fei that a calamity would befall his family on this day if he did not avert it by taking all the members out to the high land, where they were to wear *wu-chu-yu* (*Evodia*

277

rutaecarpa Benth, a plant with small yellow-and-green flowers and seeds that have a very strong sweet smell) and drink chrysanthemum wine. Huan did as he was told, and he and his family passed a peaceful day on the hills. The story goes back about two thousand years and was the origin of the 'Double Nine' Festival, a day on which it was the custom for every one to go to a high place taking wine. Other legends and stories of our poets became associated with the day, every one seeking a reason to get away to the country or up on a hill. We youngsters hardly knew what we were celebrating; we were merely glad of a day's freedom.

On one 'Double Nine' Festival a young uncle took six of my generation up Yen-chih-shan. We carried with us three kites specially made by Father and this uncle. There was always rivalry in kites. One of ours was in the form of a beautiful girl, another in the form of a butterfly, and the third represented a swallow. When we reached the hill-top we could hardly find a place to stand. Scores of beautiful kites were already flying—fish, birds, crabs and shrimps. Our 'beautiful girl' looked most original when she flew up, but in such company did not attract marked attention. But my uncle had 'something up his sleeve': he had hit upon a new and most striking plan. He had bought a long string of fireworks and some incense sticks. The fireworks he tied on the kite-string, not too close to the kite, and fixed the burning incense sticks so that they would ignite the fireworks when they had burned down to them. We knew what was going to happen, of course, but no one else did. The kites flew up and up. Then suddenly the fireworks caught and began to explode: 'pi.......pa.......pi.......pa.......pi pi.......pa pa'. Every one was amazed and stared skywards. When they saw what was happening they raised a cheer. Afterwards several people came and asked us how it was done. But my uncle would not tell, and we went home feeling very proud.

Now, when I think of the bombing aeroplanes to which

my innocent fellow-countrymen are subjected by the invader, I remember our fireworks in the air and wonder why we Chinese did not follow up our invention of gun-powder by inventing bombing aeroplanes. Perhaps it was because, though we first discovered how to make gun-powder, it did not occur to us to do anything but play with it; we did not think of using it to kill others.

BAMBOO-STEM SELLER

NOTHING IS TOO REAL

Long summer evenings were always trying. Some of the elders went into the mountains for the worst of the heat, but we youngsters had to stay behind with those who could not leave their businesses. We had our ways of passing the time. In summer, trade was not so brisk as in other seasons, and my fourth uncle, coming home early, was never too tired to entertain us with tricks, folk-songs and fantastic stories. My father, too, was a good story-teller, but his stories were quiet and literary, and we preferred to listen to them in winter round the fire. My fourth uncle had not been well educated, his father (my second great-uncle) not being anxious for him to pursue a literary career ; but he possessed a great gift of humour. In the city he mixed with all types of people, and he could mimic their voices and make them the centre of amusing stories in which he himself invariably played a leading part. This made his stories all the more exciting to a youthful audience.

One hot evening he came home just after our dinner time, when we had all taken our bamboo stools and chairs to the garden to wait till it was cool enough to go to bed. Suddenly he appeared in the guise of a stage comedian, with thick white powder on his nose. We all laughed uproariously, while he kept his face as solemn as an owl's. We knew he was going to amuse us and we waited expectantly. He wore a very long thin gown, much too big for him, and this added to his clownish appearance. And he carried an enormous oil-paper umbrella under his left arm. None of us guessed what this was for. When he spoke he used the dialect and accent of the Huang-mei district of Hupeh province, which was always used by our local comedians and which interested us particularly because the teacher of our family school came from Huang-mei.

'Boys and girls,' he said, as if addressing a large audience, 'I come to play to you to make you forget the heat. I am going to take you all to a cooler place soon, but whether you will find it peaceful or not I cannot say. Keep quiet and listen attentively. I shall be with you shortly.' As he finished speaking he opened the huge umbrella and disappeared underneath it. His face, with the white blob on the nose, kept moving and changing in the most comical expressions and kept everybody laughing.

Presently we heard a sound as if two or three birds were singing, the sound rising and falling as if the birds were flying from branch to branch. Then an old man's voice issued from the umbrella, saying that peach flowers and petals were floating on the surface of running water and that it was late spring. The voice was not at all like my fourth uncle's. After the old man came a very young boy crying : ' *Kung-kung* (grandfather), I want to go over there. *Kung-kung*, I want to go over there. There are many people there.' Then the old man coughed and told the boy that the people were women gathering mulberry leaves for their silkworms. It must, he said, be about time for them to gather their last bunches of leaves, because the silkworms would soon begin to make cocoons. Then he told the boy that they would shortly have new silk to wear. But the boy was impatient and insisted on going to see for himself, and we heard him dragging the corner of the old man's robe. Then we heard the sound of steps as they walked along very steadily. The boy seemed to run from time to time ; the old man's steps went on evenly. Presently the old man chanted a poem as he walked :

With thin cloud and mild wind near the midday,
I followed the path of flowers and willows to the bank of the
    stream.
Passing men cannot know the joy in my heart,
They'll probably say I idle about like a feckless youth.

This was one of the T'ang poems which we youngsters had
to learn by heart before we could actually read the characters, so we all knew what it was. The old man chanted
the poem as slowly as he walked, so it took a little time.
In due course they evidently arrived at the spot, for the
boy told the old man that he would like to pick some of
the mulberry leaves. We heard the sound of the leaves
dropping to the ground and of basket scraping against
basket. There seemed to be a number of women there and
some young children too. One of the women began to
sing the *Song of Gathering Mulberry Leaves* and others
followed in chorus. Each of the women's voices was dis-
tinct. Amid the songs, a young man's voice broke in and
asked : ' *Ta chieh* (young girls), how many leaves have you
gathered ? Can I be of any help to you ? ' Then he began
to sing. He sang only the first two lines, which said that
he admired the charming white faces and tender, slender
fingers of the women and did not like them to be spoiled
by the hot sunshine and the thorns of the trees, so he
suggested gathering the leaves for them. But the women
and girls seemed to be very respectable and brought up in
good Confucian thought, for one of them found the man's
suggestion insulting and began to scold him, just as we
had heard many a young girl scolding noisily. A second
girl joined in, then a third. At last they all climbed down
from the trees to scold the young man. Then we heard the
sound of steps as if the young man was running. The
women began to chase him. The faster the young man
ran, the more noise his pursuers made. In the end the
young man reached the stream and was obliged to plunge
in. We heard a big splash and then we realized that my

fourth uncle had come out from under the huge umbrella and had thrown a stone into the little pond in our garden.

We had not the habit of clapping hands to express appreciation, so we all laughed our applause. The fourth uncle finished by telling us that the old man who had taken the little boy to the scene did not like the incident; he thought it would be a blot upon society, on Confucian principles, if this young man were not punished. So he wrote to the local authority about it. This was the end of the story.

We all gazed at the fourth uncle in wonderment. How had he made so many different sounds and voices at the same time? After washing the white spot off his nose he tried to explain his technique. ' Nothing in the world is too real,' he said, and then showed us two pairs of soles which he had flapped on the ground for the sound of footsteps; a few bamboo chopsticks which he used for the breaking of the branches; and some papers to produce other noises. It seemed simple enough when he explained, but it had had a magical effect on us. We all went to bed in a good humour and slept soundly.

Among all my fourth uncle's many tricks, games and stories I remember two in particular because I helped him with them beforehand. On the first occasion he gave me a cup of clean water and a new brush and asked me to paint a lotus flower for him. When I had painted it and the paper had dried, there was no trace of the flower. He told me to keep the secret so that he could play the trick on all the other youngsters. Bringing two other cups of water with him he pasted my invisible painting on the wall. Then he took a mouthful from one of the cups and blew the water skilfully on to the paper. At once the lotus flower appeared in red. Then he blew water from the third cup in the same way, and the lotus flower disappeared. This he called *Kou-tu-lien-hau* (Spitting a lotus from his mouth). We were most intrigued. Later I learnt that I had painted the lotus with *Chien-shui* (water impregnated with carbonate of soda); the second cup contained *Chiang-huang-shui* (*Curcuma longa* water); and the third, *Pai-Fan-sui* (alum water). Apparently they produced some chemical change upon each other.

The second time I helped him he gave me a special sheet of soft Chinese paper and asked me to cut it into many small butterflies. He put these in the scorching sunshine and after a while they all flew up into the air. This he called *Chun-tieh-fei-wu* (a group of butterflies flying and dancing together). The paper had been covered with the fine white powder of *Yang-chi-shih* (a kind of Chinese mineral drug) which is said to vaporize in the heat.

I remember another experiment somewhat like this carried out by my father. Father was not a landscape painter, but he sometimes did a landscape for fun. On this occasion, after painting one he ground a piece of the dried gall-bladder of a goose into very fine powder and dissolved it in pure water, which turned a bluish-grey colour. Then he brushed this fluid over the hill-tops and tree leaves. He had made his painting in black ink and it represented a man holding a folded umbrella on his shoulder. He now, with the gall-bladder fluid, added a few strokes on each side of the umbrella. When the painting was dry, the parts painted with the gall-bladder fluid were invisible. Then Father explained that the object of this painting was to act as a weather-glass. In fine dry weather only the black landscape and figure showed. In wet or humid weather the bluish-grey colour of the gall-bladder fluid appeared, like rain, all over the hills and trees and the man was found to be carrying an open umbrella. As a weather-glass the picture worked fairly well but never perfectly. Father told me that it was an old method invented by a painter of the Sung period, but he did not know his name.

These tricks made me see very clearly that indeed 'nothing is too real'.

- 45 -

GREEN-HAIR TURTLES

ONCE WHEN my father went sightseeing to Chi-chou, in the province of Hupeh, he brought back a real *Lu-mao-kuei*, a green-hair turtle. Chi-chou was not far from my city, being situated between Hankow and Kiu-kiang, farther up the Yangtse River. It could be reached in those days in less than a day's journey by small steamer. This tiny freshwater turtle was also cultivated in Hunan, but Chi-chou produced the best specimens. The green-hair turtle owes its name to the fact that on its carapace grows a cluster of green filaments, the central ones of which measure two or three inches and the outer ones about an inch. Father kept his in a big porcelain bowl-shaped dish filled with clear water. All the filaments stood up in the water giving a wonderful green effect against the greyish porcelain background. The tip of each filament was a shining golden colour. The turtle kept quite still in the bowl, except when it stretched out its head to eat something, such as small insects or rice powder, or when occasionally it extended its legs to move its body slightly. The creature was so small that it looked like a water plant. Its plastron was ivory coloured and kept the bowl clean-looking for a long while. As I had a passion for the turtle, Father sometimes let me change its water and look after it.

When it was first brought home it was taken to my third great-uncle because he had a comprehensive knowledge of trees, flowers, insects, birds and animals. He told Father that the turtle was a genuine specimen of the green-hair variety, and explained that there were a great number of imitation ones sold in the market. The species was always in demand for decorative purposes as well as for pets, and, moreover, these turtles were credited with the power to keep away poisonous snakes and insects.

Chi-chou was a small district, and green-hair turtles were not found in all its streams and canals, so that, even allowing for the turtles produced in Hunan, it was not possible to supply the whole demand from places as far away as Peking. Hence a method of growing the green filaments on the carapaces of ordinary turtles was developed. The juice of the ginger root was rubbed on the carapace, which was covered with mud, and the turtle put into a little water for about a month. The green hair did grow, but the filaments were never very long, usually less than an inch, and easily broken ; also they had not the same brilliant green colour, being sometimes even brownish. The body of the genuine green-hair turtle never grew any bigger, whereas the body of the fake one kept on growing. Furthermore, the plastron of the ordinary turtle is always brown or black, and it has not the three ridges along the surface of the carapace which mark the genuine green-hair. The best green-hair turtles are very small ; they can be the size of a coin, though specimens as small as that are rare and fetch a big price. The longer the green hair the better.

The one Father bought was not very small, but smaller than a full-grown ordinary turtle, and it never grew any bigger while we had it. For most of the year it was kept in Father's study, but in winter it was put into a wooden case without any water at all. When spring came it was replaced in the water-bowl, none the worse for its months of ' drought '. I derived much pleasure from observing it. What became of it after my father's death I do not know ; it was not, I am certain, in our house any longer.

My knowledge of green-hair turtles came in handy once a few years later. As Chi-chou was so near Kiu-kiang, dealers came to visit my city with their turtles. One spring day a dealer called at our house and showed a number of turtles to some of my aunts and older girl-cousins. They had just agreed the price for two when I came home from school. I told my aunts to select the smallest turtle instead of taking two larger ones for the same money. And I also insisted on the dealer showing me the plastron of the turtles. When he saw that I knew something about green-hair turtles he quickly packed up his belongings and went away. The fact was that the price that had been agreed for the two big turtles was not big enough for the smallest turtle. It was clever of the dealer to bring some good small turtles among the larger ones, and to know that people would probably choose the bigger ones, but on this occasion the trick did not succeed. Large numbers of people in big cities must have been fooled by these dealers at different times.

FISH SELLER

46

UP THE PAGODA

I NEVER UNDERSTOOD why it was the custom at Kiu-kiang to visit the pagoda at the Mid-Autumn Festival, for I found that elsewhere in China they did not do so though they held the Mid-Autumn Festival in the same manner and on the same day. The pagoda is of Indian origin. The first

NEN-JEN-SZU PAGODA

Chinese pagoda is said to have been built in the third century. In Kiu-kiang there were two pagodas. I do not know when they were built, but they looked very old and had probably stood for over a thousand years.

One of them stood by the river a mile or so from the city wall and was a landmark to ships approaching from the lower Yangtse. To me, returning for holidays from college at Nanking or Shanghai, it seemed to offer a greeting. I found myself looking forward to the sight of it a whole day beforehand, and my heart lightened when it came into view. It was called the Pagoda of Su-Chiang-Lu. Actually this was the name of the adjoining building and meant 'Locking-the-river Loft', for the building and pagoda stood where the river narrowed and rumour had it that in the second century, during the war between the states of Wu and Wei, a heavy iron chain had been stretched beneath the water to prevent the passage of fighting junks, and thus the river had been 'locked'. The site was some distance from the city and was seldom visited. The loft was small, old and out of repair. Its only resident was a Taoist priest, and it was not open to the general public. I occasionally visited it with a few classmates from the middle school and enjoyed the wide prospect of the river and city wall.

The second pagoda in Kiu-kiang, the Pagoda of Nen-Jen-Szu, was situated inside the city wall. It was a Buddhist temple, and it was this which was open to the public for the Mid-Autumn Festival. The date was the fifteenth day of the eighth month, when the sweet-laurel trees were in full blossom, their tiny yellow flowers smothering the twigs and branches. Every house was decorated for the occasion with the same blossom, so a few days beforehand farmers would bring supplies into the city for sale. The yellow flowers and deep green leaves looked very effective in 'ox-blood'-coloured vases. The scent, too, was extremely fragrant. On the day of the festival girls would wear little sprays of it in their hair. Every one wore new clothes, and dinner took place at one o'clock in order to allow plenty of time for visiting the pagoda. The dinner always included baby chicken cut into small pieces and cooked with *pan-li*, a flat, smooth-fruited sweet-chestnut resembling the hazel nut. The flavour was delicious.

One occasion stands out in my memory. After dinner one of my uncles took several of us youngsters to visit the Nen-Jen-Szu. On arrival we found hundreds of people passing in and out. In a large courtyard in front of the main hall a crowd, mainly composed of children, thronged round a small pond. The pond was spanned by a stone bridge and surrounded by a low ornamental wall. The water was full of tortoises and fishes, and the crowd were leaning on the wall and throwing them food. I wanted to join them, but my uncle persuaded us to make a tour of the temple halls first.

I knew nothing of Buddhism in those days, but, young as I was, I could not help being deeply impressed by the colossal figures of Buddha and his disciples. They were not awe-inspiring but seemed to smile encouragingly and protectingly. The long, graceful draperies of the figures imparted a dignity to the hall which every one felt and which imposed quiet on the throng. It took us about an hour to make our tour, and we came out by a side door leading to the pagoda. A crowd of people were gathered at the foot; some had already ascended. There were seven storeys, and people were visible on each, but on the topmost storey only one tiny figure could be seen. The pagoda was octagonal, and at each angle of the curving roofs hung a bell which the visitors tried to beat with long bamboo sticks as they ascended. The tinkling sounds were very agreeable amid the harsh clamour of hundreds of human voices. Presently Uncle said that some of us might go up, but not the younger ones. Fortunately I was just old enough to be counted among the ' elders ', so I went up. On the ground floor was another huge figure of Buddha towering nearly to the ceiling. On either side were stair-cases leading up and down respectively. Age and lack of re-pair had reduced them to an indescribable condition. There were no railings of any kind round the parapets of the storeys, and Uncle accordingly wisely forbade us to go out on them. I went up as far as the fourth storey, and by stretching my head through the doorway on to the parapet got a view of the crowds below and of a large part of the city. I can feel now the qualms I felt at the time as I stumbled up and down those dark, rickety staircases. Once was quite enough! In any case the whole pagoda has probably now been entirely demolished in the present war.

For the children who were too young to leave the house a large paper model of the pagoda was erected in the second hall. The framework was composed of bamboo sticks, and a candle or small oil lamp was lit in each storey. The ground floor, which of course was the largest, contained

MOON-CAKE SELLER

a special lamp, called *Tsu-ma-tun* (lamp of galloping horses), the cover of which was made to revolve. Paper figures of horsemen were affixed to the frame-sticks of the shade so that as it revolved the horsemen appeared to be galloping. Children always delighted in this. The paper pagoda was burnt at the conclusion of the day's festivities.

The Mid-Autumn Festival was also called Moon Festival, because we believed that the moon was brighter and rounder on this evening than at any other time of the year. The day's ceremonies were concluded with an offering to the moon as she came up. My family always faithfully carried out this ritual. We had a short rest after visiting the pagoda, then a square table was set in the centre of the first sky-well and Grandmother arranged dishes of sweets and fruits and small cakes on it. Right in the middle she set a huge round moon-cake. Incense was burned and fire-works let off, and then one of the elder boys was chosen to kneel three times to pay the family's respects to the moon. Afterwards all the youngsters were told to stand clear of the table because the moon was coming down to eat the cakes and sweets. Crouching in corners we held our breath. Once, one of the little girl-cousins, growing impatient after a long wait, asked : 'Why does the moon come down so slowly ? And how can she eat all the cakes when every family is giving her some ? '

'She cannot, of course, eat them all,' replied Grand-mother. 'She will just come down and touch the cakes in each house, and after she has been you can eat them.' The little girl was delighted. And so were we all !

CABBAGE SELLER

47

NO WASTE

'I DON'T WANT you to be mean,' said Grandmother, 'but I want you to realize that everything has some use and that nothing should be thrown away thoughtlessly. Cultivate the habit of taking care of your things and of remembering how much trouble went to the growing or making of them.' How often we heard these words in our childhood! We were taught not to leave a single grain of rice in our bowl or to drop any on the table or floor. If we did, we were reminded that each single grain of rice had formed part of the farmer's labour during the season and caused him to worry about drought and flood. Money could not repay such labour. Moreover, we ought, we were told, to think of those who might not have had a single grain of rice to eat for some time. Some of us, however, were too young to manage the chopsticks deftly enough to get all the rice-grains safely into the mouth, and it was the parents who were subjected to rebuke. Elders always finished up the remnants in the children's bowls. My sister, before her marriage, used to help me Later, of course, I was able to manage by myself. When we had guests at table, 'finishing up' by elders naturally could not be done. It seemed a very odd rule, but it had become one of our good habits.

On the same principle of wasting nothing, the older girls in the family kept all the many small strips of silk left over after making clothes and shoes. There were consequently plenty of these strips available on the occasion on which, as described in an earlier chapter, we celebrated the Birthday of the Flowers. Sometimes these strips were given to somebody who wished to make a *Pai-chia-I* ('suit of a hundred families') for a child. Often some lady would come to our house and ask for any spare strips of coloured silk we might have. Having collected a number of these she would fit them together into a sheet from which a small child's gown for festival occasions was made. One of my youngest cousins had one such gown. A superstition alleged that the child who wore a *Pai-chia-I* would be protected by a hundred families; hence the name 'suit of a hundred families'. I thought the garment very beautiful and decorative for a child. Had my mother lived, I might have had one myself.

The principle of 'no waste'—or 'waste not, want not', as the European proverb has it—extended to everything we ate or used. From late autumn to mid-spring we used to eat a sweet orange, like a tangerine but with a red peel. We never threw the peel away but dried it in the sun and kept it until some native drug-store sent a messenger to collect it. The dried peel was used to make a sedative, carminative stomach remedy and expectorant. Sometimes we youngsters used the fresh red peel for a game. We would ask our cook for a duck's or a goose's wing-feather, strip off the feathery parts and open the two ends of the quill. Then we would press one end of it on to the red peel and use a thin stick to push the peel, cut small, into the middle of the quill. By doing this a second time and then blowing down the quill one could expel the first piece of peel at the other end with a 'pop'. We nearly always played this game after eating oranges.

In summer we used to eat a lot of fresh raw lotus seeds. Their kernels were starchy and refreshing and had a very pleasing flavour, but inside them grew a tiny soft green stick called *lien-hsin* (lotus heart) which had a bitter taste. To save trouble we might eat this too, but it rather spoilt the taste of the kernels and as a rule we tried to get it out. When we did so, the *lien-hsin* were dried and mixed with the tea-leaves in the tea-pot. This gave a new flavour to the tea and prevented summer fever. I remember helping Grandmother to dry *lien-hsin* on a sheet of white paper in a bamboo basket in one of our small sky-wells. Almost all parts of the lotus—leaf, stem and root—were used in our medicines. *Lien-peng*, the part which held the seed, resembling the broad nozzle of a watering-pot, was a popular remedy for haemoptysis.

Lien-peng was used, too, for a game. First, after eating the seed, we took the inside out, and then we slit the outer skin into very thin strips the lower ends of which were left attached to the stalk. We would toss this improvised 'shuttlecock' into the air with a palm fan and count how many times we could catch it without letting it touch the ground. There were many ways of throwing it and the player who could accomplish the biggest number was the winner. Our elders did not need to buy toys for us, there were so many natural things that we could ourselves transform into toys. We learnt how to make a horse or a buffalo with three four-horn or two-horn water caltrops. Out of fresh dates and little short sticks we could make a pagoda. We learnt how to keep the different fruits, in what ways they were best to eat, and how best to use the remnants to amuse ourselves with.

We used to plant the stones of peaches or *p'i-pa-ke* (a yellowish-brown fruit with a sweet taste and leaves similar to those of the rhododendron) after we had eaten the outer part, because these two plants were very easy to grow and did not need much tending. After they had been in the soil for a few days two young leaves would appear. We might give these away or let them grow in our gardens. Jessamine flowers were first used as hair ornaments and also dried to make jessamine tea. Dried peach flowers had laxative properties. And so on. I remember we loved to sweep together all the fallen petals and to select the good peach ones for drying. My girl-cousins were very fond of collecting the petals of white peach blossom because it could be used to make the skin of the face softer, smoother and clearer. In the third month these trees were in full bloom and my cousins were always quick to gather them before they were quite ready to fall. After washing them carefully they put them into a silk bag which was hung on the roof-beam for a time; these petals were not dried in the sun. Then they mixed the dried flowers with white of egg or chicken's blood, and pasted the result all over the face for a night or two. White pear blossom was used in the same way. The girls used the dried pear flowers to wash off traces of powder.

Almost all our plants could be put to some use after they had been employed for decoration. If we were careful and interested we could learn any amount about them, and this knowledge was given to us in support of the principle of 'no waste'. How many useful things I waste nowadays just because I have no time to care for them!

A KIND OF RICE-CAKE SELLER

48

SONG OF PEACE

At the time, I was not very conscious of the last Great War in Europe, for I could not read newspapers, and there were few or no visible signs of war about me. Teachers in the school mentioned the war occasionally, but I never felt greatly concerned about it. I had no conception of countries in other parts of the world, and had no means of realizing what was taking place. One thing, however, has remained in my memory : the ' Song of Peace '.

The song was written by my brother, who was at the time the head of the local educational authority, on the occasion of the celebration of the Armistice. China was on the side of the Allies, and when the Armistice was announced our Government ordered that a lantern procession should be held in every town and city. My city, Kiu-kiang, though small, was advantageously situated on the banks of the Yangtse River, and was a treaty port, with a small British Concession. The date of the Kiu-kiang procession was decided at a conference of all the local authorities ; amongst them the authority in the British Concession must, I now think, have taken part. Every house hung out lanterns in front of the doors, and the shops vied with one another in making beautiful decorations for the occasion. The whole city looked very gay. All the members of the different associations, societies, official authorities, schools and commercial firms gathered for the procession in a vast open space near the east gate of the city wall. There must have been twenty thousand people taking part, each with a lantern of some sort. Most of the lanterns were made in the form of flowers, birds and animals ; some represented Chinese legends. But a big lantern in the form of a huge British battleship, with about a hundred candles burning inside it, was the feature of the occasion. I believe it was specially provided by the ships' companies of two British ships stationed in Kiukiang, and was made by skilful native craftsmen. The light of the candle-flames was also made use of to suggest the movement of small figures on the ship, and smoke came out of the funnels. The model was a huge affair moving on wheels. It attracted everybody's attention. I stole a chance to look at it for a few minutes and then had to join my school group.

The procession took a long time to start. Drummers, trumpeters and other musicians led ; my school was in the middle, and my brother was in the group of local authorities. As we passed through the residential quarter, every house let off fireworks as if to join in the celebration. In the high street, big crowds lined both sides of the way and joined with us in shouting ' *Chin-hou Shih-chieh-ho-p'ing* ' (Celebrating World Peace). We students all sang loudly together my brother's song, which had been issued during the previous week to every school by the local education authority.

For months afterwards we often sang the song, but I am sorry to say that I cannot now remember the middle part of it. The rest ran :

The lantern lights make the high street gay,
The evening mist has dispersed.
The purple cloud comes from a long way
Gladly looking forward to this peaceful day.
All made great effort
To destroy the ' enemy of humanity '.

. . . .

. . . .

Lifting our heads and clapping our hands, how happy we are!
From now on we pray there will be no rough waves on the
    sea perpetually.
Let us gather and go on together,
Singing loudly the Song of Peace!

A purple cloud symbolizes a cheerful atmosphere or
happiness.

My brother has been dead now for over a year. His
hope of perpetual peace was not fulfilled. He himself took
part in the war which Japan has been waging on China
for more than two years, and the end of which I doubt
very much is even in sight. From the time of the Great
War onwards Japan seized every opportunity of creating
trouble with us, knowing that no other Power would
interfere. We Chinese have been passing through a time
of suffering. Only we ourselves know of these sufferings
in much detail. Who else in the world could realize the
depths of the issue between Japan and China?· These
troubles have made great changes in my country and its
life.

I do not think I have since enjoyed such a lantern procession as this Armistice one. A friend of mine, just after
the beginning of the present war, wondered why we
Chinese should try so desperately to resist the Japanese.
How could I tell him, in a few words, all that we stood
to lose? Now, the war itself has given the answer. I
look back at the joys of my childhood and contrast them
sadly with the present time. And now, in England, I
stand at the commencement of what may develop into a
second world war. I should like to ask my brother why
there must always be an ' enemy of humanity ', but reflect
that he can never answer me now.

CONCLUSION

THIS IS but a fragmentary account of my childhood. Many more incidents out of the years between my fifth and fifteenth birthdays crowd into my mind, but often the sweet memories they bring can hardly be explained to other people.

While I have been absorbed, in my two little rooms near Hàmpstead Heath, in writing these reminiscences, I have not been able wholly to shake off the feeling that the things I was writing about could not be true. Either the boy who lived those sheltered years within the walls of his home in Kiu-kiang was not really me, or else he has turned since into a most unexpected kind of man, for the two rooms he now occupies are so different from the rooms of his childhood. They are quite ' static '. One of them has yellowish wall-paper, a big table, a huge filing case, three bookcases and a built-in cupboard, and I see these objects in the same places morning, noon and night. I cannot change or move any of them, for I have no cousins here to give me a hand. If I sent for workmen, the whim to change the look of the room would have passed before they arrived. So I leave them as they are. And indeed where else could, for example, the two half-worn-out armchairs stand except on either side of the fireplace ?

I have always tried to find time to read books on my country by those who have had personal experience of it. For the most part I have found the authors kind and complimentary about our life. But I wish more of them could have penetrated below the surface. They generally dub us fatalists, individualists, a highly superstitious people, the ' inscrutable Chinese ' ! I admit that all these epithets are more or less apt. We are fatalists, inasmuch as there are certain things we do not try to struggle against. We are individualists, in that we want to enjoy our life through our own work rather than to exercise power over others. We are superstitious ; but who is not ? And I certainly considered the mentality of my elders ' inscrutable ' when they did not let me play as much as I liked when I was young ! But do not all these qualities make us *human* ?

My elders certainly did their best to make our home a happy one. They worked hard and, finding happiness themselves, engendered it in the household. In peaceful pursuits they passed their days. They were law-abiding creatures and what else were they to do with their lives ? Thirty years or so ago such placid existence was possible. Difficulties were, it is true, arising among the Chinese as a result of contact with other parts of the world. But we never made trouble with other nations, for we were never envious of them. As we were taught by our philosophers to be friendly with all living creatures and to realize that they are as worthy of respect as man, we could not possibly refuse friendship with human beings of other nations. This had the unexpected result of causing it to be thought that we did not love our own nation ! Oh, how strange ! Personally I deplore the habit of boasting of one's nation's strength in whatever sphere, because this is the root of all the troubles in the history of mankind. He who thinks himself better than others is apt to want to subdue them to his will. Few are willing to submit, and so the trouble starts. As human beings we are all equal. Some may be crushed for a time, but the desire to recover will always revive and bring renewed struggle. In our long history we have seen this happen many times. We Chinese strive to enjoy ourselves in Nature and to live with her as much as possible, and we look upon happiness as the greatest good. This is why my elders took such pains to create happiness in our house.

Unhappily history has come full circle again. The

period, about 500 B.C., when China was divided into many small States, each claiming to be better than its neighbours and suppressing its rivals by force, is being relived. But this time China as a whole is trying to defend herself. Our utmost effort is being made, because we are equal human beings with our enemies. For myself I am sure that we shall survive, as our forefathers survived their many difficulties. China will always be Chinese. But we must abandon any attempt to vaunt our nation at the expense of others, or we, and mankind as a whole, will never have peace. This has been our national philosophy for more than two thousand years.

There were no war memorials in China in my younger days. I saw nothing of war weapons. I heard no stories of national heroes who had fought in such and such battles. No books of war experiences were published. I did not think Genghis Khan so wonderful a person as many of my Western friends think him. But now my youngest cousins and nephews write to me in a most belligerent strain. One has become a guerrilla fighter in the rear of our enemies; another has joined the regular army as a soldier. I have just received a photograph of my youngest cousin standing by his warplane; he recently finished his training as a pilot. . . .

In speaking of the happiness of our household I do not, by the way, want to suggest that there was never any quarrelling! Being human beings, my elders sometimes quarrelled, like every one else. I do not remember any particular incident, but I know there was gossiping and discontent from time to time. As long as both my grandparents retained their vigour everything went smoothly. Whatever money was earned by any individual member of the family was given to the head, and an allowance made to all for the month. Those members with children received more. This worked out very well, for the financial condition of my family was good, and, all necessaries being provided, no one had much use for money.

Traditional thought still exercised great influence, and filial regard and industry in the interests of the whole house were esteemed. If any quarrel spread beyond our walls it was considered a blot upon the entire household. Every one tried to curb his irritation and any tendency to quarrel. In any event, our law did not provide for quarrels and we had in those days no lawyers to help one side and thus make a solution more difficult to find. Later a great change came—in my house as in the whole country. Students, returning from studying in foreign lands, where their peculiar habits and customs had been the subjects of jokes, shouted that we should adopt other ways of living. China fell into confusion. The financial position of my family declined ; my grandparents were no longer there to control matters ; and, the personal needs of some members being larger than before, frequent quarrels ensued. We still kept together, but the old happiness was gone.

Now my grandparents have been dead for nearly twenty years ; most of my elders are dead too or are getting far on in years ; and I myself have been in exile in this sea-country for over six years. And China has been invaded by enemies and is still at war. Before my brother's death, he wrote to me urging me to stay in England to gain more experience, and so be of more use to my country in the future. He said that I should not try to go back to take part in the war unless I was called-up by the Government. At the time of writing he had not long returned from the war himself, and less than a month later he was dead. Two months later my native city, Kiu-kiang, fell. I have heard that our house and garden are entirely destroyed, but I cannot tell. Recently the members of my family by whom I was surrounded in my childhood wrote that they had escaped from Kiu-kiang and were now scattered in five different places, some in Chungking, some in interior districts whence letters could not easily be sent. None of them wanted me to go back. They tell me that the young cousin whom I have described in the chapter on

the New Year Festival was shot dead by Japanese without
reason in the country near Kiu-kiang ; he was lame in
one leg. Another cousin and his wife, who had escaped
to another district, found themselves suddenly attacked by
the invaders, and they themselves were shot. My sister
had become a widow before I came to England ; I have
had only two letters from her since the war began ; she
managed to escape with her children and is living on the
side of a mountain. . . .

Sometimes I ask myself : Is it because we enjoyed such
happiness that we have now to bear such grief ? How is
it that the invaders do not think of their own cousins and
relations ? The loss of material things—our house, our
garden, our collections of paintings and books—leaves me
now comparatively unmoved, though we took such pleasure
in them. But on what principle is a civilization based
which can destroy happiness and kill fellow-beings in the
interests of some unstable dream of expansion and aggrand-
isement ? What happiness can the invaders look for ?

I hope and believe that I shall one day enjoy again some
of the experiences described in this book, even if, before
the end of the struggle, I myself take part in the war. No
matter what sufferings we endure, we shall find our way
back to happiness. For the present there keeps passing
through my mind this poem of Li Yu, a prince who was
thrown from his beautiful palace into exile :

> In silence I go to the Western Chamber ;
> Above hangs the sickle moon ;
> In the deep, lonely court of paulownia trees
> Is gaoled the chilly autumn.
>
> Cut it—yet unsevered ;
> Order it—yet more tangled :
> Such is the parting sorrow,
> That dwells in my heart,
> Too subtle a feeling to tell.

[1] Translated by Ch'u Ta-Kao.